The Catholic Holy Sites of the Mohawk Valley

fuit, pluries prestitit. Verum maturius re considerata, censuerunt seniores nihil in hac re Gallorum esse precipitandum, nosq. in concilium, ubi aduocarant, uiuere pronuntiarunt. Reliquis item Huronibus pene omnibus uitam dedere tribus exceptis, Paulo, Eustachio, et Stephano, quos tribus in pagis, qui nationem istam constituunt, occiderunt, Stephanum in eodē quo eramus pago, Andagaron appellant, Paulum in alio Onenrenon, Eustachium in Theonontogen. Et Eustachio quidem, ubi eum toto pene corpore ustularunt, cultro ceruices amputarunt, quæ omnia Christiane admodum pertulit: cumq. soleant captiui alij moriendo cum ita dicere: Exoriare aliquis nostris ex ossibus ultor, ille contra Christiano spiritu, quem a baptismo altè imbiberat, astantes Hurones conciues suos rogauit, ne ipsius consideratio stabiliendæ cum Iroquæis illis paci officeret. Paulus Ononchiraton, qui in pago Onenrenon dicto post solitas ustulationes securi percussus fuerat iuuenis erat 25. circiter annorum, et maxime animosus: hos enim potissimum occidunt, ut hostium uires succidant, is egregius mortis contemptor spe melioris uitæ, ut palam loquebatur in uia cum ad me accederent Iroquenses, ut aut mihi ungues detraherent, aut aliquid aliud agerent, se illis offerebat, rogans ut me derelicto in ipsum potius desæuirent: reddat illi Dominus centuplicia cum fœnore pro eximia illa charitate, qua animam suam dabat pro amicis suis, et ijs qui eum in uinculis in Christo genuerant. Sub uesperum Guillelmum Couture, quem iuuenem prestantem uiribus intuebantur, in ultimum regionis pagum Theonontogen dictum, deducunt, eumq. cuidam barbarorum familiæ adscribunt. Solemne est his barbaris, cum captiuo alicui dant uitam, eum in familiam aliquam allegare, in qua demortui alicuius locum supplet, in cuius etiam iura quodadmodo succedit, nec quispiam alius ipsius Dominus est, quam is, qui familiæ illius caput est: ob id enim munera aliqua exhibet. Me uerò, et Renatum, quos non ita firmis uiribus conspiciebant, deducunt in pagum primum, in quo ij, qui nos captiuos ceperant, manebant: ibiq. nos quoad aliud statueretur, constituunt.

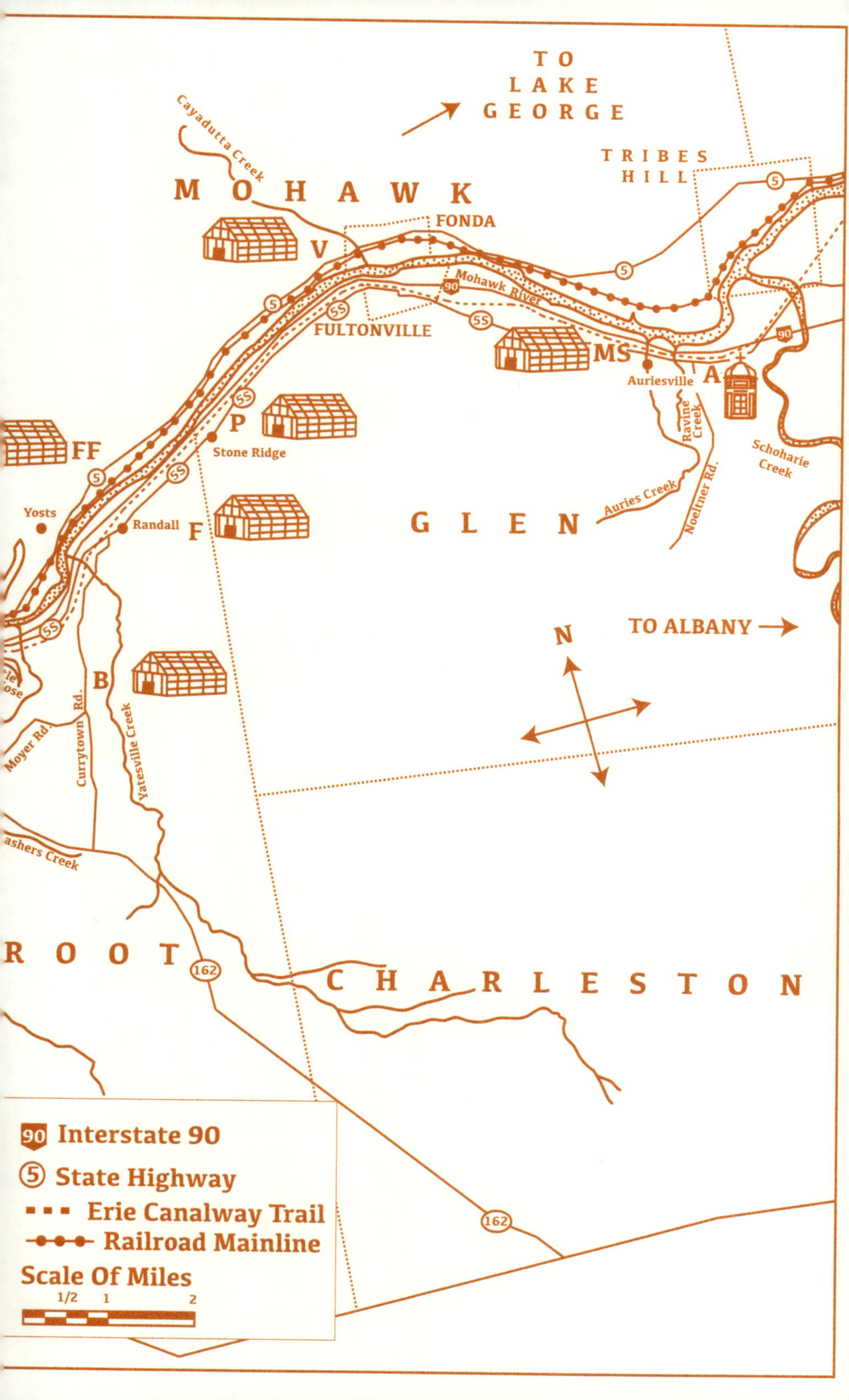
TO LAKE GEORGE
Cayadutta Creek
TRIBES HILL
MOHAWK
FONDA
V
Mohawk River
FULTONVILLE
MS
Auriesville
A
Ravine Creek
Schoharie Creek
P
Stone Ridge
FF
Yosts
Randall
F
Auries Creek
Noeltner Rd.
GLEN
TO ALBANY
N
B
Currytown Rd.
Moyer Rd.
Yatesville Creek
ashers Creek
ROOT
CHARLESTON
Interstate 90
State Highway
Erie Canalway Trail
Railroad Mainline
Scale Of Miles
1/2
1
2

The Catholic Holy Sites of the Mohawk Valley

The True Locations of the Deaths *of the* JESUIT MARTYRS and of the Birth and Upbringing *of* ST. CATHERINE TEKAKWITHA

Richard Upsher Smith Jr.

FRANCISCAN UNIVERSITY PRESS

Franciscan University Press
1235 University Boulevard
Steubenville, OH 43952
740-283-3771

Distributed by:
The Catholic University of America Press
c/o HFS
P.O. Box 50370
Baltimore, MD 21211
800-537-5487

Cataloging-in-Publication Data available from the Library of Congress

Cover and Interior Design: Reflective Book Design

Cover Image: Mouth of Yatesville Creek at the Mohawk River.
Photo by the author, 22 June 2022.

Frontispiece: Leaf from "Epistola Patris Isaaci Jogues in noua Francia inter Iroheos captiui ad Prouincialem Francię," Folio 373 of MS Pra A9, Collection du P. Prat, SJ. The name of the easternmost Mohawk Castle in the Mohawk River Valley is spelled Ossenrenon on lines 6 and 13. Reproduced with permission of the Archives françaises de la Compagnie de Jésus, Vanves, France.

Printed in the United States of America.

ISBN: 979-8-89372-116-4

To my friend and collaborator, Deanna J. Smith

CONTENTS

List of Illustrations ix

List of Maps x

Acknowledgments xi

Introduction 1

The Problem 1 / The Evidence, Method, and Genre of This Book 2 / The Documents 5 / Mourning War among the Iroquoian Peoples 14 / A Preliminary Note on Ossenrenon 16

Chapter 1. Background on the Lives of Saints René Goupil, Isaac Jogues, Jean de Lalande, and Catherine Tekakwitha 19

Chapter 2. Evidence for Auriesville as the Site of the Martyrdoms with Initial Observations 33

Chapter 3. The Martyrdom of St. René Goupil at the Bauder Site 42

Archeological Evidence 42 / Documentary Evidence with Translations 53 / Commentary 80 / Summary 98

Contents

Chapter 4. The Martyrdoms of St. Isaac Jogues and St. Jean de Lalande at the Bauder Site 101

Documentary Evidence with Translations 101 / Archeologists' Arguments against the Martyrdoms of St. Isaac and St. Jean at the Bauder Site, with Rebuttals 110 / Conclusion 124

Chapter 5. The Locations Where St. Catherine Tekakwitha Lived in the Mohawk Valley 125

Documentary Evidence with Translations 126 / Archeological Evidence 134 / Conclusion 144

Chapter 6. A Narrative Presentation of the Research Results 146

Conclusion. The Continuing Significance of the Shrine of Our Lady of Martyrs and of the St. Kateri National Shrine 151

Appendix. What Did St. Isaac Do with St. René's Bones? 157

Bibliography 161

Index 173

ILLUSTRATIONS

Figures

FRONTISPIECE: Leaf from "Epistola Patris Isaaci Jogues in noua Francia inter Iroheos captiui ad Prouincialem Francię"

Following Page 184

1. Plateau of the Shrine of Our Lady of Martyrs from the Mohawk River
2. Auriesville #1, showing the shrine gift shop
3. Auriesville #2, showing the torture platform crucifix
4. Auriesville Hill from the shrine plateau
5. Ravine Road and brook at Auriesville
6. Brook as it flows through the Auriesville meadow
7. Junction of the brook and Ravine Creek at the edge of the Auriesville meadow
8. Looking down Ravine Creek from the Auriesville meadow
9. Bauder Site and Bauder Graveyard fields
10. Bauder Site field
11. View of the northern ravine down to Yatesville Creek from the Bauder Site
12. View from the Bauder Site up the field to the ridge
13. Ridge between the Yatesville's mouth and the Bauder Site
14. Mouth of Yatesville Creek at the Mohawk River

15. Side channel of Yatesville Creek below the Bauder Site looking downstream

16. Main channel of Yatesville Creek below the Bauder Site looking upstream

17. View downstream from the union of the two Yatesville channels below the Bauder Site

18. Union of the two Yatesville channels below the Bauder Site at the end of the island of scree

Maps

ENDPAPERS FRONT AND BACK: Some Mohawk archeological sites, 1635–1700. Based on Paul H. Clayburn, Commissioner of Public Works, *Montgomery County Highway Map* (Erlanger, KY: Universal Map Enterprises, 2007), and the author's own research. Drawn by Roddy Lowder.

FOLDOUT: Auriesville Shrine with environs. Based on USGS Historical Map, Tribes Hill, New York, and on maps drawn by Gen. John S. Clark, 22 November 1881 (2 maps), Rufus A. Grider, 16 June 1888, and J. Franklin Ewing, SJ, August 1951. The elevation lines are approximations of those on the USGS map. The numerals designating elevations are exact, however. Courtesy of Wayne Lenig. Drawn by Roddy Lowder.

FOLDOUT: Bauder Site with environs. Based on USGS Historical Map, Randall, New York, and on original field mapping of the Bauder Site by Donald A. Rumrill on file at the New York State Museum in Albany (used with permission). The elevation lines are approximations of those on the USGS map. The numerals designating elevations are exact, however. Courtesy of Wayne Lenig. Drawn by Roddy Lowder.

ACKNOWLEDGMENTS

I WOULD LIKE TO THANK Deanna J. Smith for her help with the research for this book. A professional genealogist and fellow Catholic, she graciously donated her time to working on this book. I dedicate this book to her. Wayne Lenig has kindly shared his careful, detailed reports on the various sites associated with the Auriesville Shrine, the Bauder Site, the Levi Dillenbeck Site, and the Fox Farm Site. These have been crucial in nuancing and correcting the major published reports on these sites, and they have saved me from a couple of mistakes and a major blunder. I must also thank William Maring, the town historian of Root in Montgomery County, New York. He kindly gave me a tour of the archeological and historical sites of the Town of Root, for which I am grateful. I also thank Terry McMaster, who made some inquiries for me.

I must also thank Kelly Yacobucci Farquhar, the county historian and records management officer, and her assistant, Earlene F. Melious, in the Montgomery County History and Archives Department for their kind and efficient assistance. It was a pleasure working in their sanctum. Montgomery County officials at the County Clerk's Office, the County Surrogate's Court, and the County Tax Maps and Real Property Office were also extremely helpful and generous with their time.

Joannie Lajeunesse and her student assistant at the Archives des Jésuites au Canada, Montreal, deserve my most humble thanks not only for their archival expertise, but also for their good-humored patience with my poor French, and for their readiness to switch to English whenever my Gallic sails began to luff. Michael Knox, SJ, DPhil (Oxon), former director of the Shrine of the Canadian Martyrs in Midland, Ontario, granted me a lengthy interview without an appointment, and his staff, both clerical and lay, especially my former student Daniel Devine, were very helpful.

I must also thank Benjamin Ravier-Mazzocco, Conservateur des bibliothèques, Bibliothèque municipale de Lyon, and François Dubois, Adjoint à la responsable des Archives, Archives françaises de la Compagnie de Jésus à Vanves, for their cordial and extremely competent handling of my request for a copy of St. Isaac's "Letter to His Provincial."

Gerard "Roddy" Lowder, a 2022 graduate of Franciscan University of Steubenville, drew the maps. It was his second such effort for me, and the results are excellent.

Rebecca Schreiber, book designer for Franciscan University Press, has been extremely helpful and competent. I am very grateful to her. I am also grateful to copy editor Ashleigh McKown for editing a difficult manuscript brilliantly. Last but not least, I am much obliged to Sarah K. Wear, editor-in-chief of the Franciscan University Press, for accepting this unusual book for publication.

The Catholic Holy Sites of the Mohawk Valley

Introduction

The Problem

I FIRST VISITED Our Lady of Martyrs Shrine at Auriesville, New York, in 2016. I knew little about the Jesuit Martyrs of New York or about St. Catherine Tekakwitha.[1] Nevertheless, the stories about the martyrs and St. Catherine moved me deeply, as did walking the grounds of the site. Especially striking was the old sign in the ravine telling the pilgrim that he was standing in a reliquary. When I returned home, I wrote up my experiences, and the piece was published as "Nature's Own Reliquary" in *Crisis Magazine* on 11 August 2016.

My interest in and devotion to the martyrs and to St. Catherine increased, and in 2018, I undertook a pilgrimage and research trip to New York and the Canadian provinces of Quebec and Ontario. At that point, I had already read archeological reports on Mohawk Valley excavations that contradicted the traditional Catholic recognition of Auriesville as the site of the martyrdoms and as St. Catherine's birthplace. They also contradicted

1. "Catherine" was Tekakwitha's baptismal name. Her patroness was St. Catherine of Sienna. The supposed Mohawk pronunciation of Catherine—"Kateri"—was invented by Ellen Walworth in the nineteenth century. See Allan Greer, *Mohawk Saint*, xi, who observes that the saint was always known as "Catherine" until Miss Walworth's 1891 biography and concludes, "Since 'Kateri Tekakwitha' was born in an atmosphere of fin de siècle primitivism, I prefer to call her 'Catherine.'" I agree. For more on Miss Walworth and her uncle Fr. Clarence Walworth, and on primitivism, see Greer, *Mohawk Saint*, 195–97.

the traditional understanding of the Saint Kateri National Shrine and Historic Site in Fonda, New York, as the place of Catherine's conversion and baptism. The results of my research were published in two parts in the *New Oxford Review* in 2019.[2] I made a few mistakes in that article, which have been silently corrected in this book.

In 2019, 2021, and 2022, I again made research trips to the Mohawk Valley, in order to discover the exact locations of the sites which archeologists proposed as the places of the martyrdoms and of St. Catherine's early life. This had to be done because the archeologists' descriptions of the site locations were often unclear. I have since learned that this lack of clarity was deliberate, for they wished to prevent the sites from being plundered. These three trips reinforced my conviction that the archeologists are right that Auriesville and the Saint Kateri Shrine are not the locations of the events that they have been believed to be. The arguments contained in this book will demonstrate the truth of my conviction.

Nevertheless, as I shall explain in more detail in the conclusion to this book, I do not think that these discoveries of recent archeological investigation in any way diminish the significance of the two great Mohawk Valley shrines. In fact, I think they may enhance their significance. Please study the arguments of this book carefully, and see if you do not agree.

The Evidence, Method, and Genre of This Book

The argument of this book will show that the martyrdoms of St. René Goupil, St. Isaac Jogues, and St. Jean de Lalande in 1642

2. Richard Upsher Smith Jr., "Preludes and Points—Part I. On the Trail of the Jesuit Martyrs of North America and St. Catherine Tekakwitha," *New Oxford Review* (June 2019): 18–26, and "Preludes and Points—Part II. The Final Journey of the Jesuit Martyrs of North America and the Birthplace of St. Catherine Tekakwitha," *New Oxford Review* (July–August 2019): 20–26.

and 1646 did not occur at the location of the Shrine of Our Lady of Martyrs at Auriesville, New York. Their deaths happened about seven miles away, up the Mohawk River at what archeologists call the Bauder Site in Root Township, Montgomery County, New York. The present argument will also demonstrate that the birth of St. Catherine Tekakwitha in 1656 did not occur at the Auriesville location, but about five miles upriver at what is called the Printup Site in Glen Township, Montgomery County. In addition, I show that St. Catherine was converted, catechized, and baptized not at the location of the St. Kateri National Shrine and Historic Site north of the river in Fonda, but about two miles upriver at what is called the Fox Farm Site. The evidence on which these conclusions are based is documentary, archeological, and visual. Each category must be briefly explained here.

The documents are all of the seventeenth century, except one that dates to 1715. They were composed by well-informed contemporaries of the events under consideration, sometimes by those involved in the events. While most of the documents for our investigation were studied in modern critical editions, the originals reproduced in these editions were either handwritten letters, journals and other texts, or printed reports that went through the press almost four hundred years ago. They were composed in Latin, French, or Italian. A translation into English of many of these documents exists, made in the late nineteenth century. A more detailed account of the documents will be given below.

The identification of the Auriesville Shrine as the location of the martyrdoms of St. René, St. Isaac, and St. Jean, and of the birth of St. Catherine, was based largely on a reading of the documents and on a cursory inspection of the site in the late nineteenth century. The situation at the Fonda Shrine is somewhat similar. Thus a close examination of the documents is essential for the purposes of this book, and so a critically informed and up-to-date narrative of the martyrdoms and of St. Catherine's early life will be postponed until the end of the book. The tedious preliminary work of studying the documents in the original languages, of translating them carefully, and of commenting on them must come first. It is the necessary first step in reassessing the traditional interpretation of the documents and identification of the sites, and the only sure way of persuading readers that another interpretation of the documents than the traditional does exist.

To be sure, knowledge of the classical languages and also of modern languages has fallen so dramatically in the United States in the past half century, even among scholars, that one might wonder whether it is worthwhile to present the documents in the original languages. Exact knowledge of the problem, however, depends on a close reading of the documents in the original, and enough readers will have knowledge of one or more of the relevant languages that they will be convinced by the arguments in this book. They will be able to affirm that this is what the documents say, and not just what the author imagines they say.

The work of twentieth-century archeologists, both avocational and professional, made the traditional interpretations of the Auriesville and Fonda Shrines impossible. Excavations at Auriesville and Fonda have not produced artifacts of the correct dates in sufficient types and quantities to demonstrate that towns of the sort reported in the documents existed at those sites when they should have. Therefore in this book the archeological evidence must also be examined in some detail for the arguments to be persuasive. Only then can the story of the martyrs and of St. Catherine be narrated anew.

The identification of Auriesville as the site of the martyrdoms was made, as noticed above, after a cursory comparison of the documentary evidence with the terrain at Auriesville. We shall look into this in more detail shortly. For now, we must simply note that the evidence of the eyes and of the feet is also part of the evidence for the argument of this book. To put it simply, the terrain of the

Bauder Site, which this author has seen and walked thrice, fits the picture one builds up from the documents much better than does Auriesville.

This book, then, is a history book, but of a special kind. First, it is narrow in focus and might be classified as local history. Second, the argument focuses on minute details of old documents, artifacts, and landscape, and might be called antiquarian. Antiquarianism has a bad name nowadays for being shortsighted,[3] but in its accumulation and handling of evidence at least, it is close kin to the modern "genetic or evolutionary concept of history."[4] Third, since the topic has to do with Catholic martyrs and saints, the book might be categorized as religious history or martyrology. At bottom, this book contains the raw material of history, presented as such because only a detailed analysis of documents, artifacts, and terrain will be persuasive to those attached to the traditional interpretations that they must adjust their beliefs.

Professional historians might also object to the formatting of the book, particularly to the use of boldface type, lemmata, and long nonnarrative sections of text. As a classicist by training and profession, I find such techniques natural and helpful. They are common in classics in this sort of book.

The Documents

In obedience to the Constitutions of the Society of Jesus, the superior of the Jesuit mission in New France compiled an annual *relation* or report for his superior in France. He drew his material from reports made at least annually to him by the superiors of

3. Garraghan, *Guide to Historical Method*, 10.

4. Garraghan, *Guide to Historical Method*, 15–16: "The merit of having introduced the genetic concept and of making it the basis of a new school of historiography belongs to a group of German scholars ... who at the turn of the eighteenth century began to apply the law of development to history.... [I]t stresses cause and effect and the slow process of social evolution from past to present." See also pp. 67–69.

the various Jesuit posts throughout the colony.[5] Between 1632 and 1673, these *Relations* were edited and published in France for the reading public, in order to win support for the Jesuit mission in North America.

The *Relations* were republished in three volumes in Quebec in 1858.[6] Between 1896 and 1901, the *Relations* were published with a great deal of related source material and with English translations in seventy-three volumes by Reuben Gold Thwaites and a team of collaborators. It was entitled *The Jesuit Relations and Allied Documents*, or *JR*.[7] This was the standard edition used by scholars throughout the twentieth century, and it still is to a large extent. A modern critical edition of the same material, however, with much additional material as well, was produced by Lucien Campeau, SJ, entitled *Monumenta Novae Franciae* (*MNF*). He was able to publish nine volumes before his death in 2003, covering the years 1602–61.[8] Wherever possible, I have used the texts in *MNF*.[9] In

5. See Padberg, *Constitutions*, 326 and 328. A description of how the *Relations* were compiled can be found in Pouliot, *Étude sur les Relations*, 20–22.

6. *Relations des Jésuites contenant ce qui s'est passé de plus remarquable dans les missions des Pères de la Compagnie de Jésus dans le Nouvelle-France* (Québec: Augustin Coté, 1858). See True, "Is It Time?," 272–73, for an assessment of this edition. In True's estimation, it comes in third among the available modern editions.

7. Thwaites, *Jesuit Relations and Allied Documents*.

8. Campeau, *Monumenta Novae Franciae*.

9. For the superiority of *MNF* to *JR*, see True, "Is It Time?," 261–79, esp. 264: "Thwaites's rapidly produced edition could not stand in starker contrast to Campeau's much larger collection of documents . . . In addition to the missionary reports, Campeau's volumes contain hundreds of letters, journals, and other materials related to the New France mission, far surpassing the smaller collection of supplementary documents in the Thwaites edition . . . In contrast to his predecessor, Campeau was a trained, professional historian and his work is without doubt the most rigorous scholarly edition of the texts available. Nonetheless, most scholars have neglected it. One does not have to look very hard for factors that may account for the continued preference for the earlier edition. Where Thwaites provides facing-page translations in English of the Relations and other documents, Campeau presents them in their original languages only . . . and if Thwaites's *Jesuit Relations* is easily available on the Internet and in most research libraries, *Monumenta Novae Franciae* is found in approximately one hundred libraries worldwide,

fact, most of the sources used in this book are contained in *MNF*. But some texts are not found therein, namely, those that appeared after the *MNF* cutoff date.

In this book, relevant passages from the source texts will be quoted in the original languages with English translations of my own following them. In order to make the presentation of these texts below less cluttered, a bibliographic review of the texts will be made here. Note that in terms of narrative time, I proleptically award the title "St." to those here and throughout this book who would later earn it.

Document 1. The most important account of the martyrdom of St. René Goupil, as well as of the captivity of St. Isaac Jogues, was written in Latin by St. Isaac, the "Epistola Patris Isaaci Jogues in Nova Francia inter Irohaeos captivi ad Provincialem Franciae," or "Letter of Father Isaac Jogues Captive among the Iroquois in New France to the Provincial of France."[10] Fr. Campeau's source

---

and is not available electronically. [The latter is no longer true.] Further limiting the more recent edition is the fact that the editor's death in 2003 left the final twelve years of published reports unaccounted for, not to mention the letters and other supplementary documents for those years." See also Codignola, "CAMPEAU, Lucien," passim. While this is a review of *MNF* 4, nevertheless Codignola comments on all four volumes of *MNF* in print at the time, and assesses Campeau's work highly, although he sees him as a partisan Jesuit and quibbles with some of his opinions on historiography. In mentioning that Campeau provided no translations of the documents, Codignola wisely warns: "Historiens unilingues, prenez garde! Désormais, il sera difficile d'écrire sur les Jésuites en Amérique sans être capable de travailler dans ces langues" (99). He concludes his review in the same vein: "Les documents sont en eux-mêmes une mine d'or et, sous la direction de Campeau, ils deviennent accessibles à tous ceux qui sont capables de lire d'autres langues que leur langue maternelle" (103).

10. In *MNF* 5, *La bonne nouvelle reçue (1641–1643)*, Document 115, 592–625. This text can also be found in Alegambe, *Mortes Illustres*, 619–32, on which see also "Preliminary Note on Ossenrenon" below. A portion of the letter was copied in Ragueneau, *Mémoires*, held in the Jesuit Archives in Montreal. The *Mémoires* were published under the title above—transcribed by William Lonc, SJ, and edited by Steve Catlin—at Ottawa by Early Jesuit Missions in Canada in 2013. The letter is Document 5, 43–50, in that edition. A translation of this text into English by Sr. M. Renelle, SSND, can be found in Roustang, *Jesuit Missionaries to North America*.

for his edition of this letter was a seventeenth-century copy of the original. He dated the letter to 5 August 1643 at Rensselaerswick, a Dutch village on the Hudson River.

Document 2. A rather free Italian translation of the preceding letter of St. Isaac, with some substitutions from Document 3, was published by Francesco Gioseppe Bressani, SJ, in Macerata, Italy, in 1653. It was entitled "Lettera del Padre Isaac Iogues al Padre Provinciale della provincia di Francia," or "Letter of Father Isaac Jogues to the Father Provincial of the Province of France," and was included in Bressani's *Breve Relatione d'alcvne missioni de' PP. della Compagnia di Giesù nella Nuoua Francia*, or *A Brief Report about Some Missions of the Fathers of the Society of Jesus in New France*. Fr. Campeau's source for this document was a copy of the original edition of the book.[11] Fr. Bressani (1612–72) served in New France from 1642 to 1644, and from 1645 to 1650. He was captured by Mohawks on his way to the Huron Mission in 1643 and tortured in the same village where St. René had been killed and St. Isaac had been tortured. He was held in servitude, but his owner, thinking him a useless slave, ransomed him to the Dutch in 1644. He sailed to France, and then immediately returned to New France, and reached the Huron Mission at last.

Document 3. At the order of his superior, Jérôme Lalemant (1593–1673), SJ, St. Isaac wrote an eyewitness account of St. René's ordeal, "Le martyre de René Goupil par les Iroquois," or "The Martyrdom of René Goupil by the Iroquois."[12] Fr. Campeau's source was Fr. Paul Ragueneau's 1652 *Mémoires*.[13] Campeau reckons St. Isaac wrote the narrative at Montreal in 1646.[14] (Fr. Ragueneau's dates were 1608 to 1680.)

11. In *MNF* 8, *Au bord de la ruine* (*1651–1656*), Document 103 III, 483–502. One can find this document also in *JR* 39.175–224. Campeau also mentions an edition by Fr. Félix Martin, SJ, which I have not tracked down.

12. Document 80 in *MNF* 5.284–91.

13. See note 10 above.

14. It appears as Document 28, 144–50, in the Lonc-Catlin edition. It also is found

Document 4. Quite complicated is the case of the fourth document: Jogues and Lalemant, *Relation de ce qui s'est passé en la Nouvelle-France en l'anné 1647*, chapters 4–5.[15] Fr. Campeau's source was a copy of the original printed edition of the *Relation*. Fr. Campeau notes, "Two principal accounts exist of the captivity of Fr. Jogues among the Mohawk.[16] The oldest was written in Latin by the captive himself as a letter addressed to his provincial, 5 August 1643 [Document 1] ... Another [Document 5] was composed by Fr. Jacques Buteux, who had lived with Fr. Jogues at Montreal in 1644–1645. The present narrative [Document 4], [while] in agreement with the substance of the others, is not a copy or an extract of the one or the other. It seems to have been a French draft by Fr. Jogues, obtained by Fr. Lalemant during the stay of the confessor of the faith at Montreal. This version contains some points and details completing the content of the others, but, if it has given the audience some important parts of the story, they are still only some excerpts."[17] Fr. Lalemant himself notes, "What has been said about his [Fr. Jogues's] toils in the preceding *Relations* came forth for the most part from certain savages, companions

---

in *JR* 28.116–35. An edition is found in *Rapport de L'Archiviste de la Province de Québec* (1924–25), 89–93. An English translation is provided in Ragueneau, *Memoirs*. A translation of this text into English by Sr. M. Renelle, SSND, can be found in Roustang, *Missionaries*. The detail about Fr. Lalemant's order appears at Lonc-Catlin's Ragueneau, 150.

15. In *MNF* 7, *Le Témoignage du sang* (1647–50), Document 35, 96–114. The document is also printed in *JR* 31.16–69.

16. Campeau excludes Document 3 because it is an account not of St. Isaac's own ordeal, but of St. René's.

17. *MNF* 7.97n3: "Il existe deux principaux récits de la captivité du P. Jogues chez les Agniers. Le plus ancien a été écrit en latin par le captif lui-même sous forme de lettre adressée à son provincial, le 5 août 1643 ... Un autre a été composé par le P. Jacques Buteux, qui a vécu avec le P. Jogues à Montréal en 1644–1645. Le présent récit, d'accord avec la substance des autres, n'est pas une copie ou un extrait de l'un ou de l'autre. Il semble avoir été une rédaction française du P. Jogues, obtenue par le P. Lalemant durant le séjour du confesseur de la foi à Montréal. Cette version contient des précisions et des détails complétant le contenu des autres, mais, s'il en a donné au public des tranches importantes, elles ne sont encore que des extraits."

of his afflictions. But what I am going to set down has come from his pen and from his own mouth. It was necessary to use a superior's authority and a sweet skill in more private conversations to discover what the very low estimate he possessed of himself kept hidden in a deep silence."[18] Lalemant therefore draws on St. Isaac's new account of his captivity, written in French; on his own conversations with the saint; on Document 1; and on Fr. Paul Le Jeune's additions to the 1643 *Relations*.[19] By and large, therefore, the contents of chapter 4 of this *Relation* were written newly by St. Isaac in French.[20] Chapter 5 is in the third person, narrated by Fr. Lalemant from the sources mentioned above.[21]

Document 5. Fr. Campeau identifies this document as the second of the "principal accounts . . . of the captivity of Fr. Jogues among the Mohawk," as we saw above. It is entitled "Narré de la prise du Père Isaac Jogues, par le P. Jacques Buteux," or "Narrative of the Capture of Father Isaac Jogues, by Father Jacques Buteux."[22] Fr. Campeau's source for this document was Fr. Ragueneau's 1652 *Mémoires*.[23] Fr. Buteux (1600–1652) and St. Isaac were both assigned to Montreal during the period 1644–45. St. Isaac regarded Fr. Buteux "as his best friend and his most trusted spiritual adviser."[24] Fr. Campeau dates this narrative to the fall of 1645.[25]

18. *MNF* 7.96: "Ce qu'on a dit de ses travaux dans les Relations précédentes provenoit pour la pluspart de quelques sauvages, compagnons de ses peines. Mais ce que je vais coucher est sorty de sa plume et de sa propre bouche. Il a fallu user d'authorité de supérieur et d'une douce industrie dans les conversations plus particulières pour descouvrir ce que l'estime très basse qu'il faisoit de soy-mesme tenoit caché dans un profond silence." The reports of the Native Americans mentioned by Lalemant can be found at *MNF* 5.761–66.

19. *MNF* 7.96n1. For Fr. Le Jeune's additions, see *MNF* 5.772n1.

20. *MNF* 7.96–108.

21. *MNF* 7.108–14.

22. In *MNF* 6, *Recherche de la paix (1644–1646)*, Document 67, 273–306.

23. Document 1 in Lonc-Catlin edition, 1–35. See comments above on Document 4 for Fr. Campeau's judgment on the relationship among Documents 1, 4, and 5.

24. Talbot, *Saint among Savages*, 348. Note that the Ignatius Press reprint of Father Talbot's book omits most of the references.

25. *MNF* 6.273.

With the following document, we turn to texts that have to do with the martyrdoms of St. Isaac and St. Jean de Lalande.

Document 6. "Le P. Isaac Jogues au P. André Castillon," or "Father Jogues to Father André Castillon."[26] Fr. Campeau transcribes the autograph copy of the letter. It is dated Montreal, 12 September 1646.

Document 7. "L'Interprète Labatie à Jean de la Montagne," or "The Interpreter Labatie to Jean de la Montagne."[27] Fr. Campeau's source is Ragueneau's 1652 *Mémoires*.[28] The letter is dated 30 October 1646 from Fort Orange. Jan Labatie was a Flemish interpreter residing at Fort Orange. Jean de la Montagne was a Flemish resident of New Amsterdam, who was a counselor to the director-general of the colony, Willem Kieft.[29]

Document 8. "Willem Kieft, Dir., à Charles Huault de Montmagny, Gouv.," or "Willem Kieft, Director, to Charles Huault de Montmagny, Governor.[30] Fr. Campeau's source for this letter is Ragueneau's 1652 *Mémoires*.[31] The letter is dated 14 November 1646 from New Amsterdam. Document 7 was enclosed with this letter.

Document 9. Fr. Jérôme Lalemant, *Relation de ce qui s'est passé en la Nouvelle-France ès années 1645 et 1646*, chapitre IV, "De la Mission des Martyrs commencée au pays des Iroquois," or *Report of What Happened in New France in the Years 1645 and 1646*, chapter 4, "Concerning the Mission of the Martyrs Begun in the Land of the Iroquois."[32] Fr. Campeau's source was a copy of the original printed edition.

26. Document 121 in *MNF* 6.512–14. It is found also in *JR* 28.136–41.

27. Document 132 in *MNF* 6.527–28; also Document 35 in *MNF* 7.130. The letter is also found in *JR* 31.116–19.

28. Document 8A, in Lonc-Catlin edition, 59–60.

29. *MNF* 6.527, 527n2.

30. Document 137 in *MNF* 6.539–40; also Document 35 in *MNF* 7.129. The letter is found in *JR* 31.114–15, too.

31. Document 8B in Lonc-Catlin edition, 60–61.

32. Document 140 I in *MNF* 6.568–76. The document is found, too, in *JR* 29.44–63.

Document 10. "Le Père Jacques Buteux au P. Jérôme Lalemant, Sup.," or "Father Jacques Buteux to Father Jérôme Lalemant, Superior."[33] Fr. Campeau's source for this letter is Ragueneau's 1652 *Mémoires*.[34] The document is dated 6 June 1647, Trois-Rivières.

Document 11. "Le P. Jacques Buteux au P. Jérôme Lalemant, Sup.," or "Father Jacques Buteux to Father Jérôme Lalemant, Superior."[35] Fr. Campeau's source for this letter is Ragueneau's 1652 *Mémoires*.[36] The document is dated 29 July 1647, Trois-Rivières.

Document 12. Fr. Jérôme Lalemant, "Lettre au R. P. Estienne Charlet, provincial de la Compagnie de Jésus en la province de France," or "Letter to the Reverend Father Étienne Charlet, Provincial of the Society of Jesus in the Province of France," in *Relation de ce qui s'est passé en la Nouvelle-France en l'année 1647*, or *Report of What Happened in New France in the Year 1647*.[37] Fr. Campeau's source was a copy of the original edition. The letter is a cover letter for the *Relation* of 1647. It is dated Quebec, 20 October 1647.

Document 13. Fr. Jérôme Lalemant, *Relation de ce qui s'est passé en la Nouvelle-France en l'année 1647*, chapitre I, or *Report of What Happened in New France in the Year* 1647, chapter 1.[38] Fr. Campeau's source was a copy of the original edition.

Document 14. Fr. Jérôme Lalemant, *Relation de ce qui s'est passé en la Nouvelle-France ès années 1647 et 1648*, chapitre II, or *Report of What Happened in New France in the Years 1647 and 1648*, chapter 2.[39] Fr. Campeau's source was a copy of the original edition.

We now turn to texts regarding St. Catherine.

Document 15. Fr. Claude Chauchetière, SJ, *La Vie de la B[ienheureuse]. Catherine Tegakoüita, Dite à Present La Saincte*

33. Document 20 in *MNF* 7.43–44.
34. Document 4 in Lonc-Catlin edition, 42.
35. Document 24 in *MNF* 7.48–51.
36. Document 3 in Lonc-Catlin edition, 38–41.
37. Document 35 in *MNF* 7.70–72. The text is found in *JR* 30.218–25, too.
38. Document 35 in *MNF* 7.72–82. The text is also found in *JR* 30.226–53.
39. Document 77 in *MNF* 7.299–308. The text is found in *JR* 32.143–71 as well.

Sauuagesse, or *The Life of the Blessed Catherine Tekakwitha, Called Currently the Holy Woman of the Wilds* (Manhattan: Presse Cramoisy de Jean-Marie Shea, 1887). A note initialed "F. M." (= Felix Martin, SJ, undoubtedly), on the third page of the reprint edition held in my hand as I write (University of California Libraries), reads, "This Life is owed to Fr. Claude Chauchetière, and still exists in his own autograph. It was given to the Jesuits upon their return to Canada in 1842, by the Religious of the Hotel-Dieu of Quebec. They had received it from the Rev. Fr. Cazot, an old Jesuit, who died at Quebec in 1800."[40] Felix Martin, SJ (1804–86), was a French Jesuit, antiquarian, and architect who spent almost twenty years in Canada rebuilding the Jesuit order. To him more than any other is due the salvation of the history of the order in Canada, and much of the early history of New France.

Document 16. Fr. Pierre Cholenec, SJ, *La Vie De Catherine Tegakouita Première Vierge Irokoise*, or *The Life of Catherine Tekakwitha, First Iroquois Virgin*. This French text is contained in a separately paginated appendix of an English translation of Fr. Cholenec's biography of St. Catherine by William Lonc, SJ.[41] Fr. Lonc made his translation from "a xerographic photocopy of a typewritten transcription of a Document—presumably based on Fr. Cholenec's original Autograph . . . Our Document is found in the Vanier Library, Loyola Campus of Concordia University in Montreal." The transcription was compared both with "a similar document . . . at the Woodstock Theological Center Library at Georgetown University in Washington, D.C.," and "with a xerographic copy of Fr. Cholenec's Autograph as found at the

40. "Cette Vie est due au Pere Claude Chauchetiere, et existe encore dans son autographe meme. Il a ete donné aux Jésuites revenus en Canada en 1842, par les Religieuses de L'Hotel-Dieu de Québec. Elles l'avoient reçu du R. P. Cazot, ancien Jésuite, mort à Québec en 1800." On the last page of the original text in this reprint edition, one reads, "Achevé d'imprimer à Albany par les Fils de feu Joel Munsell, après le manuscrit autographe conservé au College Ste Marie, à Montréal, le 28 de Mars 1887."

41. Cholenec, *La Vie De Catherine Tegakouita*, Appendix [in French], separately paginated, 1–67, in Lonc, *Catherine Tekakwitha*.

Hôtel-Dieu Archives in Quebec."[42] This must be the document described by Allan Greer as "'La vie de Catherine Tegakouita, première vierge Iroquoise,' Archives de l'hôtel-dieu de Québec."[43]

Document 17. "Lettre du Père Cholenec, missionnaire da la Compagnie de Jésus, au Père Augustin le Blanc, de la même Compagnie, Procureur des missions du Canada," or "Letter of Father Cholenec, Missionary of the Society of Jesus, to Father Augustin LeBlanc of the Same Society, Procurator of the Missions in Canada." The letter is dated at the Sault de Saint-Louis (= Mission de Saint-François-Xavier-du-Sault), 27 August 1715. There is no note on its provenance. One assumes that the editors discovered the original or a copy in a Jesuit archive in France.[44]

Mourning War among the Iroquoian Peoples

One aspect of the religion of the Iroquoian peoples, among whom are included not only the Five Nations of the Iroquois but also most notably the Huron-Wendat, is what one historian has called the "warfare-torture-sacrifice-cannibalism complex."[45] This complex is much in evidence in this book and will disturb many readers. A brief explanation follows.

42. Cholonec-Lonc, *Catherine Tekakwitha*, i.

43. Greer, *Mohawk Saint*, 208n1.

44. Charles Le Gobien and several other Jesuits compiled thousands of documents from the Jesuit missions around the world and published them in thirty-six volumes at Paris between 1703 and 1776 as the *Lettres édifiantes et curieuses écrites des missions étrangères* (4.25–61).

45. Tuck, "Northern Iroquoian Prehistory," writes, the "warfare-torture-sacrifice-cannibalism complex seems intimately bound up with the development of Northeastern horticultural peoples. Although its origins are obscure, its presence is well attested to before the fourteenth century; and the fear of reprisals in this never-ending pattern of blood revenge was probably a major factor in the formation of large villages, tribal units, and ultimately the several historic confederacies ... The blood revenge patterns of a single lineage segment or village of the thirteenth century were transferred to tribal units and finally to allied tribes" (330).

The "warfare-torture-sacrifice-cannibalism complex" had its religious roots in the Iroquoian belief in the interdependence of all things in the Holy Circle of life. It developed from the necessity of replacing deceased members of the various institutions that composed the community, beginning with the particular lineages of the several clans in the various villages and rising all the way up to the chief magistrates of the nation and confederacy. In this way, the grief of the relatives of the deceased might be assuaged by condolence ceremonies, and the virtues of the deceased might not be lost, but "requickened" and perpetuated by the award of his or her name to another person. At least at the subsidiary levels of Iroquoian societies, the replacement person was usually a captive taken in warfare. Thus the term "mourning war." Taking captives was more important in Iroquoian warfare than winning glory or snatching booty. As demographic decline accelerated rapidly in the seventeenth century, mourning war became endemic and self-defeating.[46]

All of the captives of mourning war were tortured. After their ordeals, most captives were awarded to families in mourning. The matrons of the families would then decide whether to keep the captive in place of their deceased or to kill the unfortunate person. Sometimes an unsatisfactory captive was even sold away, as was Fr. Bressani. One or two of the captives, always magnificently stoic warriors, were sacrificed, butchered, boiled, and ritually eaten by the villagers. This ritual cannibalism also served as a kind of requickening, as the virtues of the sacrificed person enriched the personalities of all the villagers who participated in the feast.[47]

It seems probable that all Americans feel the taboo against

46. Richter, *Ordeal of the Longhouse*, 32. The term the "Holy Circle of life" comes from Sioui, *Pour une autohistoire amérindienne*, 3 and passim. Sioui, a Huron-Wendat, is the first aboriginal Canadian to have earned a doctorate in history in Canada.

47. The account of mourning war in Richter, *Ordeal*, 32–37, is excellent. Also helpful are Fenton, *The Great Law and the Longhouse*, 259–61, and Snow, *The Iroquois*, 109–11.

cannibalism. Given this widespread feeling, it is natural to feel horror at the rituals involved in "requickening." This reader feels it himself. However, the historian Georges E. Sioui, an aboriginal Canadian, would have us view these rituals as the actions of people who believed in the Holy Circle of life as well as in the dignity of the human person, but who were trying to defend their peoples and cultures against catastrophic population loss to European diseases and to the encroachment of European traders, soldiers, missionaries, and settlers.[48] This reader is not persuaded by the details of Sioui's argument but believes understanding, not disgust, is owed to the ancient Iroquoian peoples.

A Preliminary Note on Ossenrenon

The first or easternmost Mohawk village or castle[49] on the Mohawk River, where St. Isaac Jogues, St. René Goupil, Guillaume Coûture, and their Huron companions were taken after their capture in 1642, has been called Ossernenon since Philippe Alegambe (1592–1652), SJ, published a transcription of St. Isaac's "Epistola P. Isaaci ad Prouincialem Francia [*sic*]" in his *Mortes Illustres et Gesta Eorum de Societate Iesu*, printed at Rome by the Typographia Varesii in three continuously paginated volumes dated 1657, 1659, and 1660.[50] St. Isaac's epistle is in the third volume on pages 619–32. On page 624, line 55, one reads "Ossernenon," and on page 625, line 1, one reads "Ossenreron." Neither spelling is correct.

One cannot now check the spelling of Alegambe's book against the original manuscript. During the sixteenth and seventeenth centuries, English printers usually destroyed the manuscripts

48. Sioui, *Pour une autohistoire amérindienne*, 57–80.

49. "Castle" is a traditional English designation of a principal Mohawk village, usually surrounded with a palisade. Unfortified hamlets and annual fishing and fowling camps were associated with the castles. Hunting camps were established anew each winter, and were located far from the castles.

50. The date of the third volume is given as "MDCXL," but given the dates printed in the other volumes, this is clearly a mistake for MDCLX.

from which their compositors set the type.[51] One presumes this was true in France as well. At any rate, only one manuscript of St. Isaac's epistle seems still to exist, which bears no indications that it was used by a compositor or pressman.[52]

This manuscript, entitled "Epistola Patris Isaaci Jogues in noua Francia inter Iroheos captiui ad Prouincialem Franciȩ," is found today in the Archives françaises de la Compagnie de Jésus in Vanves, France, in the Collection du Père Prat, SJ. It is PraA9, folios 361–92. On folio 373, one finds the passage transcribed in Alegambe's *Mortes Illustres* on pages 624 and 625. The handwriting in PraA9 is a simple, legible, seventeenth-century semi-cursive in the humanistic and *italienne* tradition.[53] The minuscule vowels are all much like those in modern italics, as are the *n* and the *r*. Few abbreviations are used, and only an occasional tilde.

In this manuscript, the name of the first Mohawk castle is spelled "Ossenrenon" in both places where it occurs, on folio 373 at lines 6 and 13. The reader may verify this claim by looking at the reproduction of this folio in the frontispiece.

The spelling "Ossernenon" in Father Alegambe's publication

51. I base this statement on observations made on the printing history of Richard Hooker's *Laws*. Books I–IV were published in 1594, Book V in 1597, and Books VI–VIII in 1648, well after Hooker's death in 1600. Only one printer's copy survives of the texts of all these books, that for Book V. "As such, it is one of a handful of Elizabethan manuscripts to have gone through the printing house and survived." See Hooker, *Of the Laws of Ecclesiastical Polity*, xv. Given the loss of the printer's copies of Books VI–VIII, it appears that the practice of discarding the printer's copy continued well into the seventeenth century in England, and one assumes in France, too. Cf. Reynolds and Wilson, *Scribes and Scholars*, 139 and 40: "It should be remembered … that the humanists also had a capacity for losing texts … Nor does the situation appear to have been much better in the sixteenth century. Manuscripts were often treated with scant respect by the printers to whom they had been entrusted and faced an uncertain future when they had served their purpose. There were some sad casualties."

52. On printer's markings in printer's copies, cf. Hooker, *Of the Laws of Ecclesiastical Polity*, xxiv: "The use of the Pullen manuscript as printer's copy for the first edition of 1597 is evident from the printer's markings in the margins for signature and page and in the text for page breaks."

53. See Buat and Van den Neste, *Manuel de paléographie française*, 45.

most probably resulted from a compositor's transposition of the *nr* group to *rn*, an easy transposition to make. The spelling "Ossenreron," which is so very close to the spelling of the name in PraA9, could have come from a misreading of the second *n* in Ossenrenon as *r*. An *n* with a short second leg (or minim), which makes the letter look like an *r*, can be seen in PraA9 on folio 372, on the second line in the word *remitterent*.

Therefore St. Isaac's spelling of this village name was quite clearly "Ossenrenon." This spelling will be used in the text of this book, except in quotations of sources that use the spelling "Ossernenon." St. Isaac's spelling of the other two Mohawk castles in PraA9, Andagaron and Theonontougen, will also be used.

One only wonders why Fr. Lucien Campeau, who transcribed this very manuscript and published it for the first time,[54] still spelled the name Ossernenon in each occurrence. It may be that his eye, like mine at first, refused to read anything but the traditional spelling.

54. *MNF* 5.607.

CHAPTER 1

Background on the Lives of Saints René Goupil, Isaac Jogues, Jean de Lalande, and Catherine Tekakwitha

THE JESUIT MISSION to the Iroquois began by accident. Although the Jesuit missionaries in New France had dreamed of carrying the Gospel to the Five Nations of the Iroquois League, a constant state of warfare and predation had prevented the fulfillment of this dream. In 1642, however, Fr. Isaac Jogues, SJ, two lay associates, and several Huron Catholics were captured by a Mohawk war party and taken to the Mohawk castle named Ossenrenon on the Mohawk River. This was the inauspicious and accidental beginning of the Jesuit mission to the Iroquois.

Since the 1880s, Catholics have believed that Ossenrenon stood a musket shot east of the little town of Auriesville, New York. Over the years, an impressive shrine was erected at the supposed site for the Jesuit martyrs and for the Mohawk saint, Catherine Tekakwitha, who was thought to have been born there. Moreover, Catholics believed that St. Catherine Tekakwitha was catechized and baptized in a village named Caughnawaga at what is now the St. Kateri National Shrine and Historic Site in Fonda, New York, and an impressive shrine developed there, too. Twentieth-century archeology, however, has undermined the claims of Catholic tradition for Auriesville and for Fonda. This book contains an examination of these competing claims.

The events and places investigated in this book have a historical background. If they are to be understood adequately, that background must be supplied. Moreover, not every reader will know the basic facts of the martyrdoms and of St. Catherine's life. These must be given, too. Here, then, in a brief and selective narrative, is the most necessary information.[1] An effort has been made to avoid controversial designations of places, to be noncommittal. At the end of the book, the story of the saints will be told again in brief with the results of our investigations incorporated into the narrative.

Normans, Bretons, Basques, and Portuguese were fishing for cod from the shores of Newfoundland in 1497, shortly after the discovery of North America. Jacques Cartier (1491–1557) explored the Gulf of St. Lawrence, the Bay of Chaleur, and the St. Lawrence River in three voyages between 1534 and 1542, and the French fishery soon extended throughout these seas. Around the middle of the century, these fishermen learned to trade with Native Americans for furs and became an early conduit by which European trade goods reached Native Americans. They were also a conduit for European diseases.[2]

French merchants in 1600 established a station at Tadoussac, on the north bank of the lower St. Lawrence River at the mouth

1. The narrative is derived from Bradley, *Onondaga and Empire*; Grumet, *Historic Contact*; Innes, *Cod Fisheries*; Lenig, "Patterns of Material Culture"; Provencher, *Chronologie du Québec depuis 1534*; Richter, *Ordeal of the Longhouse*; Talbot, *Saint among Savages*; and Greer, *Mohawk Saint*, unless otherwise noted.

2. On the introduction of disease through these contacts, see Sioui, *Pour une autohistoire amérindienne*, 59–62.

of the Saguenay River, to trade for furs with the Montagnais, a nomadic people living north of the St. Lawrence, and with other Native peoples. In 1604, the settlement of Port-Royal was established in Acadia on the Bay of Fundy near the present town of Annapolis Royal, Nova Scotia. The first Jesuit missionaries to the aboriginal peoples of New France came to Port-Royal in 1611.

Meanwhile, on 3 July 1608, Samuel de Champlain (1567–1635) had established Quebec City, at the head of navigation for large seagoing vessels on the St. Lawrence River. In 1609, Champlain entered into an alliance with the Huron or Wendat people, a great agricultural and trading nation located between Lake Simcoe and the Georgian Bay in what is now the Province of Ontario. In 1611, he discovered Lake Champlain (for Europeans) and fought a portentous battle with the Iroquois. Champlain visited Huronia in 1615, taking the route that the Jesuits would later take: up the Ottawa River to the Mattawa River, then the length of Lake Nipissing and down the French River to Georgian Bay.

Five Jesuit missionaries came to Quebec in 1625, including St. Jean de Brébeuf (1593–1649). Brébeuf went to Huronia the following year. Brébeuf and the other Jesuits (and Récollets) were deported to France in 1629, when the English captured Quebec and held it briefly. By 1634, however, Brébeuf was back in Huronia.

For thousands of years, aboriginal bands had summered at what is now called Trois-Rivières, on the north bank of the St. Lawrence about halfway between the future cities of Quebec and Montreal. The Algonquin, Montagnais, and Huron had traded there with the French during the early seventeenth century. The Algonquin, some of whom were sedentary, lived on the Ottawa River and north of the upper St. Lawrence. In 1634, the French established a trading post at Trois-Rivières. In 1636, St. Isaac Jogues (1607–46) arrived in New France and was sent to Huronia. The Ursuline Order established a seminary for girls, including aboriginals, in Quebec in 1639, and Ville-Marie or Montreal was established by a pious sodality of French men and women on Montreal Island in 1642.

Meanwhile, the Dutch, a Protestant people, had founded the colony of New Netherland (in Latin *Novum Belgium*) in 1614 on the coasts of what are now the mid-Atlantic states, and up the Hudson River to the present Albany. At the latter place were founded the village of Rensselaerswyck and Fort Orange. In 1628, the Mohawk, the easternmost nation of the Iroquois League of Peace, having conquered their competitors the Mahicans, became the major fur-trading partner of the Dutch, and in 1639 the Dutch began trading harquebuses to their Native partner. Since the French did not at that time permit the trading of firearms to their Indian allies, this new development gave a great military advantage to the Mohawk and the other Iroquois nations: the Oneida, Onondaga, Cayuga, and Seneca, from east to west.

And so began the Beaver Wars, which ran intermittently from 1638 to 1701. On one side were the Dutch and their Iroquois allies. After the English took the Dutch colony for good in 1674, they entered into a similar alliance with the Iroquois. On the other side were the French and their Huron, Algonquin, and Montagnais allies. At stake for the European governments and merchant companies was the lucrative trade in beaver pelts, along with international prestige and power. At stake for the aboriginal peoples were not only the trade in European goods, but also the settlement of national animosities, the capture of slaves, the "requickening" of the dead, and the prestige of individual warriors. At stake for the Jesuits was the salvation of souls: of those of the aboriginals by conversion and baptism, of their own by heroic self-sacrifice in God's service, even martyrdom. Some historians see the Beaver Wars as chiefly commercial wars. Others see them as primarily mourning wars. Dr. Georges Sioui sees them as an attempt at aboriginal self-preservation by the Iroquois League.[3]

3. Sioui, *Pour une autohistoire amérindienne*, 57–66, reviews the theories on the

In the spring of 1642, St. Isaac Jogues went as a volunteer from the Jesuit mission in Huronia to Quebec City, the capital of New France, with a party of mainly Catholic Huron traders. The journey was predicted to be dangerous because the Iroquois had gone to war again against the French and their allies the previous year. St. Isaac carried his superior's annual report, and he intended to bring back supplies on his return trip in the summer. The Hurons meant to trade beaver pelts for French goods. The journey to Quebec went well.

On 28 July, St. Isaac and his party left Quebec in twelve canoes for Trois-Rivières via the St. Lawrence River. René Goupil (1608–42) went with him as surgeon for the Huron Mission. St. René was a *donné*, a skilled worker under contract to the Jesuits. The contract required a religious commitment of the workman. Guillaume Coûture (1617–1701), a brave man of many parts, also accompanied the party as a *donné*. A Huron girl named Thérèse headed home with her relations from the Ursuline Seminary in Quebec. On 30 July, they beached their canoes at Trois-Rivières.

Early in the morning on 1 August, St. Isaac said the Mass of St. Peter in Chains. St. Isaac and his companions then pushed off from Trois-Rivières, and paddled upriver into Lac Saint-Pierre, a widening of the St. Lawrence itself, where they landed and spent the night.

Despite signs of an Iroquois war party, they continued up Lac Saint-Pierre on 2 August to the islands at its head. There, threading the narrow channels, they were set upon, captured, and tortured by Mohawk warriors. The Mohawk, with their captives and booty, paddled across the St. Lawrence to the mouth of the Richelieu River, known then as the River of the Iroquois, where they

causes of the Beaver Wars and presents his own theory. Richter, *Ordeal of the Longhouse*, 65, argues that while economics was one cause of the Beaver Wars, demographic collapse was the major cause, so that the Beaver Wars were primarily mourning wars and secondarily economic wars.

camped for the night. The next day the party began making its way south up the Richelieu toward the foot of Lake Champlain. They entered Lake Champlain 6 August. Three days later they encountered a party of two hundred Iroquois warriors heading north on the lake. The captives were tortured by all these warriors on Jogues Island, a little south of today's Westport, New York. On 11 August, the party reached the head of Lake Champlain and began the overland march to Ossenrenon, the first castle of the Mohawk.

The party reached Ossenrenon on 14 August, and the captives were "welcomed" both with informal violence and with the more organized running of the gauntlet. It was the Vigil of the Assumption of the Blessed Mother. Torture was semicontinuous over the next two days. During the day, the captives were held on a platform or stage in the middle of the village, where they were tortured by all and sundry. At night the prisoners were pegged down on the ground in the various longhouses, and the children tormented them with live coals from the fires. On 17 August, the captives were marched to Andagaron, the second castle, and compelled to run the gauntlet again. Again, the torture continued almost constantly over the following days. Two days later, the captives were marched to Theonontougen, the third of the principal Mohawk villages. They were spared running the gauntlet this time, as it was feared that they would not survive. Otherwise, the torture was ongoing over the next couple of days.

On 21 August, the captives were marched back to Andagaron, where their fates were deliberated and decided by the Mohawk leaders in council. St. Isaac and St. René were sent back to Ossenrenon on 23 August, though they were not awarded as slaves to any particular families. Guillaume Coûture was sent to Theonontougen as a family slave. Among the Huron captives, only Eustace Ahatsistari, a great war chief, Stephen, and Paul Ononchouraton were sentenced to death. All were notable Catholics. One was allotted to each of the castles for more torture, for sacrifice, and for ritualized cannibal consumption. At Ossenrenon, St. Isaac was lodged with a powerful matron who grew to admire him and to think of him as a nephew. He reciprocated by calling her aunt.

On the Feast of St. Michael the Archangel, 29 September, the martyrdom of St. René Goupil occurred at Ossenrenon, where the members of the Bear clan hated the French and Catholicism. St. René had made the sign of the Cross on a child's forehead. The child's grandfather was frightened and furious. He sent two young warriors of his clan to kill St. René. They found him as he returned to the village with St. Isaac from prayer on a nearby hill. They split his skull, stripped his body, and dragged it through the village and down a ravine. At last, they cast his body into a creek. The next day, St. Isaac found St. René's naked body where the youths had abandoned it. The dogs and birds had already been at it. He concealed the body in the creek with stones.

The following day, although St. Isaac wished to descend again to the creek to bury St. René's body properly, his adoptive aunt sent him out to her plot in the surrounding fields to protect him from the Francophobes in the village. A heavy rain fell that night. On 2 October, St. Isaac descended surreptitiously into the ravine. He could not find St. René's body, though he searched diligently in difficult conditions. He was told mendaciously that youths had dragged the body to a faraway stream, which he had never heard of.

St. Isaac passed the winter of 1642–43 in a hunting camp, possibly in the Adirondacks. Back in the village in early March, St. Isaac was told where St. René's remaining bones were. He found them, offered prayers, and concealed them. In August, St. Isaac was at a fishing camp on the Hudson River with his aunt. She naively permitted a small party of young warriors to take him back to Ossenrenon. Along the way, he learned that he would be executed when they reached the village. He escaped to the Dutch, who hid him during August and September at Rensselaerswyck and Fort

Orange. On 5 August, St. Isaac wrote his letter to Fr. Jean Filleau, the provincial in France (Document 1). The Dutch Reformed clergyman Johannes Megapolensis (1603–70) was instrumental in his escape, even debating the ethical question with him. The barber-surgeon Harman Meyndertsz van den Bogaert (ca. 1612 to ca. 1648) tended his wounds. Finally, he escaped down the Hudson River on a Dutch sloop. On 25 December, St. Isaac landed in France. It was Christmas Day, and he made his confession and heard Mass for the first time in many months.

On 28 April 1644, Fr. Francesco Gioseppe Bressani (1612–72) was captured by the Mohawk on Lac Saint-Pierre. He was taken to Ossenrenon, where he was tortured and given to an old woman as a slave. In November 1644, Fr. Bressani, having proved a useless slave, was traded by his mistress to the Dutch. He returned to France and then to New France the following year.

In the first week of May 1644, St. Isaac sailed from La Rochelle for New France, having received a papal dispensation to say Mass with maimed hands. In late June, he reached Tadoussac and Quebec. During the first week of July, he sailed to Montreal, where he was now stationed until spring 1646. Fr. Jacques Buteux (1600–1652) was his colleague during the winter of 1644–45. Both Fr. Jérôme Lalemant (1593–1673) and Fr. Buteux talked about his captivity with St. Isaac during this period, and what they learned was included in later writings (Documents 4 and 5).

On 12–14 July 1645, the governor of New France, Charles Huault de Montmagny (1601–54), held a peace conference at Trois-Rivières with representatives of the Mohawk, Huron, and Algonquin nations. Fr. Jogues was present, as was Honatteniate, son of his adoptive aunt.

In the spring of 1646, St. Isaac composed his "Le Martyre de Renè Goupil par les Iroquois" (Document 3), probably at Montreal. A peace council was held over 7–13 May by Governor Montmagny with representatives of the Mohawk, Algonquin,

Montagnais, and Huron nations. A peace treaty was made, including the French, Algonquin, and Mohawk. St. Isaac, Jean Bourdon (1601–68)—an engineer, surveyor, and important figure in the colony—and two Algonquin chiefs were chosen as ambassadors to the Mohawks to formalize the treaty.

The ambassadors departed from Trois-Rivières for Iroquoia by canoe 16 May. On 20 May, the party of ambassadors celebrated the Feast of Pentecost at the mouth of the Richelieu River at the ruins of the French fort there, Fort Richelieu. On 27 May, they camped on Jogues Island, and on 28 May, they made the Ticonderoga portage and began paddling up what is now called Lake George. Two days later, they reached the head of the lake. It was the Feast of Corpus Christi. St. Isaac named the lake, hitherto unknown to Europeans, Lac du Saint-Sacrement. On 1 June, they reached a Mohawk fishing camp on Saratoga Lake. St. Isaac encountered Thérèse, the Huron school girl who was captured with him in 1642. She was now 17 years old and married, but she still said her Rosary.

The next day, they departed in borrowed canoes for the Hudson River. On 4 June, they reached Rensselaerswyck, and two days later departed for Ossenrenon. On 8 June, they landed at the first Iroquois village, "Oneugi8ré, jadis Osserrion," which translates to "Oneugiouré, formerly Osserrion."[4] People came from far and wide to welcome them. A council was held with the ambassadors by Mohawk chiefs and elders on 10–12 June. At the end of the negotiations, St. Isaac displayed a small coffer containing kit for Mass that he intended to leave behind as a pledge of his intention to return. The chest caused much concern, for many suspected it

4. We shall see later that "Osserrion" is a misreading of "Ossenrenon." Note too that seventeenth-century French orthography contained a ligature which stood for the diphthong "ou." In this book it occurs only in the Mohawk name Oneugi8ré, but this name occurs frequently in some of the original texts. Following current French book-making practice, I have represented this ligature with the numeral "8," which resembles the ligature closely.

contained a devil. During the next two days, St. Isaac was busy with pastoral work among the Mohawk and the Huron slaves of the Mohawk.

The ambassadors departed for home on 16 June. On 27 June, they reached the mouth of the Richelieu, and two days later, they reached Trois-Rivières. On 3 July, they reached Quebec City, where they were debriefed by the governor. M. Bourdon produced a map of their route.[5]

St. Isaac completed his *Novum Belgium*, an account of the Dutch colony, on 3 August 1646 at Trois-Rivières, where he was spending a few days. He then returned to Montreal, where on 12 September he wrote his letter to Fr. André Castillon (Document 6).

On 17 September, Governor Montmagny convened a council at Trois-Rivières with a number of Huron chiefs. They agreed to join the peace with the Mohawk, and to send an embassy to them. On 19 September, St. Isaac reached Trois-Rivières and agreed to accompany the Huron ambassadors. However, while on the last embassy he had consented to go in mufti to avoid stirring up Mohawk religious sentiment, this time he agreed to go only if he could wear his habit.

Before departure, St. Isaac picked a young *donné* from Dieppe, France, named Jean de Lalande (1615–46), to accompany him. St. Jean was a skilled woodsman, and the ideal companion for the missionary. On 24 September, St. Isaac, St. Jean, the Huron ambassadors, and some Mohawks departed from Trois-Rivières in three canoes. On 25 September, they reached the ruins of Fort Richelieu, where they camped. Around the campfire that night, the Hurons expressed forebodings of Mohawk treachery. St. Isaac could not inspirit them with his reassurances. The next day, all but one Huron paddled off toward Huronia in one canoe. The Mohawks paddled off on an enterprise of their own in the second

5. St. Isaac also seems to have drawn a map of Iroquoia in 1644. See *MNF* 6.529–36.

craft. St. Isaac, St. Jean, and the lone Huron, named Otrihouré, began their long journey up the Richelieu and Lake Champlain by themselves. They took the Ticonderoga portage, paddled up Lake George, and, leaving their canoe, continued overland toward Ossenrenon-Oneugiouré.

Near the confluence of the Hudson River and the Sacandaga River on 14 October, the three men met a Mohawk war party quite unexpectedly, as the Mohawks were supposed to be at peace. The warriors, members of the Bear clan at Ossenrenon, seized, stripped, and beat the three men, and began driving them toward Ossenrenon-Oneugiouré. They reached the village on 17 October. It is plausible, as Father Talbot imagines, that the prisoners were rescued from their captors by St. Isaac's aunt and lodged in her longhouse. At any rate, a council was called at Theonontougen to discuss what to do with the prisoners.

The events of 18–19 October unfolded rapidly. The Theonontougen council voted to spare the prisoners to avoid conflict with the French. In the evening, however, a Bear clan warrior invited St. Isaac to a feast in a Bear longhouse. As St. Isaac entered the porch of the dwelling, he was ambushed by a hidden assassin, and struck dead with a hatchet. A warrior—Honatteniate, Fr. Talbot suggests, the son of St. Isaac's aunt—was wounded trying to protect him. The same warrior tried to keep St. Jean from harm, probably by returning to the longhouse inhabited by St. Isaac's aunt's, and compelling Jean to stay there. At some point during the night, St. Jean, "slipping away," the warrior later said, "to look for I don't know what that he had brought, was felled by a blow of a hatchet, by those who were spying on him." The bodies of the saints were beheaded, the heads mounted on poles at the gate of the village, and the bodies thrown into the river. As to Otrihouré, one account reports that he was killed at Ossenrenon-Oneugiouré. Another says he was sent back with messages to New France but was killed on the journey.

During the 1640s, the Iroquois League began to focus its violence on its Native rivals, especially on the Huron. The Iroquois destroyed the Huron Confederacy and scattered its peoples in a process that ended in 1649. In that year, they also destroyed the Jesuit mission in Huronia, killing St. Jean de Brébeuf, St. Gabriel Lalemant (1610–49), St. Noël Chabanel (1613–49), and St. Charles Garnier (1606–49). St. Antoine Daniel (1601–48) had been martyred the year before. An uneasy peace reigned between the Iroquois and the French from 1653 to 1658, while the Iroquois mopped up their other rivals.

Fr. Bressani, having returned to Italy, published his *Breve Relatione d'alcvne missioni de' PP. della Compagnia di Giesù nella Nuoua Francia* (Document 2) in 1653. In 1656, St. Catherine Tekakwitha was born in Ossenrenon-Oneugiouré.[6] About 1659, Catherine's community built a new castle, which they named Gandaouagué. During 1661–63, a smallpox epidemic raged in Iroquoia and struck St. Catherine's village. Her mother and brother, and possibly her father, died. She was scarred for life, and her eyesight was damaged.

With the temporary capture of New Netherland by the English in the Second Anglo-Dutch War (1665–67), the trading relationship with the Dutch was disrupted for the Iroquois. In addition, the four western nations of the Iroquois League were embroiled in a life-or-death war with the Pennsylvania nation of the Susquehannocks. Therefore the western Iroquois nations negotiated a peace with the French in 1665, which was confirmed in 1666. The Mohawk were not party to the treaty. In September 1666, the French under the Seigneur de Tracy (1596–1670) invaded Mohawk territory and destroyed St. Catherine's castle, as well as the other fortified Mohawk towns. The Mohawks rebuilt north

6. See in this volume chap. 4, "Archeologists' Arguments against the Martyrdoms of St. Isaac and St. Jean at the Bauder Site, with Rebuttals."

of the Mohawk River. Catherine's new village was also called Gandaouagué.

The Mohawks made peace in 1667 and accepted Jesuit missionaries into their villages. An intense missionary effort began throughout Iroquoia. But the animosity of the Francophobes and traditionalists caused a steady stream of Catholic Iroquois of all five nations to begin a migration north to New France.

In 1667, too, the Jesuits encouraged French pioneers to settle on property belonging to the order at La Prairie-de-la-Magdeleine, across the river from Montreal. Moreover, the Jesuits permitted the settlement of seven Catholic Oneidas, who "laid the foundations of the whole mission of St. Francois Xavier" ("jetterent les fondements de toute la mission de St. francois Xavier").[7] The Christian Indian village that grew there was called Kentake.

By 1672, the Mohawk had become the most numerous of the nations at Kentake, and among them, the most numerous were former residents of Gandaouagué, where the Jesuit mission had been very successful.[8] In 1673, the Mohawk, Onondaga, and Huron, the most multitudinous nations in Kentake, were at loggerheads. The Jesuits arranged councils of the three nations to elect a chief for each. This probably was meant to complement or replace the current system of two chiefs elected at large for the whole village. The Hurons felt slighted during the procedure and left the village. They reestablished themselves across the river.[9] In July 1676, in the second year of an extreme "poverty," the St. François-Xavier Mission was reestablished on Jesuit property upriver from La Prairie at the Sault Saint-Louis or Lachine Rapids across from Montreal Island. The village established there was named Kahnawake, often called the Sault.

The same year, St. Catherine was baptized on Easter Day at

7. Chauchetière, "Narration annuelle," 150.

8. Chauchetière, "Narration annuelle," 168–69.

9. Chauchetière, "Narration annuelle," 162–63, 180–81.

Gandaouagué by Fr. Jacques de Lamberville (1641–1710), the Jesuit missionary in the village. In 1677, St. Catherine emigrated, or rather fled, to Kahnawake with the encouragement of Father Lamberville. The Sault would remain her home for the rest of her short life. The Jesuit missionaries Claude Chauchetière (1645–1709) and Pierre Cholenec (1641–1723) were her pastors and confessors at the Sault, and later wrote the first biographies of the saint.[10]

On 17 April 1680, St. Catherine died. As she expired, her countenance was healed of its smallpox scars. Fr. Chauchetière was convinced of her sainthood at her deathbed. Miracles were attributed to her almost immediately.

10. See in this volume chap. 5, "The Locations Where St. Catherine Tekakwitha Lived in the Mohawk Valley."

CHAPTER 2

Evidence for Auriesville as the Site of the Martyrdoms with Initial Observations

THE SITE of Our Lady of Martyrs Shrine in Auriesville, Montgomery County, New York, was identified as the location of the Mohawk village of Ossenrenon in 1881 by General John S. Clark (1823–1912), a Union veteran of the Civil War. Thus originated the National Shrine of the North American Martyrs and Birthplace of St. Kateri Tekakwitha, the full name of the shrine.

The story of Gen. Clark's identification of the site is told by Thomas Egan, SJ, from unpublished letters between Clark and the Catholic historian John Gilmary Shea (1824–92) deposited in the archives at the Auriesville Shrine.[1] Fr. Egan describes Clark's 1877 discovery of the site of Gandaouagué on the west bank of Cayadutta Creek in Fonda, New York, on the north side of the Mohawk River, the site of the present St. Kateri National Shrine and Historic Center, as well as his discovery, as he thought, of the site of Theonontougen "on the north bank [of the Mohawk]

1. Egan, "The General and the Professor."

a little to the west of Fort Plain."[2] That same year, Clark also speculated to Shea that the location of Ossenrenon, the site of the martyrdoms, was only a mile or so upstream on the Cayadutta.[3]

Shea encouraged Clark to study several seventeenth-century maps of the Mohawk Valley, including one in the 1660 *Jesuit Relations*, that placed the three major Mohawk villages on the south side of the Mohawk River. "Finally," says Fr. Egan, "a map attributed to Joliet [*sic*] in 1673 … showed a village in the angle formed by the Schoharie Creek as it flows into the Mohawk from the south."[4] His enthusiasm stirred by these maps, Clark returned to the Mohawk Valley in November 1881. In a letter written to Shea, Clark reported that he made this exploration of the south bank of the Mohawk "in the company of Samuel D. Frey of Palatine Bridge, who is greatly interested in anything relating to Jogues."[5]

Frey also left an account of this expedition. As it has not been published, we shall base our account of the exploration on his report. The report exists in an unsigned account dated 22 November 1881. A photocopy of this twelve-page document, written in a nineteenth-century hand, is held in the Montgomery County Department of History and Archives. Its identification number is HF 14-A-5, its cataloging title "Work with Gen. Clark re: 3 Towns." The pages were photocopied out of order. (I penciled in

2. Egan, "The General and the Professor," 2.

3. Egan, "The General and the Professor," 3.

4. Egan, "The General and the Professor," 3.

5. Egan, "The General and the Professor," 3. Even on this evidence alone, it is certain that Clark's companion was Samuel Ludlow Frey of Palatine Bridge, a noted collector of Mohawk relics. Egan probably read Clark's majuscule *L* as a *D*. Moreover, Lenig, Auriesville Shrine I," fig. 2, reproduces notes of Clark's that clearly mention "Mr. S. L. Frey." On Frey (1833–1924), see Snow, *Mohawk Valley Archaeology: Collections*, 29–35. Lenig, "Auriesville I," 2, mentions that Adelbert G. Richmond (d. 1899), a banker in Canajoharie and a fellow collector and close friend of Frey's, accompanied Clark and Frey on this expedition. (On Richmond, see Snow, *Mohawk Valley Archaeology: Collections*, 119–27.) This is correct, if one notes as done below, that Frey went with Clark on the first day of exploration, and Richmond on the second.

the page numbers on the archives' copy for ease of study for myself and others.) No information on the provenance of the document was available when I was reading it at the archives in August 2021, but comparison with Egan's account of the expedition and quotations from Clark's letter to Shea make the identification certain. Moreover, in 2022, I was able to compare the hand in this document with examples of Frey's hand in the Montgomery County Department of History and Archives Archival Collection file entitled "Frey Correspondence." The file contains many letters to Frey as well as a number of unsigned notes on historical subjects in the same hand as seen in HF 14-A-5. The majuscule *V*, *S*, and *W* are quite distinctive. These notes can only be notes by Frey himself. Unfortunately, the original of HF 14-A-5 was not included.

Frey, Gen. Clark's host in Palatine Bridge in late November 1881, indicated that while all interested in the Mohawks at that time, including Clark, supposed that the Mohawk towns were north of the Mohawk River in 1642, Clark had come upon a map in the *Jesuit Relations* on 3 January 1881 that showed the towns on the river's south side. He now wanted to locate them, with Frey's help.

Certain details in St. Isaac's account of St. Rene's martyrdom led Gen. Clark "to believe that we shd be able to find the 1st town at least without much trouble" (p. 4). Frey mentioned these details: (1) the village was located at "the top of a hill"; (2) it was "5 or 6 miles from Andagoron [*sic*]"; (3) a nearby hill "commands the town," the hill where he and St. René went to pray the day of the latter's murder; (4) a ravine existed "at a considerable distance" where St. René's body was thrown; (5) a stream flowed through the ravine, in which St. Isaac tried to hide the body; (6) there was "quite a distant river"; (7) or a river "a quarter of a league away," of which St. Isaac was ignorant; and (8) a "torrent ran" at the foot of the town" (pp. 3–4).

Numbers 1–2 are found in Document 2, Fr. Bressani's "Lettera del P. Isaac Jogues al P. Prouinciale della Prouincia di Francia." Numbers 3–6 are found in Document 1, "Epistola Patris Isaaci Jogues in Nova Francia inter Irohaeos captivi ad Provincialem Franciae." Numbers 7–8 are found in Document 3, St. Isaac's "Le martyre de René Goupil par les Iroquois."

At Auriesville, Clark and his associate found a site that seemed to fit these details (Figure 1). In Frey's words,

> We took the [railroad] cars [from Palatine Bridge] at 8 a.m. and went to Tribes Hill, crossed the suspension bridge to Fort Hunter … We then walked up the tow path [of the Erie Canal] to a point a little east of Auriesville where we crossed the canal, where we met a man, Mr D. A. Quackenbush[6] … he knew something about Indian relics and told us that considerable quantities of beads &c had been found exactly at the point where we were on the top of the hill. We went up this hill rising probably 150 ft above the river. and in a few minutes decided that we were precisely on the site of the ancient Indian town of Ossernenon. (4–5)

Clark's notes indicate that he and his companion determined that the western part of the shrine plateau where the gift shop and parking lot now stand was the site of Ossenrenon. The eastern portion of this land was then "covered with a most luxuriant growth of wheat."[7] This is the site of what archeologists call Auriesville #1 (Figure 2). Clark also noticed that "relics have been found both east and west of the road" (Noeltner Road or CR-164). East of the road is the site of what is now known as Auriesville #2 (Figure 3). Excavations of Auriesville #1 in 1950 by J. Franklin Ewing, SJ, of Fordham University uncovered little. Of Auriesville #1, Wayne

6. David A. Quackenbush of Auriesville, as Clark states in his notes as reproduced by Lenig in his communication mentioned in note 5 above. This meeting could have been arranged beforehand or could have occurred by chance at Mr. Polheimus's local store, where Indian relics could be purchased. See Lenig, "Auriesville I," 2; "Auriesville II," 1–2.

7. Lenig, "Auriesville I," fig. 2.

Lenig concludes, "Probable multi-component prehistoric campsite based on Ewing's finds of a hearth and single biface [chert blade] as well as sporadic documented finds of debitage, chipped and ground stone tools in other collections. No European artifacts are documented in this locus."[8]

Clark and Frey explored Auriesville #1 and Auriesville #2, climbed the hill south of Auriesville #2 (Figure 4), and followed a tiny brook (Figures 5 and 6) down into the nearby ravine to a larger creek (Figures 7 and 8). Clark and Frey then continued up the towpath to Yatesville (now Randall), "which we reached about four o clock. having walked about 15 miles." There they crossed the Mohawk "to the depot at Yosts in a row boat, and reached home about 8 o clock" (9). On their way west along the towpath, they identified the site, as they thought, of the second or middle village, Andagaron, on Mr. Wormuth's farm about three miles west of Fultonville (8).[9] The following day, Frey being "busy," Richmond accompanied the general to "the site of the large town at Sprakers Basin which I had discovered in the fall of 1878. and which we concluded must be the 3rd castle site Teonontogen [*sic*]" (10).[10]

8. Lenig, "Auriesville I," 1.

9. A New York State historical marker used to stand on the south side of NY 5 South, about two miles west of Fultonville. I do not know the history behind this marker, or what has happened to it, but the description of the site in Frey's narrative says the Andagaron site lay three miles beyond Fultonville, which corresponds exactly with Clark's description of the site as being six miles from the Auriesville Site (Egan, "General," 5). Frey also says that the site was on a Mr. Wormuth's farm, which as we will see is the location of the archaeologists' Printup Site. Thus what Clark and Frey thought of as the Andagaron Site was at what is now called the Printup Site. See also note 10 below.

10. Egan, "The General and the Professor," 5, reproduces a map drawn by Clark to show the locations of the three Mohawk castles. Clark's Andagaron seems to be about halfway between Fultonville and Yatesville, today's Randall. This fits the location of Stone Ridge and the archeologists' Printup Site. His Theonontougen appears to be the Mitchell Site above Sprakers. Snow, *Mohawk Valley Archaeology: Sites*, 36, seems to be correct in his opinion that Clark identified the Printup Site as Andagaron (and the Milton Smith Site as Gandaouagué, on which more later). Snow notes, too, that Frey knew

Gen. Clark wrote Dr. Shea, "I have succeeded in determining beyond a reasonable doubt the sites of Ossernenon, Andagaron and Tionnontogen."[11]

Egan notes further that in June 1884, Clark returned to the valley and identified another village site "a mile west of Ossernenon on the west bank of Auries Creek where the Turtle Clan had an intermediate settlement from at least 1659 to 1666 between their stay at Ossernenon and their residence at Gandawague." After de Tracy's raid of 1666, Clark reckoned that the people of Gandaouagué rebuilt their village on the north side of the river above Cayadutta Creek.[12]

One admires Clark and his associates for their willingness to test a new theory with fieldwork and shoe leather. One also realizes that Mohawk Valley archeology was still in its infancy, and the study of beads and other artifacts had hardly been undertaken. Nevertheless, one marvels at the boldness of their conclusions on such a cursory survey of Mohawk sites and relics. At any rate, Joseph Loyzance, SJ (1820–97), a parish priest in Albany, New York, who was already saying annual Masses in Tribes Hill on the day of St. Isaac's martyrdom, welcomed Clark's conclusions,

---

the Mitchell Site well (375). Snow states that the Mitchell Site was occupied from 1646 to 1666 and was the second successor village to Rumrill-Naylor (more on this later). Apparently, the Rumrill-Naylor community moved to a location near Canajoharie (the Van Evera-McKinney Site) toward the end of the 1635–46 period and remained there only a short time (Snow, *Mohawk Valley Archaeology: Sites*, 322). If this is correct, then the castle at Printup was contemporary with the Mitchell castle. The Mitchell Site lies under NY-162 "just east of Flat Creek" (Snow, *Mohawk Valley Archaeology: Sites*, 375) on an uphill slope from the Flat Creek Ravine. The location is only around a half a mile from Rumrill-Naylor, so one wonders if the community dwelt in Canajoharie long enough for the fields and forests to regenerate around Rumrill-Naylor.

11. Egan, "The General and the Professor," 5.

12. Egan, "The General and the Professor," 5. See note 10 above for the identification of Gandaouagué with the Milton Smith Site. Loyzance reckoned that the people of Andagaron crossed the river and established themselves three miles west of Gandaouagué. See "Kateri Tegewitha." Roughly three miles west of Gandaouagué is what the archeologists now call the Fox Farm Site. See Snow, *Mohawk Valley Archaeology: Sites*, 415.

and in 1884 he was able to purchase the Auriesville Site, ten acres, where he built up the shrine as a pilgrimage center.[13]

In 1945, an article was published in the shrine's magazine, *The Auriesville Pilgrim,* under the title "How We Know: Auriesville Is Ossernenon."[14] The facts adduced are similar to Clark's.

First, it is argued, several contemporary maps and letters place the Mohawk villages south of the Mohawk River. One of the maps, Louis Jolliet's, shows Ossenrenon "in the angle between the Mohawk and Schoharie rivers, where Auriesville railway station is now."

Second, other evidence confirms this location south of the river. St. Isaac writes, "We arrived at a small river distant about a quarter of a league from the first Iroquois village" (Documents 4 and 5); "we reached a river which flows by their first village" (Document 2); and "On the other side of this river there were many Iroquois" (Document 5).

Third, Jogues writes, "They told me that the body [of St. René] had been dragged to a river a quarter of a league distant, with which I was not acquainted" (Document 3). This could only have been the Schoharie, as Jogues already knew of the Mohawk, the article asserts. Thus Ossenrenon had to have been on a hill between the junction of the Mohawk and the Schoharie. The hill at Auriesville, where Indian artifacts had been found abundantly, fits this description.

Fourth, several details found in Buteux's narrative (Docu-

13. Artur Melançon, SJ, archivist at St. Mary's College in Montreal (1918–41), resisted the identification of Ossenrenon with the Auriesville Site. The Jesuit Archives in Montreal contain an undated letter of Fr. Melançon to an unnamed fellow priest (the author of a "Vie de Catherine," influenced by the work of Ellen Walworth published in the 1890s). Melançon argues strenuously, if ineffectively in my view, for the location of Ossenrenon north of the Mohawk River on Cayadutta Creek, which enters the Mohawk at the present town of Fonda. See Jesuit Archives, BO-80-K, 17.

14. "How We Know," 10–11. I am indebted to Beth Lynch, the current shrine pilgrimage coordinator and museum manager, for PDFs of the pages of this article.

ment 5) support the identification of the Auriesville Site: a steep bank at the riverside; St. Isaac and his companions had difficulty in climbing this bank; St. René's body was found at the confluence of "a small watercourse with a rivulet," and the hill where Jogues and Goupil went to pray was an harquebus shot from the village. Fifth, precise distances are given between Ossenrenon and the other two Mohawk castles (Documents 1 and 2), where in fact villages have been found. Sixth, Indian relics have been "constantly found at Auriesville, especially in the excavations of 1930 and 1943."

Before examining the archeological evidence more carefully, one may make the following observations. Regarding the first point, while no dissent exists today about the location of the Mohawk villages at that time south of their eponymous river, no great weight can be placed on Jolliet's map, as seventeenth-century maps of the Mohawk Valley are unreliable.[15] Regarding the second point, only the third quotation seems to confirm the location of the villages on the Mohawk's south side, not that it matters to this argument. Regarding the third point, this argument has the form of begging the question or assuming the conclusion. The river unknown to Jogues could have been the Schoharie, only if one assumes that Ossenrenon was between the Mohawk and the Schoharie. Regarding the fourth, these details that fit the Auriesville Site may fit other sites, too, and better. Regarding the fifth, the existence of these Indian sites at certain distances from Auriesville will only support the claim that Auriesville is Ossenrenon, if they can be shown to have been the sites of Andagaron and Theonontougen. The argument is circular. Regarding the sixth, artifacts dug from the earth have to be analyzed

15. Snow, *Mohawk Valley Archaeology: Sites*, 362: "Van der Donck [who made a map of the valley in 1656] was probably using garbled and partly out-of-date data, a problem that is common on virtually all maps of the Mohawk Valley produced through the remainder of the century."

to determine the time and place of their origin, as well as their suitability to the place where they were discovered.

Which means we must attend more closely to the discoveries of archeology in the last half of the twentieth century. We must also closely read the documentary evidence.

CHAPTER 3

The Martyrdom of St. René Goupil at the Bauder Site

Archeological Evidence

THE Mohawk Valley Project was begun in 1980 as an archeological study of Native American prehistory and history in the Mohawk Valley. The study ended in 1995, and that year one of the initiators of the project, Dean R. Snow, published a two-volume compendium of the project's results, *Mohawk Valley Archaeology: The Collections*, and *Mohawk Valley Archaeology: The Sites*.[1] Auriesville is studied on pages 451–54 of the latter volume.

Snow confines his study to what he identifies as Auriesville #1 and Auriesville #3. As for Auriesville #2, which he identifies as a location on the shrine property adjacent to that which Gen. Clark identified as Ossenrenon, Snow observes cryptically that "this component probably does not exist except in the site file."[2]

1. See Lenig, *Prehistoric Mohawk Studies*, 3–8, for a history of the Mohawk Valley Project. The point of Lenig's book is to rectify mistakes regarding prehistoric Native American sites in the valley by the Mohawk Valley Project. Wayne Lenig is the son of Donald Lenig.

2. Snow, *Mohawk Valley Archaeology: Sites*, 36, 454.

According to Snow, Auriesville #1 is the site of a Mohawk village, while #3 is the site of an associated cemetery. Snow mentions excavations at "the Auriesville Shrine" in 1931, and at Auriesville #1 in 1950.[3] Auriesville #3 was excavated by Donald Lenig, he says, but Snow gives no date.[4] He remarks, "There are artifacts from this site in the Frey, Hartley, Mohawk-Caughnawaga Museum, Richmond, and Smithsonian collections."[5] As to the age of the site, Snow observes, "Glass beads, iron tools, copper alloy kettle fragments, and other key trade artifact types date the Auriesville Site to the first quarter of the eighteenth century." Again, "The Auriesville #1 site . . . was estimated to date to A.D. 1700–1712 by Donald Lenig."[6] Finally, as Snow says, "There is no surviving evidence of a palisade, houses, or features for either of the two loci."[7]

Wayne Lenig has called many elements of Snow's study of Auriesville into question. First, Auriesville #1 is prehistoric, according to artifacts found during Fr. Ewing's excavations of 1950. Second, Auriesville #2, Lenig says, is in the northwestern section of the Shrine grounds east of CR-164, between east-southeast and south-southeast of the first chapel's original location, where the Martyrs/Kateri Chapel now stands.[8] It was also partially excavated by Fr. Ewing. Third, Auriesville #3 has four components, some prehistoric, others eighteenth-century, none a cemetery.[9] Fourth, neither Donald Lenig nor Wayne Lenig ever worked on these

3. Snow, *Mohawk Valley Archaeology: Sites*, 453.

4. Snow, *Mohawk Valley Archaeology: Sites*, 453.

5. Snow, *Mohawk Valley Archaeology: Sites*, 451.

6. Snow, *Mohawk Valley Archaeology: Sites*, 451, 454.

7. Snow, *Mohawk Valley Archaeology: Sites*, 454.

8. The 1885 chapel has been moved south on the shrine grounds. The Martyrs/Kateri Chapel stands in its former location. This is shown by a comparison of an early picture of the 1885 chapel in Lynch, *Our Lady of Martyrs Shrine*, 12 and 13, and of the Grider sketch of the ditches/earthworks (mentioned in the next paragraph of the text above), with the map on the back cover of Lynch's book.

9. Lenig, "Auriesville III," 1.

sites.[10] Other errors will come to light if we look more closely at Auriesville #2.

Auriesville #2 is also called the Victor Putnam Site because a farmer of that name owned the land before the Jesuits. At some point prior to the purchase of the shrine grounds by the Jesuits, Putnam filled in an eighteenth-century cellar hole at the site. The cellar had belonged to a European-style Mohawk house. After the sale to the Jesuits, a Canajoharie "artist and antiquarian," Rufus A. Grider, discovered "ditches and earthworks" on the shrine plateau east of CR-164. They form an almost rectangular enclosure, the sides of which Grider and Putnam stepped off in 1888. Wayne Lenig reckons the enclosure contained about two-thirds of an acre of land. The northern earthwork of the enclosure extends east from the vicinity of the chapel about 175 feet (72 steps) to the eastern earthwork, and then beyond to the edge of a small ravine. The eastern earthwork extends south about 165 feet (68 steps), where it meets the southern earthwork. The southern side extends westward 175 feet (72 steps) to the western earthwork. It also extends eastward beyond the enclosure almost twice the length of the extension of the northern side. The western earthwork is about 151 feet long (61 steps). Grider drew a map of the earthworks "in order to record their size & that the fact may be perpetuated."[11]

Fr. Ewing came back to the Mohawk Valley in 1952 and excavated at Auriesville #2. He sought the palisade of Ossenrenon but found only post molds of houses. Post molds are discolored patches in the soil that indicate that house posts have rotted there. These molds were found outside the palisade, by which, it seems, he means the rectangular enclosure. Ewing says, "Work was suspended after we had found a large number of … posthole molds, but had not found the palisades … We … came to the conclusion that

10. Lenig, "Auriesville III," 5.

11. Lenig, "Auriesville II," 1–2, fig. 1. The cellar hole that Putnam filled in was in the northwest corner of the enclosure.

we had discovered the evidence of houses outside the palisade." He then surmises, "At this period of Mohawk history, it would seem, much of the town was outside the palisade."[12] While Ewing does not mention the ditches and earthworks in his 1953 article, he does seem to assume them in speaking of inside and outside the palisade. Moreover, newspaper articles cited by Lenig mention them explicitly and claim, "[It has been] commonly believed since the shrine has been in existence ... that these mounds represent the line of the once palisaded village to which the French missionaries were brought as prisoners."[13] In fact, the current Stations of the Cross pathway roughly follows the line of the earthworks.

Lenig reports that "early-to-mid 17th century" and eighteenth-century artifacts were discovered in this area of the shrine.[14] In addition, many "native-manufactured items" found on the shrine grounds "most likely originated with a proto-historic village or hamlet at the site."[15] Lenig concludes that Auriesville #2 contained three components: a sixteenth-century component (ca. 1560–1600), a seventeenth-century component ("the 1640–1655 era"), and an eighteenth-century component. Lenig speculates that the enclosure might have been associated with the middle component, while the post molds outside the enclosure might have belonged to the first component.[16]

What do we make of this evidence? It certainly muddies the clear waters of Snow's report by showing that seventeenth-century artifacts did exist at the Victor Putnam Site, as did post molds for Indian dwellings.[17] In fact, one wonders why shrine historians have not made anything of the 1952 excavations. They contain some promising evidence for the traditional account of

12. Ewing, "First Note," 390. Cited in Lenig, "Auriesville II," 5.
13. Lenig, "Auriesville II," 4.
14. Lenig, "Auriesville II," 1, 3–4.
15. Lenig, "Auriesville II," 5–6.
16. Lenig, "Auriesville II," 5–6.
17. Ewing, "First Note," 390, fig. 136.

Ossenrenon. One regrets that Fr. Ewing did not return to continue his work in 1953, as he intended.[18]

Nevertheless, Lenig does not believe that these Mohawk finds indicate that this was the site of Ossenrenon.[19] His reasons are that it appears to be "a small outlying village or hamlet," that other known sites fit better with "the limited historical record," and that "the geographic setting" does not fit written descriptions.[20] My own reasons are similar.

First, the archeological evidence we have, as Lenig says, suggests "a small outlying village or hamlet." Unfortunately, we do not know the number or the dimensions of the dwelling places discovered by Ewing. Second, the topography of the Bauder Site fits the written evidence much better. Third, the "limited historical record," insofar as it is documentary, will also be seen to support other sites than Auriesville. Fourth, the evidence of the ditches and earthworks is ambiguous. We do not know how deep and wide the former were, or how tall and wide the latter. Nor do we know whether the ditches were outside or inside the earthworks. If they were outside, they would have been defensive; if inside, ceremonial.

We do not know the height of the earthworks either, but for the sake of argument, let us assume that the earthworks were originally, say, six feet high, a decent height for a tall fence or a wall. We know that Native Americans were able to erect such structures, and even bigger ones. Indeed, the hunter-gatherers of what is now northeastern Louisiana constructed large mounds and earthworks for their mortuary practices 5,500 years ago. They dug mud from the river bottoms, carried it in baskets to the burial site, and heaped up the mud to enormous heights over successive generations of the dead laid there to rest. They probably used the same

18. Ewing, "First Note," 390.

19. Lenig, "Auriesville II," 6.

20. Wayne Lenig, email to the author, 8 September 2022.

tools as the later Hopewellians: "sharpened sticks, antler picks, bone and shell hoes, and baskets," tools similar to the wooden hoes, fire-hardened sticks, and animal scapulars used in traditional Iroquois construction work. Later cultural complexes like the Adena, the Hopewell, and the Mississippian accomplished even greater feats of construction. Moreover, we know that the Adena and Hopewellian cultures influenced Native American cultures in what is now New York State. So, it might be worth exploring the possibility that these earthworks—though no others like them have been discovered in the Mohawk Valley, to my knowledge—were built by pre-Iroquoian people for their mortuary practices. [21]

But we could also assume that the earthworks were originally only about two feet high and accommodated a palisade on top. This hypothesis fails both because, as we have seen, Fr. Ewing discovered no evidence of a palisade and because the Iroquois do not seem to have built their palisades on top of earthworks.[22]

The remaining possibility is that these ditches and earthworks were of European construction or were built by a local Mohawk farmer who had adopted European technology. If we assume they are the product of a Mohawk farmer, the assumption is absurd, for

21. On the implications of the placement of ditches in relation to walls, see Martin, *The Land Looks after Us*, 16. On the earliest earthworks, see Pauketat, *Cahokia*, 17 and 138. On Hopewellian tools, see Hancock, "Earthworks," 162. On Iroquois tools, see Grumet, *Historic Contact*, 337. On the Adena, Hopewell, and Mississippian cultures, see Tuck, "Regional Cultural Development," 43, and Fitting, "Regional Cultural Development," 44–57. On Adena and Hopewellian influences in New York, see Ritchie, *Archaeology of New York State*, fig. 1 (xxx–xxxi) and 179–253.

22. The claim above regarding Iroquois palisades rests both on Snow, *Mohawk Valley Archaeology: Sites*, passim, and on Bradley, *Onondaga and Empire*, passim. Speaking of Iroquois construction techniques, it is interesting that European shovels do not show up on Iroquois sites, although Wayne Lenig, "Bauder," 5, mentions a piece of a possible shovel. Indeed, one finds frequent mention of axes, hoes, adzes, saws, knives, and awls among European tools that could have been used in construction, but not shovels. It should be noted, too, that the Iroquois, in the early period of contact with Europeans, usually adapted European tools to other purposes than the intended use. See Bradley, *Onondaga and Empire*, 224–25.

it would have been far easier to enclose the space with a wooden fence. What more would have been needed to keep some animals in and other animals out? If we assume European construction, then we may be looking at the location of a small fort. But why would a fort have had extensions of the northern and southern sides of the earthworks beyond the corners of the enclosure? They would have provided cover for an attacker. So, it seems that the hypothesis of European construction is far-fetched.

Furthermore, the area enclosed by these structures is not only nearly rectangular, but the sides are also straight, and all but one of the corners are constructed at ninety-degree angles. To be sure, the architects of the earlier mound-building cultures were able to build structures in various precise geometrical shapes. Until the last quarter of the seventeenth century, however, the palisades of Iroquois villages followed the contours of the land upon which they were built. They were irregularly shaped and only became neatly geometric under European influence.[23]

Moreover, the enclosure at Auriesville is only about two-thirds of an acre in area. That is small for a Mohawk castle, even after the epidemic of the 1630s. Even the Bauder Site, the smallest of the three castles of the 1635–46 period, probably encompassed 2.15 acres. Additionally, the three undoubted Mohawk castles of the period—at the Bauder, Rumrill-Naylor, and Oak Hill #1 archeological sites—were built on steep, high ridges around a mile south of the Mohawk River.[24] Auriesville #2, however, stands on a low, narrow plateau near the Mohawk and is easily accessible from it.

23. Bradley, *Onondaga and Empire*, 290–91, 428, and Snow, *Mohawk Valley Archaeology: Sites*, fig. 11.3, 434, a map of the excavations at Caughnawaga, the Veeder Site (ca. 1679–93). Grumet, *Historic Contact*, 366, mistakenly reprints this map as a map of the Fox Farm Site. On the geometric achievements of the Hopewellian architects, see Hancock, "Earthworks," 164–65.

24. Snow, *Mohawk Valley Archaeology: Sites*, 301, 304–5, 308–9. On the preferred terrain for castle sites, see the articles on the various castles in Snow, *Mohawk Valley Archaeology: Sites*.

Lastly, we know that Fr. Ewing found no evidence of a palisade at Auriesville #2, but Mohawk castles of this period were fortified.

It seems unlikely, then, that the enclosure in the northwestern section of the Auriesville Shrine grounds east of CR-164 was the site of Ossenrenon in the "1640–1655 era." In consequence, it is also all but impossible that Auriesville was the site of the martyrdoms of 1642 and 1646, or the place of St. Catherine's birth in 1656, since the documentary evidence places her birth in a castle. Therefore another location or other locations must be found to fit better the documentary evidence to be examined.

Such locations have been proposed by the archeologists. In 1985, Donald A. Rumrill, an accomplished avocational archeologist, published an overview of Mohawk settlement in the Mohawk Valley from 1595 to 1785.[25] He argued that evidence existed for only three Mohawk castles in the Mohawk Valley from 1630 to 1650: the Bauder Site, the Rumrill-Naylor Site, and the Oak Hill #1 Site, or Ossenrenon, Andagaron, and Theonontougen.[26] The first is near Randall, the second near Sprakers, the third near Fort Plain, each one on the hills and ridges roughly a mile south of the Mohawk River.

The Bauder Site lies east of Currytown Road, which runs south into the hills from Randall to Currytown. The site stands at roughly 574.48 feet of altitude in a field above Yatesville Creek. It lies in tax parcel 82.–1–46, behind 421 Currytown Road. William Maring, town historian of Root Township, kindly pointed out the site to me from Currytown Road on 9 August 2021. This confirmed what I had surmised and felt on a walk around this site on 24 October 2019.

I located the site tentatively in 2019 through an entry in "Some Small Cemeteries, Town of Root, Montgomery County, NY." The entry was written by Albert Elswick in 1967 for the Caughnawaga

25. Rumrill, "Interpretation and Analysis."

26. Rumrill, "Interpretation and Analysis," 11.

Chapter of the Daughters of the American Revolution. It is entitled "Bauder Burial Lot, Town of Root, Off Currytown Road on the Land of Winford Peck, Randall, Root Twp.," and reads,

> This abandoned family lot is located in a clump of trees in an open field about 800 feet east of Currytown Road. A wagon track runs from the road, at the base of the hill, below the house of Robert Minch to the field. Near the plot is an old well. This field is just north of the field where the Mohawk Castle, Onekajonka (sp?), was located.[27]

Research into county records relating to the Bauder family led me to what I thought must be the site (Figure 9).

To confirm my Bauder research, I drove up Currytown Road and walked east through two fields behind 451 Currytown Road, the old Robert Minch house, which was built over the foundation of the Bauder farmhouse. As I wrote at the time,

> I noticed a four-wheeler track through the weeds at the eastern end of the [second] field. I followed it, and came out in the woods above a ravine leading down to the Yatesville. The ravine was formed by a running stream. On my side, the southern side, the irregularity [of the declivity] of the bluff became clear, but on the other side [behind 421 Currytown Road] the field fell off in an almost sheer drop. I decided to explore that field, and followed the four-wheeler track across the stream and up to the next field.
>
> The field was shaped like a thumb viewed from above, the rounded tip in the east [Figure 10]. I followed the edge of the field on the south side. All along the drop-off seemed close to sheer. When I reached the rounded end of the field, I made my

27. At Elswick, "Bauder Burial Lot." The name "Onekagoncka" was applied to the Bauder Site in the early twentieth century. See Lenig, "Bauder," 2. The name occurs in a list of Mohawk habitations in 1634. It probably was the so-called Cromwell Site. See Snow, *Mohawk Valley Archaeology: Sites*, 309.

> way through the weeds to a strip of woods at the edge of the bluff. Again, the drop was precipitous. I followed the track of a collapsed stone wall around the rounded end of the top of the bluff, and found the drop off precipitous, until I began to curve back along the northern edge of the field.
>
> There I discovered another dramatic ravine, cut by a stream that again flowed down to the Yatesville [Figure 11]. Here the descent was slightly less precipitous than the descent of the stream on the southern side, and I imagine this is where the village children [and young warriors] dragged the body of St. René down to the Yatesville.[28] Returning to the field, I saw that the field was on the flank of a steep ridge that rose to the west [Figure 12]. This could be the hill that Jogues and Goupil climbed, in order to pray.

While in the field, I felt the presence of the martyrs. I wrote, "It occurred to me later that I may well be the first Catholic to have stood on the site of the martyrdoms and prayed to the martyrs, since the martyrs themselves prayed for each other. What a blessing!"

Be that as it may, one can agree with Donald Rumrill, "One in-person visit to this site will confirm that which Jogues describes—the nearby hill overlooking the small village, the hill through the fields down to the creek below which is ever running and torrential at times, and the woods on the opposite bank are still not cleared off."[29] Mr. Rumrill confirmed his dating of the three 1630–50 villages—Ossenrenon, Andagaron, Theonontougen—in an exhaustive study of Mohawk beads published in 1991.[30]

Regarding the Bauder Site, Dean Snow observes, "The site has been surveyed by Donald Rumrill and by University at Albany

28. In 2021, I climbed down this ravine fifty yards or so but could push my knees no farther without planning and proper equipment. In 2022, I made the descent, on which see below.

29. Rumrill, "Interpretation and Analysis," 17.

30. Rumrill, "Mohawk Glass Trade Bead Chronology."

crews. However, no formal excavations have been carried out on the Bauder site." Again, "Only the village locus is known. If there are cemetery loci, they have escaped notice. No structures or features are known for the site."[31] Rumrill, however, states that "there are four middens and one possible,"[32] and in fact Rumrill drew a map of the Bauder Site, dated 1 April 1983, that indicates his view, based on the distribution of metal artifacts, that the village contained nine longhouses.[33]

The site can be dated with fair accuracy to 1635 through 1646. As Snow notes, "According to John McCashion, the trade pipes all indicate that the Rumrill-Naylor, Bauder, and Oak Hill #1 sites date to the same decade, that is to 1635–1646. Furthermore, these three cross-date with Thurston (Oneida) and Shurtleff (Onondaga). All of them have produced pipes bearing the diamond fleur-de-lis stamp. Finally, all of them lack the diagnostic EB pipe that sets the 1646 terminus ante quem."[34]

Artifacts from the Bauder Site are contained in several collections. They are "the Brown, Hartley, Hagerty, Klinkhart, Mohawk-Caughnawaga Museum, Montgomery County Historical Society, and Jackowski collections."[35] Thus one can say with confidence that, based on the archeological evidence, the Bauder Site was the location of Ossenrenon, the easternmost Mohawk castle, in 1642.

31. Snow, *Mohawk Valley Archaeology: Sites*, 305.

32. Rumrill, "Interpretation and Analysis," 12.

33. Lenig, "Bauder," 3. Others believed themselves to have discovered the outlines of eleven longhouses. See Lenig, "Bauder," 7. See also the Bauder foldout map in this book.

34. Snow, *Mohawk Valley Archaeology: Sites*, 307–8. Regarding the pipe types: "The EB heel mark belonged to Edward Bird, who produced pipes in Holland from 1630 to 1665. However, the EB pipes do not begin showing up on Mohawk sites until after 1644 ... [I]t is enough to say that the fleur-de-lis design came into use after 1635 and that most of the pipes bearing it and its variants were made by 1647" (43). Lenig, "Bauder," 6–7, however, dates the site to ca. 1635–45. The latter date is that of the expiration of the original charter of the Dutch West India Company, and in his "Patterns of Material Culture," Lenig argued for the periodization of Iroquois material culture according to the periods of Dutch trade.

35. Snow, *Mohawk Valley Archaeology: Sites*, 305.

We shall see in the commentary later in this chapter that it also fits the documentary evidence better than Auriesville does.

Documentary Evidence with Translations

Here follows all the documentary evidence on the martyrdom of St. René Goupil that contains references to time and place.[36] Given that focus and limitation, the reader should not expect a continuous narrative, although some details have been provided with the texts. The texts are given in the original languages, so that readers who are able may check my translations against the originals and determine for themselves whether I have been faithful to the evidence. For bibliographical details, see the introduction. All of this testimony is St. Isaac's directly or indirectly.

Document 1. "Epistola Patris Isaaci Jogues in Nova Francia inter Irohaeos captivi ad Provincialem Franciae," or "Letter of Father Isaac Jogues in New France Captive among the Iroquois to the Provincial of France."

St. Isaac has already described the capture and torture of himself and his companions by a Mohawk war party on the St. Lawrence River, as well as their journey up the Richelieu River and Lake Champlain. Well up the lake they encounter another war party going north and undergo more torture.

1. "Octavus dies venerat, cum in turmam ducentorum barbarorum qui ad bellum proficiscebantur advenientes."[37] [*MNF* 5.598]

36. The translations are my own and are quite literal. In particular, I have followed the original texts in their use of the historical present, which will seem odd to the English reader, since we do not use it except in certain dialects; e.g., "A few weeks ago I get this email from my sister," a phrase used just the other day by a Yinzer friend of mine.

37. This meeting and the following session of torture occurred at Jogues Island, now commonly called either Albany or Cole Island. It is owned by the state of New York. It is in a cove some three miles south of Westport, off the Camp Dudley beach. One could reach it by water from Westport or by car south on 9 North to Dudley Road and the camp beach, and thence by water in one's own boat. I presume one would need permission from a camp official. After visiting the beach in 2018, I wrote, "There was

Translation. "The eighth day had come, when coming upon a crowd of 200 barbarians who were setting out for war."

The journey by water ends, and the party sets out overland.

2. "Tandem decimo die, sub meridiano, canoas reliquimus et reliquum iter quod quatuor dies tenuit pedites confecimus." [*MNF* 5.600]

Translation. "Finally, on the tenth day, at noon, we left the canoes and made the rest of the journey, which took four days, on foot."

The war party arrives at Ossenrenon with its captives.

3. "Tandem decimo tertio die, qui in vigiliam Assumptionis Beatae Mariae incidebat, ad primum pagum Irokensium pervenimus." [*MNF* 5.600]

Translation. "At last, on the thirteenth day, which fell upon the Eve of the Assumption of Blessed Mary, we came to the first cantonal village of the Iroquois."

4. "Vigilia igitur Assumptionis, circa horam tertiam, ad amnem[38] illorum pago vicinum pervenimus. Nos ex utraque fluvii[39] ripa præstolabantur, cum veteres captivi Hurones, tum Irokei; et illi pro salute nos vivos lento igne comburendos admonuerunt; hi vero nos baculis, pugnis et lapidibus exceperunt." [*MNF* 5.601]

Translation. "Therefore, on the Vigil of the Assumption, about the third hour, we came to a stream near the village of those men. On each bank of the stream were waiting for us both old, captive Hurons and the Iroquois, and the former for a salutation warned

---

something very moving about the island: small, uninhabited, hidden in a small cove, the great lake lying beyond, its history unknown to locals, its existence unknown to Catholics, yet it is the site of one of the great Christian contests between the demons and God's saints."

38. According to Lewis and Short, *Latin Dictionary*, s.v. *amnis*: "any broad and deep-flowing rapid water; a stream, torrent, river (hence, esp. in the poets sometimes for a rapidly-flowing stream or a torrent rushing down from a mountain = *torrens*)."

39. According to Lewis and Short, *Latin Dictionary*, s.v. *fluvius*, this word can mean either "river" or "stream."

us that we would be burned alive by means of a slow fire, but the latter received us with sticks, fists, and stones."

5. "Ubi satis ad fluvii ripam illorum crudelitati datum est et ludibrio patuimus, nos ad illorum pagum in edito colle positum deducunt. Ante pagum nos totius regionis iuventus fustibus armata, hinc et inde, ex utraque viae parte expectabat." [*MNF* 5.601]

Translation. "When enough had been paid to their cruelty at the bank of the stream, and we had been exposed to derision, they lead us to their cantonal village, built upon a lofty hill. In front of the village, the youth/braves of the entire region, armed with clubs, awaited us, on this side and on that, on each side of the road."

The captives are led to Andagaron the next day.

6. "Postera die, quae erat Assumptionis Beatae Virginis ... circa meridiem nos in alium pagum duobus milliaribus a primo illo distantem deducunt." [*MNF* 5.603]

Translation. "The next day, which was the day of the Assumption of Blessed Mary ... about noon they lead us to another cantonal village two thousand paces distant[40] from the first village."

They are led to Theonontougen two days later. They are not made to run the gauntlet again.

7. "Tertium [pagum] quidem pacifice sumus ingressi." [*MNF* 5.604]

Translation. "We entered the third cantonal village peacefully."

After two days of torture in Theonontougen, the captives are led back to Andagaron.

8. "Ubi duos dies itidem in illo pago degimus, nos in pagum illum quem secundum ingressi eramus, ut tandem de nobis

40. The distance was two Roman miles, or 10,000 Roman feet. A *passus* was 5 Roman feet, and a mile was *mille passuum*. The Roman mile is estimated to have been 426 English feet shorter than the English mile, i.e., 4,854 English feet. See Lewis and Short, *Latin Dictionary*, s.v. *passus* and *mille*. The site was the Rumrill-Naylor Site, as we shall see below.

statueretur, deducunt. Iamque septimus dies venerat ab eo tempore quod de pago in pagum ... deducebamur." [*MNF* 5.606]

Translation. "When we have passed two days in that cantonal village in the same way, they lead us to that village which we had entered second, in order that finally it might be decided about us. And already the seventh day had come from that time when we began to be led from cantonal village to cantonal village."

The head men decide the fates of the prisoners. Most of the Hurons are spared.

9. "Reliquis item Huronibus paene omnibus vitam dedere, tribus exceptis: Paulo, Eustachio et Stephano; quos tribus in pagis qui nationem istam constituunt occiderunt: Stephanum in eodem quo eramus pago Andagaron appellant; Paulum in alio, Ossernenon; Eustachium in Thenont8gen." [*MNF* 5.607]

Translation. "They gave life also to almost all the remaining Hurons, three men excepted, Paul, Eustace, and Stephen, whom they killed in the three cantonal villages which make up that nation: Stephen in the same village where we were, which they call Andagaron; Paul in another, Ossernenon; Eustace in Thenontougen."

Guillaume Coûture is sent to Theonontougen, while St. Isaac and St. René are sent back to Ossenrenon.

10. "Sub vesperum Guillelmum Cousture[41] ... in ultimum regionis pagum Theonont8gen dictum deducunt eumque cuidam barbarorum familiae adscribunt ... Me vero et Renatum, quos non ita firmis viribus conspiciebant, deducunt in pagum primum, in quo ii qui nos captivos ceperant manebant, ibique nos quoad aliud statueretur constituunt." [*MNF* 5.607]

Translation. "At dusk they lead Guillaume Coûture ... to the last cantonal village of the region, called Theonontougen, and

41. Guillaume Coûture (1618–1701) was a *donné* captured with St. Isaac and St. René. A native of Rouen, devout Catholic, skilled carpenter, expert shot, and accomplished speaker, he had a noteworthy career in New France.

assign him to a certain family of barbarians ... But René and me, whom they saw not of such solid strength, they lead to the first cantonal village, in which dwelt those who had taken us as captives, and there they establish us until something should be decided."

The war party of two hundred men which was met on Lake Champlain returns and argues for the death of the Frenchmen.

11. "Ducenti illi barbari ... igitur redibant et ... nos qui adhuc vivebamus ad mortem deposcebant." [*MNF* 5.608]

Translation. "Those two hundred barbarians ... therefore were coming back ... and they began to claim us who were still alive for death."

A Dutch magistrate intercedes for St. Isaac and St. René.

12. "[U]nus ex praecipuis Batavis, qui in colonia viginti tantum leucis[42] ab his barbaris dissita manent." [*MNF* 5.609]

Translation. "[O]ne of the chief Dutchmen, who dwell in a colony situated only twenty leagues from these barbarians."

The fate of the Frenchmen is debated inconclusively. St. René is assassinated privately without a decision of the council.

13. "Sed, sub finem septembris ... ubi peracto commeatu destinatisque iis qui nos reducerent, extremum de rebus nostris consilium agitur. Igitur truculentorum hominum saevitiae relicti, ubique ad necem querimur. Ii securibus instructi domos lustrant ut inventos occidant. Forte, sub finem consilii, nescio quam mihi tunc mentem Deus iniecerat, socios meos in suburbanum agrum domus in qua degebam deduxeram, ubi ignari eorum quae agebantur tuti quodam modo delitescimus. Turbo ille, interim, qui nos omnes si in pago fuissemus sustulisset, paululum conquievit.

42. A French league was roughly 2.4 miles. See Rowlett, *How Many?*, s.v. "lieue." Thus twenty leagues would have been roughly 48 miles. By modern measurement, the distance from Albany to Auriesville is 40.5 miles, while the distance from Albany to Randall is 48.1 miles. A *leuca* or *leuga*, according to Lewis and Short, *Latin Dictionary*, was a Gallic mile, which was the equivalent of 1,500 Roman paces. The French word *lieue* (or league) comes from this Gallo-Roman word.

Postea, reducto a suis in suum pagum Guillelmo, ego et Renatus, ubi de reditu nostro conclamatum esse cognovimus, in collem vicinum qui pago plurimus imminet orationis causa secedimus ... In itinere pagum versus coronam beatae Virginis recitamus iamque quatuor decades percurreramus, cum iuvenes duos obvios habemus ... Orantes ad pagum perveneramus, cum in ipso aditu unus ex his duobus quos obvios [p. 610] habueramus, extracta quadem [ex] veste ... securi, tam validum in Renati caput ictum impegit." [*MNF* 5.609–10]

Translation. "But, at the end of September ... when the supplies had been finished, and those men had been appointed to escort us home, a last council about our affairs is held. Therefore, abandoned to the cruelty of the ferocious men, we are being sought everywhere for death. Those men, provided with hatchets, go around the houses to find and kill us. By chance, at the end of the council—I don't know what idea God had then inspired in my case—I had led my companions into the nearby field of the house in which I was dwelling, where, unaware of those things which were being done, we hide away safely for a while. That tornado, meanwhile, which would have swept all of us up had we been in the village, quieted down a little bit. Afterward, when Guillaume had been led back to his own cantonal village by his family, René and I, when we recognized that an outcry was being made because of our return, withdraw for the sake of prayer to the nearby hill, which, very large, overhangs the village ... Upon our way toward the village, we are reciting the Rosary of the Blessed Virgin, and already we had run through four decades, when we met two young men who admonish us that we should return to the village ... We had reached the village praying, when at the very entrance one of these two whom we had met, having pulled from his clothes a sort of ... hatchet, struck so strong a blow on Rene's head."

St. René's body is thrown in a creek near the village, and St. Isaac covers it with a barrow of stones.

14. "Illud [corpus] autem nudatum omnino indigne, ligato circa collum fune per pagum pertractum in torrentem sat longe proiecerant." [*MNF* 5.611]

Translation. "Moreover, they had thrown it [the body] naked entirely unworthily, which they dragged through the cantonal village by a rope tied around its neck, into the torrent a sufficiently long way off."

15. "Huius igitur auxilio repertum corpus ... in ipsomet torrente ubi erat profundior, lapidum acervo tumulo." [*MNF* 5.611]

Translation. "Therefore the body, found with the help of this man, I heap with a barrow of stones in the very torrent, where it was rather deep."

St. Rene's corpse is hidden by the Indians.

16. "[S]ubsequentis diei mane, accepto ligone seu sarculo ut corpus humo defoderem perrexi. Sed tulerunt fratrem meum. Eo redeo, montem ad cuius radices torrens ille decurrit abscendo,[43]

43. This word, which I have verified at PraA9, folio 378, line 14, is not found in any of the several dictionaries of classical, late, medieval, and neo-Latin that I have on my shelves. Nor does the Sorbonne's searchable online edition of Du Cange's *Glossarium* call it up. Moreover, no derivative of it exists in French or Italian that I can find. It would be easy to emend it to *abscedo*, "I depart, I disappear." The eye of a copyist could easily have picked up the letter *n* from the next word and added it here. *Abscedo* would fit the context well enough. However, textual criticism contains several fundamental rules, one of which is the rule of the *lectio difficilior*, the rule of the more difficult reading. See Maas, *Textual Criticism*, 13, 27, 31. This rule means that a textual critic normally must consider the more difficult reading in a doubtful passage to be the more probable reading. Thus because *abscendo* does not exist elsewhere in Latin, as far as we know—making it a more difficult reading than the possible emendation—we must reckon it the correct reading and assume that St. Isaac, fluent in Latin, coined it. But why would he have felt the need for a new word? I can vouch from experience (2021) that the south or village side of the ravine at the Bauder Site down which the young warriors and children probably hauled St. René's body is somewhat steep and rough at first, and then becomes much more so. When I climbed down the upper portion of the ravine, I felt strongly that I was *climbing away* from the field above, and I kept glancing back at it. When I saw the narrowing of the ravine below and its growing steepness, my orientation shifted, and I realized I could not *climb down* there. Perhaps St. Isaac felt the same difference in perspective and coined a word to express the former perspective.

descendo, saltum[44] qui est altera parte lustro, sed frustra. Torrentis qui ex nocturna pluvia plurimum increverat fundum cum baculo, cum pede pertento, non prohibitus aut aquae altitudine, quae ad medium corpus pertingebat, aut frigiditate … si forte illud vis torrentis alio tulisset. Obvios quosque interrogo numquid de illo sciant. Sed … in fluvium remotissimum protractum esse mentiuntur." [*MNF* 5.612]

Translation. "[E]arly the next day, having taken a mattock or hoe, that I might bury the body in the ground, I proceeded. But they had carried away my brother. I return there. Away from the mountain at the roots of which that torrent flows I climb, down I climb, I search the steep woods which are on the other side, but in vain. The bottom of the torrent, which had increased very much because of the nocturnal rains, with stick and foot I thoroughly test, not prevented either by the depth of the water, which reached the middle of my body, or by the cold … if by chance the violence of the torrent had carried it elsewhere. I ask everyone I meet whether they know about it. But … they feign that it has been dragged to a very remote stream."

St. Isaac finds St. René's remains in the spring.

17. "Verum ubi liquefactae sunt nives, audivi ab adolescentibus videri sparsa defuncti Galli ossa. Itaque eo me conferens semirosa ossa, reliquias canum, vulpium et corvorum, et praecipua ea terrae mandavi." [*MNF* 5.612]

Translation. "But when the snows had melted, I heard from the young men that the scattered bones of the dead Frenchman were being seen. And so, going there, I committed to the earth these eminent things, the half-gnawed bones, the leavings of the dogs, foxes, and crows."

44. In general, a *saltus* is a woodland pasture, the sort of place pigs might be allowed to forage for acorns. But as Lewis and Short, *Latin Dictionary*, s.v. 2, note, "Esp., a narrow pass, ravine, mountain valley." I think my "steep woods" captures the meaning in this context.

Document 2. "Lettera del Padre Isaac Iogues al Padre Provinciale della provincia di Francia," or "Letter of Father Isaac Jogues to the Father Provincial of the Province in France," included in Fr. Francesco Gioseppe Bressani's *Breve Relatione d'alcvne missioni de' PP. della Compagnia di Giesù nella Nuoua Francia*, or *A Brief Report about Some Missions of the Fathers of the Society of Jesus in New France.*

The stopover in Lake Champlain.

1. "L'ottava del nostro viaggio incontrammo ducento barbari." [*MNF* 8.486]

Translation. "The eighth day of our journey we met two hundred barbarians."

The party lands at the head of Lake Champlain and continues on foot.

2. "Il decimo dì, dopo mezzo giorno, lasciammo le canoe per fare il resto del viaggio di quattro giornate à piedi." [*MNF* 8.487]

Translation. "The tenth day, after midday, we left the canoes, in order to do the rest of the four-day journey on foot."

They reach Ossenrenon.

3. "Finalmente, il 18[45] dì, vigilia dell' Assuntione della Beatissima Vergine, arrivammo alla prima terra degl' Hirochesi." [*MNF* 8.487]

Translation. "Finally, the 18th day, the Vigil of the Assumption of the Most Blessed Virgin, we arrived at the first canton of the Iroquois."

4. "Dunque la vigilia dell' Assuntione, circa alle venti hore, arrivammo al fiume che passa longo al lor castello. Ci aspettavano dell' una e l' altra riva del fiume i vecchi schiavi huroni e gl' Hirochesi, quelli per avvertirci che fuggissimo, ch' altrimente saremmo brugiati, questi per batterci con bastoni, pugni e sassi come prima." [*MNF* 8.488]

45. A misreading of the translator, or a misprint by the printer, for "13," according to *MNF* 8.487n133. Cf. Document 1.3.

Translation. "So, the Vigil of the Assumption, around about twenty hours, we arrived at the river that passes beside their castle. Here we saw on one bank of the river and the other the old Huron slaves and the Iroquois, the former to warn us that we should flee, that otherwise we would be burned, the latter to beat us with sticks, fists, and stones as at first."

5. "Stemmo ivi esposti alquanto a' loro scherni, poi ci condussero al castello situato in un' alto colle. Prima d' arrivare incontrammo i giovani del paese in ala, armati di bastoni come prima." [*MNF* 8.488]

Translation. "We stayed there exposed a little while to their mockery. Then they led us to their castle situated upon a high hill. Before arriving, we encountered the young men of the region in an aisle, armed with sticks as at first."

They are led to Andagaron.

6. "Il dì seguente, festa della Beata Vergine ... ci condussero in un' altro castello 5 ò 6 miglia lontano dal primo." [*MNF* 8.489]

Translation. "The following day, the Feast of the Blessed Virgin ... they led us to another castle, 5 or 6 miles distant from the first."

They enter Theonontougen.

7. "Nel terzo castello entrammo con gran pace." [*MNF* 8.490]

Translation. "We entered the third castle in great peace."

They are led back to Andagaron, to wait while deliberations are made.

8. "Due dì doppo ci condussero nel secondo castello per deliberare finalmente di noi. Erano già sette dì che ci conducevano di castello, in castello."[46] [*MNF* 8.491]

Translation. Two days later, they led us to the second castle to deliberate at last about us. It had already been seven days that they had been leading us from castle to castle."

46. Bressani omits the names of the castles given by St. Isaac in this section.

9. "[M]a à i Francesi et à quasi tutti gli altri Huroni fù concessa la vita. La costanza di quest' huomo [Eustace] fù maravigliosa … Uccisero anche Paolo Onnonhoaraton, giovane di 25 anni in circa." [*MNF* 8.491–92]

Translation. "[B]ut to the French and to practically all the other Hurons was granted life. The constancy of this man [Eustace] was glorious … They also killed Paul Onnonhoaraton, a young man of about 25 years."

The dispersal of the Frenchmen.

10. "Guglielmo [Coûture] fù dato ad una famiglia Hirochese … Ma di Renato [Goupil], edi me, per non esser sì forti, non si prese l' ultima risolutione, ma ci lasciorno insieme come in una libera schiavitudine." [*MNF* 8.492]

Translation. "Guillaume [Coûture] was given to an Iroquois family … But concerning René [Goupil] and me, because we were not so strong, a final decision was not taken, but they left us together as if in a free servitude."

A Dutch magistrate intercedes.

11. "[U]no de' principali tra gli Olandesi, che hanno una colonia circa 40 miglia lontano da Barbari." [*MNF* 8.492]

Translation. "[O]ne of the chief men of the Dutch, who have a colony about 40 miles distant from the Barbarians."

The return of the two hundred warriors, deliberations about the fate of the Frenchmen, and the assassination of St. René.

12. "Ritornarono intanto quei 200 … Onde cominciò di nuovo a trattarsi di ucciderci … Ma nel ultimo conseglio che per questo si radunò, il populo et i più turbolenti n' impedirno l' esecutione [a resolution to send the captives back to the French] e se per providenza particolare di Dio, noi non fossimo stati fuori del borgo, finito il consiglio, ci haverebbero uccisi. Ma havendoci un pezzo cercato, invano si ritirorno finalmente ciascuno alla sua terra. Renato e io essendo ritornati et avvertiti del pericolo,

ci ritirammo fuori verso una collina, per far con più libertà le nostre devotioni ... Eravamo alle quarta posta [of the Rosary], quando incontrammo due giovani che ci comandorno di ritornare al borgo ... In fatti, alla porta del borgo, uno di questi due tira un' accetta ... e ne ferisce la testa di Renato." [*MNF* 8.492–93]

Translation. "In the meantime, those 200 returned ... Whereon [the Iroquois] began again to look at killing us ... but at the last council which was assembled for this, the people, and the more unruly, prevented the execution of it [a resolution to send the captives back to the French], and if by the particular providence of God we had not been outside the village, the council ending, we would have been killed, but having sought us awhile in vain, they returned each one to his own canton. René and I, having been returning and warned of the peril, withdrew outside toward a hill, to make with more liberty our devotions ... We were at the fourth decade [of the Rosary] when we met two young men who commanded us to return to the village ... Indeed, at the gate of the village, one of these two draws a hatchet ... and wounds the head of René."

St. Isaac covers St. Rene's body with a barrow of stones from the creek bed, but the body is later hidden by the Indians.

13. "Non lasciai però il dì seguente di cercare il corpo del defonto per sepellirlo ... Gli havevano legata al collo una fune e nudo strascinatolo per tutta la terra e poì gettato nel fiume assai lontano ... lo ritrovo al lido del fiume ... et ivi nel fondo d' un torrente secco lo copro di pietri, con intentione di ritornarvi il dì seguente solo con una zappa, per sepellirlo stabilmente ... Il dì seguente ritorno con istrumenti al luogo, 'sed tulerunt fratrem meum.' Ritorno, cerco da per tutto et entro io stesso fino alla cintura nel fiume, per le piogge della notte cresciuto e freddo per essere il mese d' ottobre. Lo cerco con le mani e co' piedi. Mi dicono che la piena l' hà trasportato altrove." [*MNF* 8.493–94]

Translation. "The following day, however, I did not omit

searching for the body of the dead man, in order to bury it ... They had tied a rope around his neck and dragged him naked through the whole canton, and then thrown him in the river rather far away. I found him on the bank of the river ... and there I cover him with stones at the bottom of a dry creek bed, with the intention of returning there the next day with a hoe to bury him permanently ... The following day, I return with tools to the place, 'sed tulerunt fratrem meum.' I return, I search, and I myself enter up to the belt in the river, swollen by the rains of the night, and cold ... I search for him with my hands, and with my feet. They tell me that the flood has carried him elsewhere."

In the spring, St. Isaac is able to bury St. René's remains.

14. "[E] non ne posso haver nuova prima della primavera seguente, quando liquefatte le nevi, i giovani del paese m' avvertirono haver visto le sue ossa nell' istessa riva del fiume, le quali insieme con il capo riverentemente baciate, all' hora finalmente sepellii al meglio che potei." [*MNF* 8.494]

Translation. "[A]nd I was not able to have news of him before next spring, when, the snows having melted, the young men of the canton told me they had seen his bones on the same bank of the river, the which together with the head, reverently kissed, I buried then finally the best I could."

Document 3. Isaac Jogues, SJ, "Le martyre de René Goupil par les Iroquois," or "The Martyrdom of René Goupil by the Iroquois."

The encounter on Lake Champlain with the two hundred.

1. "Dans le lac [Champlain], nous rencontrasmes deux cents Iroquois." [*MNF* 5.287]

Translation. "In the lake [Champlain], we met two hundred Iroquois."

At Ossenrenon.

2. "A l'abord du premier bourg, où nous fusmes sy cruellement traictés." [*MNF* 5.288]

Translation. "At the approach to the first town, where we were so cruelly treated."

The assassination of St. René.

3. "Un jour donc que dans les peines de nostre esprit, nous estions sortis hors du bourg pour prier plus doucement et avec moins de bruict, deux jeunes hommes viennent après nous nous dire que nous eussions à retourner à la maison." [*MNF* 5.289]

Translation. "So, one day that, in the sorrows of our spirit, we had gone out of the village to pray more sweetly and with less noise, two young men come after us to say that we had to return to the house."

4. "Nous nous en retournons donc vers la porte du bourg, récitant nostre chapelet, duquel nous avions dèsjà dict quatre dixaines. Nous estants arrestés vers la porte du bourg ... un de ces deux Iroquois tire une hache qu'il tenoit cachée soubz sa couverte et en donne un coup sur la teste de René." [*MNF* 5.289]

Translation. "We are returning therefore toward the town, reciting our Rosary, of which we had already said four decades. We having stopped near the gate of the village ... one of these two Iroquois pulled a hatchet that he had kept hidden under his blanket, and gave a blow of it upon the head of René."

St. Isaac raises a barrow over St. René's body, but the young people hide the body away.

5. "Je vais, je cherche, et à l'aide d'un Algonquin pris autrefois et maintenant vray Iroquois, je le trouve. Les enfants, après qu'on l'eût tué, l'avoient despouillé et traisné la corde au col dans un torrent qui passe au pied de leur bourg ... Je prins ce corps et à l'aide de cet Algonquin, je le mis au fond de l'eau, chargé de grosses pierres, afin qu'on ne le vît, faisant mon compte que je viendrois le lendemain, avec un hoyau ... que je ferois une fosse et que je l'y mettrois ... mais quelques-uns qui nous virent, principalement de la jeunesse, le retirèrent." [*MNF* 5.290]

Translation. "I go, I search, and, with the help of an Algonquin captured before and now a true Iroquois, I find it. The lads, after they had killed him, stripped him, and dragged [him], a rope at the neck, into a torrent which passes at the foot of their town … I took the body, and with the help of this Algonquin, I put it at the bottom of the water loaded with big stones, in order that no one might see it, reckoning that I would come the next day, with a mattock … that I might make a hole and that I might put it there … but some persons who saw us, chiefly among the youth, took it away."

St. Isaac's Mohawk aunt forces Isaac into hiding the next day. A heavy rain falls.

6. "Le lendemain, comme on me cherchoit pour me tuer, ma tante m'envoya á son champ pour esquiver, comme je pense. Ce qui fut cause que je remis l'affaire au lendemain, jour auquel il pleut toute la nuict, de sorte que ce torrent grossit extraordinairement." [*MNF* 5.290]

Translation. "The next day, as they were seeking to kill me, my aunt sent me to her field to avoid [the danger], as I think; which was the cause that I put off the affair to the next day, [a] day on which it rains the whole night, with the result that this torrent swells extraordinarily."

The third day, St. Isaac no longer can find St. René's body, for the young people have hidden it. An Indian woman misleads him. He finds the remains in the spring and buries them.

7. "J'emprunte un hoyau hors de chez nous … Mais comme j'approche du lieu, je ne trouve plus ce bienheureux dépost. Je me mets à l'eau qui estoit dèsjà bien froide. Je vais, je viens, je sonde avec mes pieds sy l'eau n'a point soulevé et entraîné le corps." [*MNF* 5.290]

Translation. "I borrow a mattock outside our house … But as I approach the place, I do not find this blessed deposit. I put myself in the water, which was already quite cold. I go, I come, I probe with my feet, if the water had not lifted up the body and carried it away."

8. "Enfin, je ne trouve rien. Et une femme de ma cognoissance, qui passa par là et me vit en peine, me dit, lorsque je luy demandé sy elle ne sçavoit point ce qu'on en avoit faict, qu'on l'avoit traisné à la rivière qui estoit un cart de lieue[47] de là et que je ne cognoissois pas. Cela estoit faux. La jeunesse l'avoit retiré et traisné dans un petit bois proche ... Le printemps, comme on me dist que c'estoit là qu'on l'avoit traisné, j'y allé plusieurs foys sans rien trouver. Enfin, la quatriesme fois, je trouve la teste, quelques os demy rongés, que j'enterray ... Je les baisé bien dévotement par plusieurs foys, comme les os d'un martyr de Jésus-Christ." [*MNF* 5.290–91]

Translation. "In short, I find nothing. And a woman of my acquaintance, who was passing by there and saw me in sorrow, told me, when I asked if she did not know what had become of it [the body], that they had dragged it to a stream which was a quarter of a league from there, and which I did not know. This was false. The youth had taken it away and dragged it into a little nearby wood ... In the spring, as they told me that it was there that they had dragged it, I went there many times without finding anything. At last, the fourth time, I find the head, some half-gnawed bones, which I buried ... I kissed them very devoutly many times, as the bones of a martyr of Jesus Christ."

Document 4. Isaac Jogues, SJ, and Jérôme Lalemant, SJ, *Relation de ce qui s'est passé en la Nouvelle-France en l'année 1647*, or *Report of What Happened in New France in the Year 1647*, chapters 4–5.

The flotilla of two hundred warriors on Lake Champlain.

1. Huit jours après nostre despart des rives du grand fleuve de Saint-Laurent, nous rencontrasmes deux cent Hiroquois." [*MNF* 7.101]

47. A quarter of a league would have been about six-tenths of a mile. Cf. Document 12 as well as the accompanying note, and commentary below under "A Quarter of a League."

Translation. "Eight days after our departure from the banks of the big river of St. Lawrence, we met two hundred Iroquois."

The journey continues overland.

2. "Le dixiesme jour depuis nostre prise, nous arrivasmes au lieu où il fallut quitter la navigation et marcher par terre. Ce chemin qui fut d'environ quatre jours." [*MNF* 7.103]

Translation. "The tenth day since our capture, we arrived at the place where it was necessary to quit going by water and to walk by land. This path, which was about four days."

They reach Ossenrenon, where they spend three days, according to this account.

3. "Nous arrivasmes la veille de ce jour sacré [of the Assumption] à une petite rivière esloignée du premier bourg des Hiroquois d'environ un quart de lieue. Nous trouvasmes sur ses rives, de part et d'autre, quantité d'hommes et de jeunes gens armez de bastons, qu'ils deschargèrent sur nous avec leur rage accoustumée ... Un Huron à qui on avoit donné la liberté ... s'escria: 'Vous estes morts, François, vous estes morts; il n'y a point de liberté pour vous. Ne pensez plus à la vie. Vous serez bruslez. Disposez-vous à la mort.'" [*MNF* 7.103–4]

Translation. "We arrived the eve of this sacred day [of the Assumption] at a stream distant from the first town of the Iroquois about a quarter of a league. We found on its banks on one side and on the other a quantity of men and of young people armed with sticks which they threw at us with their customary rage ... A Huron to whom liberty had been given ... cried out, 'You are dead Frenchmen, you are dead. There is not any liberty for you. Do not think more about life. You shall be burned. Dispose yourselves for death.'"

4. "Après qu'ils eurent assouvis leur cruauté, ils nous menèrent en triomphe dans cette première bourgade. Toute la jeunesse estoit hors les portes, rangée en haye, armez de bastons." [*MNF* 7.104]

Translation. "After they had satisfied their cruelty, they led us in triumph to this first large village. All the youth were outside the gates, arranged in line, armed with sticks."

The captives are led to Andagaron and Theonontougen.

5. "Ces trois jours [at the first large village] expirez, on nous pourmène dans deux autres bourgades." [*MNF* 7.106]

Translation. "These three days [at the first large village] having ended, they lead us to two other large villages."

6. "Au sortir de cette seconde bourgade, on nous traisne en la troisiesme. Ces bourgs sont esloignés de quelques lieues les uns des autres." [*MNF* 7.107]

Translation. "On setting out from this second large village, they lead us to the third. These towns are distant some leagues the ones from the others."

The dispersal of the Frenchmen.

7. "Ces barbares se ravisèrent, s'escrians qu'il falloit donner la vie aux François, ou plustost différer leur mort. Ils pensoient trouver plus de retenue auprès de nos forts en nostre considération. On envoye donc dans la plus grande bourgade Guillaume Cousture et René Goupil & moy fusmes logez ensemble dans une autre." [*MNF* 7.107–8]

Translation. "These barbarians changed their minds, exclaiming that it was necessary to give life to the French, or at least to put off their death. They were thinking of finding more restraint at our forts in consideration of us. They therefore send Guillaume Coûture to the biggest village, and René Goupil and I were lodged together in another."

Further deliberations on the fate of the Frenchmen.

8. "[L]es principaux du pays parlèrent de les [the Frenchmen] ramener aux Trois-Rivières pour les rendre aux François ... Mais ne s'estans pu accorder, le Père et ses compagnons rentrèrent plus que jamais dans les affres de la mort ... mais quand ils [the Iroquois] retiennent quelque prisonnier public, comme le Père, sans le donner à aucun particulier, ce pauvre homme est tous les jours

à deux doigts de la mort ... Voilà la condition en laquelle estoit le Père et l'un des François [Goupil], car l'autre [Coûture] avoit esté donné pour tenir la place d'un Hiroquois tué en guerre." [*MNF* 7.108–9]

Translation. "[T]he chief men of the country were speaking of leading them [the French] back to Trois-Rivières to give them to the French ... But they not being able to agree, the Father and his companions entered again more than ever into the throes of death ... but when they [the Iroquois] keep some public prisoner, like the Father, without giving him to any particular person, this poor man is every day within two fingers of death. There you have the condition in which the Father and the one Frenchman [Goupil] were: for the other [Coûture] had been given to take the place of an Iroquois killed in war."

St. Isaac and St. René pray at a distance from the village.

9. "Le Père Jogues, ayant eu connoissance que le dessein de délivrer les François estoit rompu ... voulut prévenir et fortifier son pauvre compagnon. Il le [St. René] conduit dans un bocage proche de la bourgade, luy déclare les dangers où ils estoient. Ils font tous deux oraison. Ils récitent puis après le chappelet de la sainte Vierge." [*MNF* 7.109]

Translation. "Fr. Jogues, having had knowledge that the design to deliver the French had been broken ... wished to forewarn and fortify his poor companion. He conducts him [St. René] to a small wood near the large village, he declares to him the dangers in which they were. They both pray. They recite the Rosary of the Holy Virgin."

The assassination of St. René.

10. "Comme ils retournoient vers leur bourgade ... le nepveu de ce vieillard [who wanted St. René killed] et un autre sauvage armez de haches ... leur vont à la rencontre. Les ayans abordez, l'un d'eux dit au Père, 'Marche devant'; et à mesme temps il casse la teste au pauvre René Goupil." [*MNF* 7.109]

Translation. "As they were returning to their large village … the nephew of this old man [who wanted St. René killed] and another Savage, armed with hatchets … go to the encounter, [and] having approached them, one of the two says to the Father, 'Walk in front,' and at the same time, he splits the head of poor René Goupil."

Although St. Isaac covers St. René's body with stones, a torrential rain and swollen stream prevent him from finding the body again the next day.

11. "[I]l [St. Isaac] se met donc a genoux … 'Faites, leur dit-il, ce qu'il vous plaira. Je ne crains point la mort.'—'Leve-toy, répliquent-ils; tu n'en mouras pas pour ce coup.' Ils traînent le mort par les rues de la bourgade, et puis le vont jetter en un lieu fort escarté. Le Père luy voulant rendre les derniers devoirs le cherche partout. Quelques enfants luy ayant enseigné, il le trouve dans un ruisseau, le couvre de grosses pierres pour le deffendre des griffes et du bec des oiseaux, en attendant qu'il le vînt enterrer. Mais il pleut toute la nuit suivante et ce torrent se rendit si violent et si profond qu'il ne peust trouver ce saint corps." [*MNF* 7.109–0]

Translation. "[H]e [St. Isaac] then drops to his knees … 'Do,' he says to them, 'what pleases you. I do not fear death.' 'Get up,' they reply, 'you will not die at once.' They are dragging the dead man along the streets of the large village, and then they are going to throw him in a place very far apart. The Father, wishing to render him the last duties, searches for him everywhere. Some lads having informed him, he finds him in a creek, he covers him with big stones, to defend him from the claws and the beak of the birds, expecting to bury him. But it rains all the following night, and this torrent grows so violent and so deep, that he could not find the holy corpse."

The next spring, St. Isaac finds the remains and hides them.

12. "Le printemps suivant, quelques enfans rapportans qu'ils avoient veu le François dans un ruisseau, le Père s'y transporte sans

dire mot, retire ces sacrez despouilles, les baise avec respect, les cache dans le creux d'un arbre." [*MNF* 7.110]

Translation. "The following spring some lads reporting that they had seen the Frenchman in a stream, the Father betakes himself there without saying a word, he withdraws these sacred remains, he kisses them with respect, he hides them in the hollow of a tree."

Document 5. "Narré de la prise du Père Isaac Jogues, par le P. Jacques Buteux," or "Narrative of the Capture of Father Isaac Jogues, by Father Jacques Buteux."

They cross paths with the two hundred warriors on Lake Champlain.

1. "L'unique consolation du Père ... estoit de ramasser le soir tous les chrestiens ... afin de les encourager à la patience. Aussy en avoient-ils bon besoin. Car quelques jours après, des avant-coureurs aportèrent nouvelle d'une band de deux cent guerriers iroquois." [*MNF* 6.278]

Translation. "The unique consolation of the Father ... was to gather all the Christians in the evening ... to encourage them to patience. They also had good need of it. For some days later, some scouts brought news of a band of two hundred Iroquois warriors."

2. "Une nuict s'estant passée seulement dans cette isle, le matin, chacun print sa route ... Chasque jour on rencontroit de nouvelles bandes ... Le troisième jour après qu'on eût laissé toutes les bandes de ces guerriers, on arriva au lieu où l'on quitte les canots. Chacun met pied à terre et se charge de ses pacquets." [*MNF* 6.279–80]

Translation. "One night only having been passed on this island, in the morning, each [group of warriors] took its own route ... Each day they encountered new bands ... The third day after they had left all these bands of warriors, they reached the place where one quits the canoes. Each one disembarked and loaded himself with his bundles."

The overland march, and the arrival at Ossenrenon.

3. "Il fallut marcher trois jours par terre ... Il fallut les [his shoes] oster et demeurer tout nud en chemise, et ainsy s'aprocher de la première des deux rivières qu'il fault traverser avant que d'arriver aux bourgs des Iroquois. Estant sur le bord de cette rivière, on commanda au Père de la passer par un certain endroict où elle estoit moins rapide. Il le fit, mais s'il n'eust sceu nager, il estoit au bout de ses souffrances. Il eschapa de ce danger et arriva à la seconde rivière, c'est-à-dire à un cart de lieue proche du premier village. A l'autre costé de cette rivière estoient plusieurs Iroquois, hommes, femmes et enfants, qui attendoient les prisonniers avec bonne volonté de ne les pas espargner. Un Huron, pris autresfoys en guerre, auquel on avoit donné la vie, se rencontra parmy les Iroquois, commença à crier tant qu'il peut: 'Vous autres, François, vous estes morts. On vous bruslera. Il n'y a pas espérance de vie' ... On ne laisse pas de passer de l'autre costé et monter avec grande peine, car le bord estoit fort escore. Le père ... fut salué de quantité de bastonnades, de coups de pied et de poins, de telle sorte qu'il estoit tout en sang. Son hoste, quoyque barbare, le voyant en sy piteux esquipage, en eut compassion et luy dit ... 'Mon frère, tu es mal accommodé.' Sy fallut-il marcher jusques au village ... il se faict une harangue à la jeunesse pour l'exhorter à saluer les prisonniers à la façon du pays. Elle ne s'y espargna pas." [*MNF* 6.280–81]

Translation. "It was necessary to walk three days by land ... It was necessary to remove them [his shoes] and to stay quite naked in his shirt, and thus to draw near to the first of two rivers that it was necessary to cross before arriving at the towns of the Iroquois. Being on the bank of this river, they commanded the Father to cross it at a certain place where it was less rapid. He did it, but if he had not known how to swim, he would have been at the end of his sufferings. He escaped from this danger and arrived at the second river, that is to say, near the first village by a quarter league. On the other side of this river, were many Iroquois, men, women, and children, who were awaiting the prisoners with a good will not to spare them. A Huron, taken before in war, to whom they had given life, was among the Iroquois, he commences to shout as much as he is able: 'You others, Frenchmen, you are dead. They will burn you. There is no hope of life' ... They do not let [them] cross from the other side and to climb with great difficulty, for the bank was very steep. The Father ... was greeted with a quantity of beatings, of blows with foot and fist, of such a sort that he was all over blood. His host, although a barbarian, seeing him in so piteous a plight, had compassion on him and said to him ... 'Brother, you are poorly adapted.' If it were necessary to march all the way to the village ... A speech is made to the youth to exhort them to salute the prisoners after the fashion of the country. The youth did not spare themselves at it."

They are taken to Andagaron.

4. "Et il fault demeurer ainsy l'espace de trois jours, au bout desquels on les meine dans d'autres villages pour y estre derechef mocqués et tourmentés." [*MNF* 6.283]

Translation. "And it is necessary to stay therefore the space of three days, at the end of which they lead them to some other villages again to be mocked and tormented."

To Theonontougen.

5. "Il reste un autre bourg plus grand que les deux autres. Il fault y aller et faire preuve de sa constance ... La cruauté de ces barbares n'a pas d'esgard à cela [St. Isaac's festering wounds]. Elle les contrainct de marche jusques à cet autre bourg." [*MNF* 6.284]

Translation. "There remains another town bigger than the two others. It is necessary to go there and make proof of his constancy ... The cruelty of these barbarians had no regard for this [St. Isaac's festering wounds]. It constrained them to walk as far as this town."

The deliberations at Andagaron and dispersal of the Frenchmen.

6. "On avoit dèsjà dict au Père que la nuict prochaine il seroit tourmenté et faict mourir. La résolution en estoit prise dans

le conseil qui s'estoit tenu à ce dessein. Dieu néanmoints renversa leurs pensées … Ces barbares changent de résolution. Ils font mourir les Hurons seulement et donnent la vie aux François. On mène Couture dans le plus grand des trois bourgs et met-on le Père et René dans une mesme cabane du premier village." [*MNF* 6.285]

Translation. "They had already told the Father that the next evening he would be tortured and killed, the resolution had already been taken for it in the Council which was being held for this purpose. God nevertheless changed their thinking … These barbarians change their resolution. They are making the Hurons only to die, and they give life to the French. They lead Couture to the biggest of the three villages and put the Father and René in the same cabin in the first village."

Further inconclusive deliberations on the fate of the Frenchmen.

7. "Les Iroquois, les voyant en estat de pouvoir marcher, résolurent de les remener aux Trois-Rivières. Les personnes qui les devoient raconduire estoient dèsjà déterminés, les vivres tous préparés et le jour pris, les prisonniers disposés à partir, lorsqu'on parle d'un second conseil ou d'une nouvelle délibération, là où il ne fut rien conclud. Et chacun se retira, laissant les prisonniers à la disposition des plus meschants, qui estoit bien le pire estat où ils pouvoient estre." [*MNF* 6.286]

Translation. "The Iroquois, seeing them in a condition to be able to walk, resolved to lead them back to Trois-Rivières. The persons who were to conduct them back had already been determined, the provisions all prepared and the day chosen, the prisoners prepared to depart, when they speak of a second council or of a new deliberation, in which nothing was concluded. And each person went away, leaving the prisoners at the disposition of the more wicked, which was quite the worst condition in which they could be."

St. Isaac and St. René pray outside the village.

8. "Aussy, quelques jeunes gens, ayant apris que les prisonniers n'avoient esté donnés á personne, les allèrent chercher à dessein d'assouvir leur rage et leur cruauté sur eux. Dieu détourna ce malheur. Car lorsque ces barbares vinrent chercher le Père et René dans leur cabane, ils ne s'y trouvèrent point. Les anciens du village qui furent advertis des desseins de ces jeunes gens firent mettre le Père dans une cabane séparée de celle de René ... Il [St. Isaac] jugea propos d'en aller donner advis à René ... Il le trouva dans sa cabane, le mène hors du village ... et, ayant donné jusques à une petite coline esloignée d'une portée d'arquebuse du village, ils montent dessus la colline, se mettent à genoux, récitent le chapelet et font quelques temps d'oraison." [*MNF* 6.286]

Translation. "Also, some young men, having learned that the prisoners had not been assigned to anyone, went to look for them with the intention of satisfying their rage and their cruelty on them. God turned aside this evil. For when these barbarians come to look for the Father and René in their cabin, they did not find them there. The elders of the village who had been notified of the designs of these young men put the Father in a cabin separate from that of René ... He [St. Isaac] judged it seasonable to go and give warning of it to René ... He found him in his cabin, leads him outside the village ... and, having gone as far as a little hill separated an harquebus shot from the village, they climb on top of the hill, throw themselves on their knees, recite the Rosary and make some time of prayer."

Two young Mohawk warriors kill St. René and discard his corpse.

9. "Leur prière finie, comme ils descendoient pour retourner au village, deux jeunes hommes iroquois les arrestent, l'un desquels, vestu d'une longue soutane de frize,[48] dict au Père Jogues:

48. The Lonc-Catlin edition of Fr. Ragueneau's *Mémoires* (13) says, "Word unknown to us." But *frize* means a "woolen cloth." See Meyer- Lübke, *Romanisches Etymologisches Wörterbuch*, no. 3518. The word *soutane* means the clerical cassock, of course, but its simplest meaning was of an "undergarment" of the sort that the cassock is in its specialized

'Marche devant; et toy demeure derrière.' L'un et l'autre obéit. A peine le Père avoit-il faict cinq ou six pas qu'il entend du bruict derrière soy. Il regarde et veoit le pauvre René renversé par terre d'un coup de hache ... ils [the two Iroquois] le [the body] prennent, le lient avec des cords, le traînent par les rues du village, et puis le vont jetter en un lieu escarté." [*MNF* 6.286–87]

Translation. "Their prayer finished, as they were descending to return to the village, two young Iroquois men stop them. One of whom, clad in a long cassock of woolen cloth, says to Father Jogues: 'Walk in front; and you [St. René] stay behind.' The one and the other obey. Scarcely had the Father made five or six steps, when he hears a noise behind him. He looks and sees poor René thrown on the ground by a hatchet blow ... they [the two Iroquois] take it [the body], tie it with ropes, drag it through the streets of the village, and then go and throw it in a place far away."

St. Isaac conceals St. Rene's body under some stones but cannot find it in the morning because of the heavy rains.

10. "Il [St. Isaac's host] le [St. Isaac] faict escorter par deux jeunes hommes jusques au lieu où il devoit aller. Il va chercher le corps, le trouve tout nud dans un petit ruisseau au bas d'un petit torrent. Tout ce qu'il peult faire pour lors fut de la [*sic*] couvrir de quelques grosses pierres qui se rencontrèrent proche de ce lieu, espérant que le jour suivant il viendroit avec une houe pour faire une fosse et l'enterrer. Ce qu'il tâcha de faire le lendemain, mais en vain. Car la pluie qui estoit tombée en abondance toute la nuict

setting, viz., one's basic, outdoor garment. See Meyer-Lübke, *Romanisches Etymologisches Wörterbuch*, no. 8402. It may be that Fr. Buteux merely means a woolen blanket wound around the warrior's shoulders and hanging to his knees, a convenient hiding place for a hatchet. Father Chauchetière drew pictures of Jesuits at the Sault in cassocks that hung only to their knees and might have resembled blankets. See Greer, *Mohawk Saint*, 21 and 136. Buteux may have had in mind a woolen garment with sleeves and open at the front, however. There is a suggestion of such a garment under the over-blankets of the two male figures in Chauchetière's drawing of the first Iroquois arrivals at La Prairie. See Greer, *Mohawk Saint*, 94.

avoit tellement faict grossir le ruisseau ou torrent qu'elle avoit emporté le corps. Sy bien que luy, revenant le matin avec un hoyau, ne vit ny corps ny pierre; l'eau avoit tout couvert ... Il se met à l'eau dans ce rapide, le cherche en ce mesme lieu et aux endroicts circonvoysins, mais il ne trouve rien ... Il va sondant hault et bas avec les pieds et un baston." [*MNF* 6.288]

Translation. "He [St. Isaac's host] made two young men escort him [St. Isaac] as far as the place where he had to go. He goes and searches for the corpse, he finds it totally naked in a little creek at the bottom of a small torrent. All that he could do for the moment was to cover it with some big stones which they found near this place, hoping that the following day he would come with a hoe to make a hole and bury it. Which he tried to do the next day, but in vain. For the rain which was falling all night in abundance had so made the stream or torrent to swell, that it had carried away the corpse. So that he, returning in the morning with a mattock, saw neither corpse nor stone; the water had covered all ... He goes in the water in this rapid, he searches for it in this same place and in neighboring places, but he finds nothing ... He goes sounding high and low with his feet and a stick."

In the spring, St. Isaac finds St. René's remains and hides them.

11. "Il fault attendre jusques au printemps. Ce fut pour lors qu'il aprit de quelques jeunes enfants que le corps du François estoit proche d'un petit boccage dans un ruisseau. Il se transporte sur le lieu, cherche longtemps et enfin le trouve, c'est-à-dire les os, qu'il ramasse décemment, les baise et les cache dans trois ou quatre creux d'arbres." [*MNF* 6.288]

Translation. "It is necessary to wait until springtime. It was then that he learned from certain young lads that the corpse of the Frenchman was near a little wood in the stream. He betakes himself to the place, he searches a long time and at last finds it, that is to say, the bones, which he gathers decently, he kisses them, and he hides them in three or four hollows of trees."

Commentary

The Journey on Foot

The war party could have left their canoes and begun their march with their prisoners and booty either at the head of Lake George or at the head of Lake Champlain (Documents 1.2, 2.2, 4.2, and 5.3). In other words, the war party could have used the Ticonderoga portage from Lake Champlain to Lake George, and then paddled to the head of the latter lake, or they could have continued up Lake Champlain to its head and continued overland from there. It would have been a three- or four-day journey to the first Mohawk castle in either case, and in either case the party would have had to cross both the upper reaches of the Hudson and Mohawk Rivers. That they took the route to the head of Lake Champlain seems most likely to this reader both because the Ticonderoga portage is not mentioned in the documents and because St. Isaac and M. Bourdon seem to have been the first Europeans to traverse Lake George in 1646, as discussed in chapter 1.[49]

Fr. Buteux (Document 5.3) provides the only information we have about the journey itself, which he may very well have gleaned from St. Isaac's stories the year they spent together in Montreal. For our purposes, two points are important: the sight of the Iroquois across the Mohawk River and the detail of the steep embankment of which the prisoners were spared the ascent.

As noted above, an argument for the Auriesville Site is the steep bank from the riverside to the intervale or flats between the river and the ridge upon which the shrine stands. In 2022, I tried to find a way from the present canalway bike path along NY-5 South, just north of the Auriesville Shrine down to the river; but the

49. Campeau, *MNF* 5.600n24, thinks the war party took the Lake George route. Talbot, *Saint among Savages*, 447, at first thought they took that route but then changed his mind to the Lake Champlain route. He gave no reason for the change.

understory of the second-growth forest appeared so badly overgrown with tall weeds and snags of vines and tangled deadfall, not to mention that the New York Thruway crosses the flats between the shrine and the riverbank, that I decided not to try it. However, an old photo exists—taken around 1885 of the new shrine chapel and down across the cleared flats to the riverbank—that shows that the ascent across the flats and up the hill to the shrine itself was not very steep. Moreover, a 1986 photograph of the shrine colosseum from out in the Mohawk River itself highlights the easy accessibility of the shrine grounds from the riverbank.[50]

In contrast, as Mr. Rumrill notices,[51] the Bauder Site can be reached from the river either by climbing over a steep ridge or by a longer, easier route, by which I believe he means a trudge east up Yatesville Creek to a point near where the bridge now crosses the creek at Currytown Road, and then south up the same ravine through which the road now travels. One can see the steep ridge from the bed of the Yatesville today (Figure 13). The steep climb over the ridge to the Bauder Site surely fits the text better than the riverbank at Auriesville.

Therefore Fr. Buteux seems to telescope the narrative. First, we see the people of Ossenrenon across the Mohawk waiting for the war party. Next, we are already on the south side of the Mohawk, probably standing in Yatesville Creek after disembarking from canoes. The Huron captive warns us. We are beaten. Nevertheless, we do not have to climb over the eminent ridge but instead are

50. See Lynch, *Our Lady of Martyrs Shrine*, 12, for a reproduction of the photo. Earlene F. Melious at the Montgomery County Archives, whose mother grew up in Auriesville, recalls that the riverbank and the flats were not steep, although the hill directly up to the shrine was a little trying. This is confirmed by USGS Historical Map, Tribes Hill, which shows an ascent from 300 feet of elevation to 400 feet in a length of 2,000 feet from the riverbank to the shrine, not an arduous ascent, not even at the end.

51. Cf. Rumrill, "Interpretation and Analysis," 11: "The Bauder site is almost one full mile (1.6km) south of the Mohawk River—by the most accessible route[,] shorter if one opted to ascend a high, almost vertical ledge face to its northwest."

led up the creek to the gentler ravine where the Currytown Road now runs.

The Initial "Greeting" of the Prisoners

The other narratives of the arrival at Ossenrenon are written from another perspective than Buteux's. These narratives show us many Iroquois and at least one captive Huron awaiting the war party and prisoners on both banks of the river or stream near Ossenrenon. St. Isaac himself uses the Latin words *amnis* and *fluvius*, on which see Document 1.4 with notes at that point. Fr. Bressani (Document 2.4) translated St. Isaac's terms with the Italian word *fiume*, meaning "river," and sometimes "stream." Fr. Lalement (Document 4.3) rendered them in French as *petite rivière*, or "little river." Although *amnis*, *fluvius*, and *fiume* can mean a river the size of the Mohawk, Lalemant's term *petite rivière* seems to fix the meaning as a smaller body of flowing water, that is, a "big stream" or a "torrent." Therefore it seems that the "greeting" of the prisoners happened on the banks of a body of flowing water smaller than the Mohawk.

Moreover, Jogues (Document 1.4: *ex utraque ... ripa*), Bressani (Document 2.4: *dell' una e l' altra riva*), and Lalemant (Document 4.3: *sur ses rives de part et d'autre*) depict Iroquois and Huron alike on one side of the "big stream" and on the other tormenting the prisoners. One wonders why the Mohawk and their Huron captives would have been waiting both on the north side and on the south side of the Mohawk, which today is about a quarter of a mile wide at Auriesville.

For one thing, the war party with its captives numbered ninety people.[52] A flotilla of canoes would have been needed to carry these people and their bundles across the river. Were enough canoes on hand both to ferry a number of people from the south

52. Talbot, *Saint among Savages*, 200.

side of the river to the north side for an initial greeting, and then to carry them and the ninety people belonging to the war party and their bundles back again?

Another thing. Would it not have been more convenient altogether to "greet" the prisoners on the south side of the Mohawk and to harry them up to the village in a festival and crescendo of violence and verbal abuse? Yet if this seems more likely, then on both banks of what stream on the south side of the Mohawk at Auriesville could they have been waiting? The only candidate is Ravine Creek, which flows up from the south alongside the present ravine clearing or meadow and monuments maintained by Our Lady of Martyrs Shrine. Why would the canoe flotilla have landed at the narrow mouth of this creek west of the hill on which the village is thought to have been built, when convenient landing places existed on the bank bordering the flats at the bottom of the village hill?

Yatesville Creek seems to fit the documentary evidence much better. Nowadays, it is about two hundred feet wide at its mouth (Figure 14).[53] The prisoners could have been made to debark and wade up the stream, with the Mohawks jumping into the water on both sides to beat and taunt them while the Hurons shouted warnings. Instead of forcing the prisoners out of the creek onto its western bank, in order to take the steep path over the ridge, their captors would have driven them up the creek to the ravine mentioned above, which would have made for a less trying ascent to the village.

A Quarter of a League

Lalemant (Document 4.3) and Buteux (Document 5.3) observe that Ossenrenon stood about a quarter of a league from the Mohawk River. This would have been about six-tenths of a mile.[54]

53. Measurement taken from USGS Historical Map, Randall.

54. Cf. Document 1.12 and note 42 at that point.

This figure does not fit either site perfectly, but it does suit Auriesville better than the Bauder Site, as the riverbank at the Auriesville Shrine is just over three-tenths of a mile from the colosseum on the shrine property, while the Bauder site is at least a mile and two-tenths from the mouth of the Yatesville. The two distances can be approximated to each other only by assuming that the quarter-league figure was a "guesstimate."

A Lofty Hill

St. Isaac (Document 1.5) and Fr. Bressani (Document 2.5) note that Ossenrenon was on a high hill. The Shrine at Auriesville stands at 122 meters or 400 feet. The Bauder Site stands at 177 meters or 580 feet.[55] The elevation at the Bauder Site suits the documentary evidence much better.

Running the Gauntlet

Lalemant reports (Document 4.4) that the prisoners were compelled to run the gauntlet outside the gates (*portes*) of Ossenrenon. Fr. Bressani (Document 2.12: *porta*) and St. Isaac (Document 3.4: *porte*) also mention that St. René was slaughtered outside the gate of the village. If there was a gate or gates, there had to have been a fence or palisade, too. It was noticed above that no traces of palisades have been discovered in digging at Auriesville, while no methodical digging has occurred at the Bauder Site. Thorough excavation of the two sites by archeologists might reveal the historical reality.

Another Large Village

The second large Mohawk village or castle was Andagaron. St. Isaac himself says (Document 1.6) that it was *duobus milliaribus*,

55. Snow, *Mohawk Valley Archaeology: Sites*, 305, 451.

"two thousand paces," from Ossenrenon, that is, two Roman miles. Fr. Bressani (Document 2.6) translated this figure as *5 ò 6 miglia*, "5 or 6 Roman miles."[56] Fr. Lalemant (Document 4.6) says, "These towns are distant some leagues (*quelques lieues*) the ones from the others." He seems to mean that each town was several leagues from the next.

As we saw above, Clark and his associates thought that Andagaron was located about 3 English miles west of Fultonville, while Theonontougen, the third castle, was farther west near Sprakers Basin (now Sprakers). Clark's identifications would place Andagaron about 6.5 English miles from Auriesville, and Theonontougen about 9 miles beyond Fultonville, or roughly 15.5 English miles from Auriesville.

We have also seen that Rumrill has identified Andagaron with the Rumrill-Naylor Site, which sits on the bluff above Sprakers, and Theonontougen with the Oak Hill #1 Site, roughly 2 English miles west of Fort Plain on a bluff above the Mohawk flats. The latter site is commemorated by a New York State Historical Marker on the northwest corner of the intersection of NY-5 South and Airport Road (CR-67). The distance from this intersection via 5 South to the intersection of Sprakers Hill Road (CR-108) and NY-162—the approximate location of the Rumrill-Naylor Site—is 9.8 English miles.[57] From that intersection to the Bauder Site is 4.3 miles, using NY-162 and Moyer Road to Currytown Road. On this route, then, the total distance from Oak Hill #1 to Bauder is 14.1 English miles.

Whether Clark is right or the archeologists, one can say at any rate that the villages were "some leagues" from each other. A discrepancy exists, however, between St. Isaac's reckoning of the distance between Ossenrenon and Andagaron and Fr. Bressani's:

56. Cf. Document 1.6 and note 40 at that point.

57. This distance, and the others given in this section of the commentary, I measured in my car in June 2022.

two Roman miles as opposed to five or six Roman miles. Can this discrepancy be resolved? It can, if one remembers that both St. Isaac and Fr. Bressani were held captive at Ossenrenon, and that Fr. Bressani translated St. Isaac's letter freely.

The shortest route from the Bauder Site to the Rumrill-Naylor Site by car is not north back to the Mohawk and NY-5 South, but south on Currytown Road to Moyer Road, and thence southwest to NY-162, where one turns northwest to Sprakers Hill and stops at the corner of CR-108, the approximate location of Rumrill-Naylor. A state historical marker just southeast of the intersection, on the north side of 162, commemorates the village and the archeological excavation. (I am grateful to William Maring for driving me to this marker in 2021, and for pointing out the village site beyond a row of trees in the middle distance to the north. He also warned me that the current owner aggressively thwarts trespassers.) The distance by this route is 4.3 English miles. This route climbs from 580 feet at the Bauder Site to about 700 feet and stays at roughly that elevation to the Rumrill-Naylor Site.[58]

Therefore Bressani's reckoning of the distance between Ossenrenon and Andagaron is correct, if we are talking of the Bauder and Rumrill-Naylor Sites. It is easy to conjecture that when he read the figure given by St. Isaac, he corrected it in his translation, knowing from his own experience that it was incorrect. In any case, neither the one figure nor the other suits the actual distance between Auriesville and General Clark's Andagaron, another point in favor of the Bauder Site.

The Nearby Hill

Three of the documents we are examining represent St. Isaac as leading St. René up a hill near Ossenrenon to pray just before the

58. Elevations taken from USGS Historical Maps, Randall, Canajoharie, and Carlisle.

latter's martyrdom. The fourth says St. Isaac led his companion to a wood near the village. The fifth mentions nothing about this prelude to the massacre.

In his letter to his provincial, St. Isaac says they withdrew to "the nearby hill, which, very large, overhangs the village" (Document 1.13: *in collem vicinum qui pago plurimus imminet*). In his translation of the preceding document, Fr. Bressani says merely that they retired "towards a hill" (Document 2.12: *verso una collina*). Fr. Lalemant mentions their seeking out "a small wood near the large village" (Document 4.9: *un bocage proche de la bourgade*). Fr. Buteux describes their retreat on "a little hill separated an harquebus shot from the village" (Document 5.8: *une petite colline esloignée d'une portée d'arquebus du village*). In his short account of St. René's martyrdom (Document 3), St. Isaac omits this incident.

Fr. Ragueneau's testimony need not contradict the other witnesses. In fact, it complements them. What are fields today at the Bauder Site would have been fields when the Mohawks were farming that land, too. What is lawn around the Auriesville Shrine today would have been producing the Three Sisters in 1642, if there was a village there. Thus the two Jesuits would have had to walk up the hill west of the Bauder Site or the hill south of the Shrine to find any woods in which to pray privately.

St. Isaac describes a hill overhanging the village. The Latin word he uses (*imminet*), which I translate as "overhanging," can mean simply "bordering on," but it can also mean "threatening," especially to readers of Virgil. St. Isaac also says the hill was "very large." Neither of these elements of the description fits the topography at Auriesville. To be sure, high ridges rise south of the shrine, as can be seen in the photograph of the colosseum taken from the Mohawk River mentioned above, but these have never been considered to be where the two Jesuits prayed. Rather, it is believed that the low hill behind Auriesville #2 and the colosseum is where they made their devotions. West of the Bauder Site, however, the land rises at first gradually and then steeply to about 750 feet of elevation, the Bauder Site being at 580. To the west-southwest it rises to 800 feet.[59] And yet, standing at the Bauder Site, one does not feel that the hill impinges, the upward slope being gradual as far as Currytown Road. It may be that Fr. Bressani, by omitting this detail of "overhanging," and simply describing a hill, was indicating that the hill did not give a fearsome impression.

In contrast, Fr. Buteux speaks of "a little hill." This seems to contradict St. Isaac quite explicitly. And one notices that the hill south of what is represented at the shrine as the village site is small. It rises to 440 feet for the most part, and 460 feet in one small area, the shrine standing at 400 feet.[60] Does Fr. Buteux contradict St. Isaac in this case? One is tempted to cry, *Absit!* "By no means!" like St. Paul (e.g., Rom 3:3), but an argument must be made.

I can only propose the following to reconcile the accounts. On the face of it, Fr. Buteux's "little hill" fits the Auriesville Hill exactly. But at the Bauder Site—it is true even today— one would have ascended a gentle, cultivated slope from the village to the woods where the hill begins to climb quite steeply. Perhaps Buteux had retained the impression from conversations with St. Isaac of this gentle slope up to the woods on the hill, the "wood" emphasized in Fr. Lalemant's account. If this be true, then the Bauder Site fits the documentary evidence better than Auriesville. If this supposition be false, then we are left with an irreconcilable contradiction between St. Isaac's account and his friend Fr. Buteux's.

Another piece of evidence seems to fit the field and hill at the Bauder Site better than the same features at Auriesville. St. Isaac states that he and St. René had time to say four decades of the Rosary as they were returning from the wood on the hill toward the village before the two warriors accosted them (Document 1.13, "In itinere pagum versus coronam beatae Virginis recitamus iamque

59. Elevations from USGS Historical Map, Randall.

60. Elevations from USGS Historical Map, Tribes Hill.

quatuor decades percurreramus"; and Document 3.4, "Nous nous en retournons donc vers la porte du bourg, récitant nostre chapelet, duquel nous avions dèsjà dict quatre dixaines"). A walk from the hill at the Bauder Site through the field toward the village would have provided more time to say four decades of the Rosary devoutly—say, fifteen minutes—than the short distance from Auriesville Hill to Auriesville #2.

The Ravine

Little has been said about the ravine at the Auriesville Shrine. From the plateau on which the shrine grounds stand at 400 feet of elevation west of CR-164, one can walk southwest down an old cinder road through a small ravine formed by a little brook. This road does not appear on the US Geological Survey map of the area because it is overhung by trees and invisible from the air.[61]

The road descends at an angle fairly easily negotiated by bad knees to a clearing or meadow that lies at 320 feet of elevation. The meadow stands in a cup formed by higher ground that falls abruptly, even sheerly, on the north and east and south. Where the road reaches the meadow, the brook turns west and trickles along at the edge of the higher ground to the north, until it meets the larger Ravine Creek, which flows north to the Mohawk. This creek forms the western boundary of the meadow. On the other side of the creek, the ground rises rather less sharply back to 400 feet, accommodating a shrine of our Lord's sepulcher at the bottom of the hill.

In the meadow are other shrines, including an altar in an open-sided chapel. Signs recounting the saints' ordeal stand along the road that descends to the meadow. A Marian shrine stands about a third of the way down the road. From the traditional site

61. USGS Historical Map, Tribes Hill. All measurements in the following discussion of the Auriesville Site are taken from this map.

of Ossenrenon to the creek in the meadow, it is about 1,000 feet. The distance of descent from 400 feet of elevation to the level of Ravine Creek—320 feet of elevation—is 400 feet. When I visited the clearing on 22 June 2022, the potential of Ravine Creek to shift stone and gravel was clear from the bed of scree at the juncture of the brook in the meadow with Ravine Creek, but no pool deep enough to conceal a body, even one covered with stones, was apparent. Moreover, Ravine Creek is considerably smaller than the Yatesville.

A little has been said about the ravines at the Bauder Site. The picture needs to be made precise. The hayfield that contains the Bauder Site slopes from Currytown Road east for about 2,000 feet from nearly 660 feet of elevation to 580 feet at the field's eastern end.[62] At the eastern end the drop is sharp. The surface plunges from 580 feet of elevation to 440 feet, the level of the creek, in about 500 feet. The brook to the south of the site falls even more steeply, from 580 feet of elevation to 460 feet—the level of the creek at that point—in 400 feet, while the brook to the north falls again from 580 feet of elevation to 440, but in 600 feet. The eastern side of the Yatesville ravine, opposite the mouth of the brook that runs down from the north side of the Bauder Site, is steeper, soaring to 600 feet of elevation in about 200 feet.

On 20 June 2022, a sunny, breezy day of 75°F, I followed the course of the brook that flows down from the northern side of the Bauder Site. I was surprised to find that this brook joins another brook that flows down from the northwest, and that the two combine to make up the brook that I had seen in 2021.[63] I followed

62. Measurements in this paragraph are taken from the USGS Historical Map, Randall; but the altitude of the Bauder Site given elsewhere in this text—574.48 feet—I measured myself with the MyAltitude app. With the same app I measured the altitude at the junction of the brook that runs down from the Bauder Site on the north with Yatesville Creek as 433.07 feet. The difference in altitude between the Bauder Site and the place where the brook and the creek meet is 141.41 feet.

63. At the time, it seemed probable to me that this second brook originated in the

the bed of the brook with considerable difficulty. I took four painful falls in the mud while clambering around fallen trees. In fact, toward the bottom, in the steepest section of the climb, several complicated tangles of downed trees, fallen branches, vines, and brambles had compressed the brook into small channels that cut little waterfalls that were hard to negotiate. These obstacles would not probably have existed in Mohawk times. They would have been cut up for firewood by the women and hauled back to the village, making the bed of the brook an easier path to travel. I have wondered why a woman should have been passing by when St. Isaac was looking for St. Rene's body in the bed of the Yatesville (Document 3.8). The answer now seems clear. She was hunting for firewood.

At the bottom of the ravine, the brook divides and enters the Yatesville through two mouths. I have given above[64] the altitude of what appeared to me as the main mouth. The brook debouches into a secondary channel of Yatesville Creek that was almost dry that day (Figure 15). In between the secondary channel and the main channel was a long, narrow islet of scree with some scrub managing to take root on it. In fact, what water there was in the secondary channel seemed to dive under the islet of sand and gravel and stones. I walked northerly down the islet to the point where the two channels met. The main channel was flowing vigorously through several pools, while the secondary channel had begun to flow again with water from the brook above. Upstream to the south, banks of scree were visible in the main channel in the distance (Figure 16), while downstream the creek had cut a high, sheer cliff out of the Utica shale that crops out unusually in this

---

northern half of the same field above, which is divided from the Bauder Site by a scrubby strip through which the brook I was following runs. I thought it likely that that field was the location of the Bauder Family Cemetery and the well mentioned above. This has been confirmed by the Rumrill map of the site. See Lenig, "Bauder," 3.

64. See note 62 above.

area (Figure 17). The meeting place of the two channels had been scoured down to the Utica bedrock, leaving a glistening shield of black-and-gray stone shot through with white. It was startlingly beautiful (Figure 18). A long embankment of scree three feet high formed the eastern side of the creek. I sat on a stone and said the Joyful Mysteries, as it was Monday.[65]

Before a difficult climb—in several places, a crawl; I had brought my gardening kneepads along—back up to the Bauder Site, I observed two things. First, while the Yatesville was low that day in June, nevertheless the creek still flowed continuously in the main channel, and pools existed of such a depth that St. Isaac could have hidden St. Rene's body under a heap of the stones which lie plentifully about. This scree, scraped up in islands and embankments, and even scattered on the floor of the woods beside the creek, provides ample evidence of the volume and violence of the waters of the creek when in spate. When at maximum volume, the creek may be 150 feet wide, including its overflow into the woods.

Second, the young warriors and children who dragged St. René's body down to the Yatesville could either have dumped their burden at the juncture of the Bauder Site brook and the dry side channel of the Yatesville, or they could have carried it onto the islet of scree. The latter seems more likely to me, as the body would have been out from under the tree canopy and completely

65. The photo in Figure 18 was taken from this point. As I was meditating, I had the unhappy thought that the Mystery of Jesus' Birth had led to this slaughter and this fanatical Jesuit mission. I felt an evil spirit loom on the island of scree, a unique experience to me. Then I recognized that Christ's birth was for the world's peace, and that the mission was to bring this good news to the Mohawk. But then I thought, Why the hierarchical, elaborately liturgical baroque Church of the missionaries? Why not a Tolstoyan sort of religion of simple, equal peacemakers? But the Presentation of Christ in the Temple and the Finding of Christ in the Temple showed that God approves of hierarchy and liturgy in order to preserve his religion. A Tolstoyan-like cult would not have persisted through time. These missionaries brought peace and good news because they were members of the Church that had persisted through the ages.

exposed to cruising vultures and crows. St. Isaac would have discovered the body where they had dropped it and carried it a few feet to the main channel of the creek where he would have found water deep enough in which to conceal his friend's remains. No doubt the locations of the islet and the embankments shift a little every year because of the force of the water, but I assume that the topographical constraints of the location keep the basic configurations the same. As we examine the documentary evidence, we must keep these terrains—these two ravines—in mind.

In his letter to his provincial, St. Isaac gives three descriptions of the surroundings into which St. Rene's body was cast. First, he says the body had been thrown "into a torrent a sufficiently long way off" (Document 1.14: *in torrentem sat longe proiecerant*). Second, he says he covered the body "with a barrow of stones in the very torrent, where it was rather deep" (Document 1.15: "in ipsomet torrente ubi erat profundior, lapidum acervo tumulo"). Finally, he gives a sense of the ravine, describing "the mountain at the roots of which that torrent flows" and "the steep woods which are on the other side" (Document 1.16: "montem ad cuius radices torrens ille decurrit . . . saltum qui est altera parte"). One can summarize these phrases into four points: a torrent ran at the foot of the mountain on which Ossenrenon stood; the torrent was rather far away from the village; the opposite side of the ravine created by this torrent was steep and forested, and the torrent was deep enough, at least in one place, for the concealment of a body under a heap of stones.

In his summary account of St. Rene's martyrdom, St. Isaac uses similar phrases: "a torrent which passes at the foot of their town . . . I put it at the bottom of the water loaded with big stones" (Document 3.5: "un torrent qui passe au pied de leur bourg . . . je le mis au fond de l'eau, chargé de grosses pierres"). One takes two points from these phrases. First, St. René's body was cast into a torrent that ran at the foot of the town. Second, the water of the torrent was deep enough for the concealment of the body under a heap of stones.

Fr. Bressani translates St. Isaac's phrase *in torrentem sat longe proiecerant* literally, *gettato nel fiume assai lontano* ("thrown him in the river rather far away," Document 2.13). Fr. Lalemant and Fr. Buteux modify this phrase slightly: "throw him in a place very far apart" (Document 4.11: *jetter en un lieu fort escarté*) and "throw it in a place far away" (Document 5.9: *jetter en un lieu escarté*). Since both Lalemant and Buteux had heard St. Isaac speak of his ordeals, perhaps this is a phrase that he used in conversation with them.

In the next detail, Fr. Lalemant sticks close to St. Isaac's letter to his provincial and his summary account of St. René's death: "he finds him in a creek, he covers him with big stones" (Document 4.11: "il le trouve dans un ruisseau, le couvre de grosses pierres").

Fr. Buteux varies the picture slightly: "he finds it totally naked in a little creek at the bottom of a small torrent ... to cover it with some big stones" (Document 5.10: "le trouve tout nud dans un petit ruisseau au bas d'un petit torrent ... la [*sic*] couvrir de quelques grosses pierres"). Recall the description of the ravines at Auriesville and at the Bauder Site above. At each place, a "small torrent" flows into a "little creek," Ravine Creek on the one hand and Yatesville Creek on the other. Buteux may well have picked up this detail from St. Isaac in conversation and included it here. That St. René was "totally naked" is not mentioned in the other narratives at this point, but it is found in Documents 1.14, 2.13, and 3.5.

Fr. Bressani varies most significantly from the other witnesses here. First, in his translation, he makes St. Isaac say, "I found him on the bank of the river" (Document 2.13: *lo ritrovo al lido del fiume*). Yet Bressani agrees with the other witnesses that the body had been cast in the creek. We have seen that the Yatesville is divided into two channels at this point in its course by an islet of scree, and that the secondary channel was nearly dry on the day I saw it. Perhaps Bressani is viewing the islet both as a part of the creek and as the bank of the creek's main channel. Second, he has St. Isaac say, "I cover him with stones at the bottom of a dry creek bed" (Document 2.13: *nel fondo d'un torrente secco lo copro di pietri*).

How can this second detail be made to agree with St. Isaac's statement that he hid the body "in the very torrent, where it was rather deep"? First, the date of St. Rene's martyrdom was 28 September. In Upstate New York, September is usually dry. It is a natural blessing that helps with the harvest. But it means that the creeks are usually low, to be filled again by the autumn rains. Second, in eighteenth-century Italian—and, one presumes, a hundred years before—the adjective *secco* could mean "dry, barren, empty, poor, low, flat, thin."[66] Bressani may have meant that the creek was not bone dry, but attenuated, low. Third, he may have been setting up a rhetorical contrast to the coming flood of water in the creek caused by the rains. Fourth, St. Isaac's statement that he covered the body "with a barrow of stones in the very torrent, where it was rather deep" may well suggest that the creek was low at the time, and that St. Isaac had to carry the body to a pool which still contained enough water in which to submerge the body. This would support Bressani's account, and we must remember that Bressani had been held captive in Ossenrenon for a summer and a fall, too. Thus once more we find that the accounts differ radically only on the surface.

Given the dryness of the season, however, it seems doubtful to me that the rather narrow, shallow Ravine Creek at Auriesville would have provided a pool where the saint's body could have been hidden. It certainly did not provide such a pool when I visited in June 2022. Conversely, Rumrill reports that Yatesville Creek flows at all seasons and is sometimes torrential, so it might well have contained such a pool even in September.[67] It certainly contained several such pools when I was there in June 2022.

66. Baretti, *Dictionary of the Italian and English Languages*, s.v.

67. Rumrill, "Interpretation and Analysis," 17.

Therefore, taking all the details together, we find a picture that supports the theory that St. René was martyred at the Bauder Site. To be sure, certain details fit both sites: a ravine, a creek, a brook that flows into the creek, and a remote spot where the body was discarded. Nevertheless, Ravine Creek does not flow at the foot of the mountain on which the shrine stands, except in the attenuated sense that the creek has cut the western edge of the low shrine plateau where Auriesville #1 stood. In contrast, Yatesville Creek runs right at the bottom of the mountain on which the Bauder Site stands. In fact, as compared with the Bauder Site, Auriesville can hardly be said to stand on a mountain at all. Moreover, no steep wood (*saltus*) stands on the other side of Ravine Creek, while one does on the opposite bank of the Yatesville. In addition, Ravine Creek is probably too shallow, except in spate, for the concealment of St. René's body. Finally, whether we compare the smaller ravines formed by the brooks at each site, or the bigger ravines formed by the creeks, we find that the terrain at the Bauder Site is much steeper and much more difficult than that at Auriesville. The nature of this terrain suits St. Isaac's narrative better than the gentler and more open topography at Auriesville.

The Rainstorm

All five witnesses (Documents 1.16, 2.13, 3.6, 4.11, and 5.10) mention a heavy rainfall that caused the creek in which St. René's body was hidden to swell to such a depth that it was plausible to think that the rushing water had carried the corpse away. Rumrill believed that such a thing could have easily happened in Yatesville Creek,[68] and I have seen with my own eyes the aftereffects of the enormous power of the Yatesville's freshet. It does seem credible, however, that it could have happened in Ravine Creek, too.

68. Rumrill, "Interpretation and Analysis," 17.

The Lie

St. Isaac mentions that he was told falsely that young people had dragged St. René's body to another stream. In the first instance he describes the stream as "very remote" (Document 1.16: *in fluvium remotissimum*); in the second he describes it as "a quarter of a league away" (Document 3.8: *à la rivière qui estoit un cart de lieue de là*). In the second passage, St. Isaac also says he did not know of the stream's existence (*que je ne cognoissois pas*). A quarter of a league was about six-tenths of an English mile.[69]

Fr. Artur Melançon took this as a telling point against the identification of Auriesville with Ossenrenon, for he thought this other river to be the Mohawk, of which St. Isaac could hardly have been unaware. Fr. Melançon says that Gen. Clark replied to this objection with an argument that a little village called "Gandaouagué," named in the documentary sources of St. Catherine Tekakwitha's life, lay just west of Auriesville, that is, what we now call the Milton Smith Site, and that the name meant *Au rapide*, "At the Rapids."[70] Melançon instead identified Gandaouagué with a village to the north of the Mohawk just west of Fonda, New York, now the Franciscan St. Kateri National Shrine, and dismissed Clark's translation of the village name.

Fr. Melançon was right that a Gandaouagué, or Caughnawaga, existed on the outskirts of Fonda, but his argument about the Mohawk River—that it is the only other body of flowing water near Auriesville—makes no sense. First, if this mysterious creek was mentioned in a lie, why could the creek not have been a fabrication, too? There need not have been a real creek at all, just an imaginary one. Second, as Auriesville's defenders have pointed

69. See commentary above under "A Quarter of a League."

70. See note 13 in chap. 2 in this volume. A New York State historical marker commemorating the location of Gandaouagué used to stand about three-quarters of a mile west of Auriesville. This identification goes back to Clark, as we have seen.

out, Schoharie Creek is nearby, and St. Isaac may well have been ignorant of its existence at the time of St. René's martyrdom, though not later on. Therefore this detail does not seem to count against Auriesville as the site of St. Rene's murder. Of course, it does not count against the Bauder Site, either, as Alston Creek runs a little more than a quarter of a league north-northeast of the Yatesville, and St. Isaac could well have been ignorant of it, too. And again, the creek may have just been made up.

Summary

Our question in this chapter has been whether the Bauder Site was the location of St. René Goupil's martyrdom. The only other candidate for the site was the traditional Martyrs' Shrine at Auriesville. The evidence has compelled us to answer the question in the affirmative.

First, the archeological evidence that has been found at the Auriesville Shrine suggests strongly that Auriesville #2 was, during the period 1645–60, an unfortified hamlet. The artifacts discovered at the Bauder Site date that site to the period 1635–46 and indicate that the locus was a castle. Thus, while the dating of certain artifacts from Auriesville #2 supports the traditional claims made for the shrine, the site is not a suitable candidate for the castle where St. René was killed.

The documents support the conclusion drawn from the archeological evidence. But how does documentary evidence speak, how do documents prove a point? Lawyers learn to weigh evidence, not to count witnesses. The students of old documents do the same. As the great philologist Richard Bentley (1662–1742) said, *Nobis et ratio et res ipsa centum codicibus potiores sunt*, "In our view, both reason and the matter itself are stronger than a hundred documents."[71] In other words, the logic of the writings under

71. Bieler, *Grammarian's Craft*, 45.

consideration and of their circumstances weighs more than the number of witnesses that can be added up in support of a certain point of view.

One point weighs heavily with this reader: the boldness and spontaneity with which Clark and Frey identified Auriesville as the location of Ossenrenon, and the alacrity with which Fr. Loyzance embraced their conclusion. Once the Martyrs' Shrine was established at Auriesville, further archeological discovery was preempted. This was neither good science nor good martyrology, both of which are normally characterized by prudence. The weak, sometimes circular, arguments used by later Jesuits to support Fr. Loyzance add to the impression of bad science and bad martyrology.

Another point that weighs heavily with this reader is the far better correlation of the Bauder Site topography with the documentary evidence. To be sure, both sites fit the evidence superficially: a river, a creek, a brook; a village on a hill; another hill nearby, a wood, a ravine. But the arguments for placing Ossenrenon at Auriesville are not nearly as strong as those that place it at the Bauder Site. Generally speaking, Auriesville's terrain is simply not rugged enough to suit the evidence.

In particular, the details of the initial "welcoming" of the prisoners to Ossenrenon gain focus and vitality—gain weight—when placed at the mouth of Yatesville Creek. In 2019 and 2022, I walked through the culverts under NY-5 South and the New York Thruway to within three hundred feet of the mouth of the Yatesville, where the water began to overtop my knee boots. It made much more sense to imagine the Mohawks on both banks of that creek, hurling abuse and jumping into the water to beat the prisoners, than to imagine the scene at Auriesville, where indeed it makes little sense.

In particular, too, is the description of the ravine at the bottom of which the youths threw St. René's corpse. It was cut by an *amnis, fluvius, torrens, fiume, torrent, petite rivière, ruisseau, petit ruisseau* at the "foot," at the "roots" of the "mountain" on which the village stood. Ravine Creek at Auriesville neither cuts a ravine at the roots of the plateau on which Auriesville #2 stands, nor does it support such a range of designations as is used in the documents, while Yatesville Creek does support them and does cut its way through the shale right at the roots of the Bauder Site mountain. Moreover, the west bank of Ravine Creek is less of a *saltus*, a "steep woods"—in my eyes, at any rate—than the east bank of the Yatesville, which, where it is not sheer, is much steeper than the bank at Auriesville.

In conclusion, it has to be said that the weight of the evidence, both archeological and documentary, whether taken together or separately, is for the Bauder Site as the location of St. René Goupil's martyrdom. Physical experience of these sites supports this conclusion.

CHAPTER 4

The Martyrdoms of St. Isaac Jogues and St. Jean de Lalande at the Bauder Site

THE EVIDENCE bearing on the martyrdoms of St. Isaac and St. Jean is very different from the evidence regarding St. René's death. It is fragmentary and based entirely on reports from Native American informants. Of course, the evidence on St. Isaac's journey with Jean Bourdon to establish peace with the Iroquois is based on the reports of those gentlemen themselves. Again, bibliographical information can be found in the introduction to this book.

Documentary Evidence with Translations

Document 6. "Le P. Isaac Jogues au P. André Castillon," or "Father Isaac Jogues to Father André Castillon."

On his diplomatic journey with M. Bourdon to the Mohawk in the late spring of 1646, St. Isaac attended to the pastoral needs of the sick.

1. "Je baptizé dans le bourg où nous demeurasmes quelques jours quelques enfants malades." [*MNF* 6.513]

Translation. "In the village where we stayed some days, I baptized some sick children."

Document 7. "L'Interprète Labatie à Jean de la Montagne," or "The Interpreter Labatie to Jean de la Montagne."

The first report of the deaths of St. Isaac and St. Jean. The source was an Indian informant.

1. "[L]es François sont esté arrivez le dis-septiesme de ce présent mois [October 1646] au for des Maquas." [*MNF* 6.528]

Translation. "[T]he French arrived the seventeenth of the present month [October 1646] at the fort of the Mohawks."

2. "Il fault que vous sçachiez que se sont esté seulement la nation de l'Ours qui les ont fait mourir, sçachant que la nation du Lou et de la Tortu ont faict tous qu'il ont pouveu pour leur sauvez la vie." [*MNF* 6.528]

Translation. "It is necessary that you know that it was only the clan of the Bear that killed them, knowing that the clan of the Wolf and of the Turtle did everything that they could to save life for them."

3. "Sçaschez donch que le dis-huittiesme au soir que ils viene appellez Isaach pour souppé. Il se leva et s'en alla avec ce barbar au logis de l'Ours. Com entrant dans le logis, il y avez un traistre avec sa hasche derrier la port, en entrant il luy fendit la teste." [*MNF* 6.528]

Translation. "Know, therefore, that the eighteenth in the evening they came to call Isaac for supper. He got up and went with the barbarian to the lodge of the Bear. On entering the lodge, there was a traitor with his hatchet behind the door, on entering he clove his head."

Document 8. "Willem Kieft, Dir., à Charles Huault de Montmagny, Gouv.," or "Willem Kieft, Director, to Charles Huault de Montmagny, Governor."

The chief magistrate of New Holland informs his counterpart in New France of the fate of St. Isaac and St. Jean. Jan Labatie's letter was enclosed in the director's.

1. "Notre ministre d'en-hault [Johannes Megapolensis[1]] s'est enquis soigneusement aux principaux de cette canaille de la cause de ce malheureux acte, mais il n'a peu avoir autre reponce d'eux que ledict Père avoit laissé le diable parmy quelques hardes qu'il leur avoit laissé en garde, qui avoit faict manger leur bled." [*MNF* 6.540]

Translation. "Our minister above [Johannes Megapolensis] has enquired carefully of the chief men of this rabble about the cause of this unhappy act, but he has been able to have no other answer than that the said Father left the devil among some old clothes which he left in their keeping, who caused the eating of their grain."

Document 9. Fr. Jérôme Lalemant, *Relation de ce qui s'est passé en la Nouvelle-France ès années 1645 et 1646*, chapitre IV, "De la Mission des Martyrs commencée au pays des Iroquois," or *Report of What Happened in New France in the Years 1645 and 1646*, chapter 4, "Concerning the Mission of the Martyrs Begun in the Land of the Iroquois."

This text gives an account of the diplomatic mission of St. Isaac and Jean Bourdon to the Mohawk. The problem of Ossenrenon's current name arises immediately. Notice, too, that a general assembly to consider peace was held at the same time as St. Isaac gave a Christian name to the village.

1. "[I]ls arrivèrent en leur première bourgade appellée Oneugi8ré, jadis Osserrion. Là il fallut demeurer deux jours pour estre considérez et bienveignez de ces peuples qui venoient de toutes

1. Johannes Megapolensis (1603–70) was the Dutch Reformed minister at Rensselaerswyck. He was involved in St. Isaac's escape from the Mohawks in 1643. See his *Short Account of the Mohawk Indians*, 43.

parts pour les voir … Le 10 de juin, honoré par le feste de la saincte Trinité, il [St. Isaac] donna ce nom sacrosainct à cette bourgade. Il se fit en mesme temps une assemblée générale de tous les principaux capitaines et des anciens du pays." [*MNF* 6.571]

Translation. "[T]hey reached their first big village called Oneugiouré, formerly Osserrion. There it was necessary to stay two days to be gazed on and welcomed by these peoples who were coming from all parts to see them … The 10th of June, honored by the Feast of the Holy Trinity, he [St. Isaac] gave this sacrosanct name to this big village. At the same time was held a general assembly of all the chief captains and of the elders of the country."

2. "Il [St. Isaac] fit en particulier un présent de trois mille grains de porcelaine à l'une des grosses familles des Annierronnons, répandue dans leurs trois bourgades … La famille dont nous avons parlé, qui se nomme la famille des Loups, asseura les François par un beau présent." [*MNF* 6.572–73]

Translation. "In particular, he [St. Isaac] made a present of three thousand beads of porcelain to one of the big families of the Mohawks, scattered in their three big villages … The family of which we have spoken, who call themselves the family of the Wolves, assured the French by a good present."

The "old clothes" mentioned by Willem Kieft.

3. "Mais quelques esprit deffians ne regardoient pas de bon oeil un petit coffre que le Père avoit laissé pour asseurance de son retour. Ils s'imaginoient que quelque malheur funeste à tout le païs estoit renfermé dans cette cassette." [*MNF* 6.573]

Translation. "But some mistrustful spirits did not regard with a kindly eye a little coffer which the Father had left for assurance of his return. They imagined that some fatal misfortune for the whole country was enclosed in this casket."

And as reported in Document 6:

4. "Il [St. Isaac] fit souvent la ronde par les cabanes, visita

les malades et envoya au ciel par les eaux du baptesme quelques pauvres créatures mourantes, mais des riches prédestinez." [*MNF* 6.574]

Translation. "He [St. Isaac] often made the round of the longhouses, he visited the sick, and dispatched to heaven by the waters of baptism some poor dying creatures but predestined for riches."

5. "Pour conclusion, le Père, nos François et leurs guides partirent du bourg de la Sainte-Trinité le 16 de juin." [*MNF* 6.575]

Translation. "To conclude, the Father, our French, and their guides departed from the village of the Holy Trinity the 16th of June."

Document 10. "Le Père Jacques Buteux au P. Jérôme Lalemant, Sup.," or "Father Jacques Buteux to Father Jérôme Lalemant, Superior."

Fr. Buteux reports what he has heard from Indian informants about St. Isaac's second trip in 1646 among the Mohawk, accompanied by St. Jean.

1. "Une autre bande [of warriors] fist rencontre du Père Jogues à deux journées du pays, laquelle le despouilla nud, luy et son compagnon [Jean] De Lalande. Il passa outre jusques dans le village, là où on tua d'abord De Lalande et un Huron qui estoit de leur canot. On différa un jour et une nuict la mort du Père Jogues, qui enfin massacré. Je n'ay peu aprendre autre circonstance de ce glorieux martire." [*MNF* 7.44]

Translation. "Another band [of warriors] met Fr. Jogues at a two days' journey from the country. They stripped him naked, him and his companion [Jean] De Lalande. He went on right into the village, where they first killed De Lalande and a Huron who was of their canoe. They put off a day and a night the death of Fr. Jogues, who finally they slaughtered. I have not been able to learn any other circumstance of this glorious martyrdom."

Document 11. "Le P. Jacques Buteux au P. Jérôme Lalemant, Sup.," or "Father Jacques Buteux to Father Jérôme Lalemant, Superior."

About seven weeks later, Fr. Buteux had learned more.

1. "Pour ce qui est des Iroquois et de la mort du Père Jogues, voicy quelques autres particularités que j'ay aprises du Huron qui s'est sauvé. Les Iroquois du premier village qui devoient deffendre le Père Jogues, et mesme le frère de sa tente ou hostesse a esté complice de sa mort. Avant que le Père fust arrivé dans le pays, les plus mutins et les plus superstitieux avoient résolu de le tuer. Ceux-là ne voulant pas de paix avec les François, ny Hurons, ny Algonquins, et ceux-cy croyant que la maladie qui régnoit dedans le pays et les chenilles qui mangeoient leurs bleds avoient esté aportées dans le coffre du Pére Jogues, qu'il avoit laissé néanmoints aux Iroquois comme gage de son affection. Ce coffre fut jetté à l'eau sans estre ouvert et plus d'un moys avant que le Père arrivast au païs." [*MNF* 7.50]

Translation. "For what concerns the Iroquois and the death of Fr. Jogues, here are some other particulars which I have learned from the Huron who escaped. The Iroquois of the first village who ought to have defended Fr. Jogues, and even the brother of his aunt or hostess, were complicit in his death. Before the Father had arrived in the country, the most mutinous and the most superstitious had resolved to kill him. The former not wishing peace with the French nor the Hurons nor the Algonquins, and the latter believing that the sickness which reigned in the country and the caterpillars that were eating their grain had been brought in the coffer of Fr. Jogues, who had left [it] nevertheless with the Iroquois as a pledge of his affection. This coffer was thrown into the water without being opened and more than one month before the Father arrived in the country."

2. "Les principaux des Iroquois n'estoient nullement d'advis qu'on fist mourir les François et surtout le Père Jogues. Pour cet

effect, ils tindrent un conseil au plus grand des trois bourgs [Theonontougen], là où on résolut de le laisser en vie et en liberté. Mais ceux qui avoient conspiré sa mort n'attendirent pas la résolution. Le coup estoit dèsjà faict, lorsque les desputés du conseil vindrent au lieu où le Père faisoit sa demeure." [*MNF* 7.50]

Translation. "The chief men of the Iroquois were by no means of the opinion that they ought to put the French and especially Fr. Jogues to death. For this purpose, they held a council at the biggest of the three big villages [Theonontougen], where they decided to let him live and leave him at liberty. But those who had plotted his death did not wait for the resolution. The blow had already been struck, when the deputies of the council came to the place where the Father was making his dwelling."

Document 12. Fr. Jérôme Lalemant, "Lettre au R. P. Estienne Charlet, provincial de la Compagnie de Jésus en la province de France," in *Relation de ce qui s'est passé en la Nouvelle-France en l'année 1647*, or "Letter to the Rev. Father Étienne Charlet, Provincial of the Society of Jesus in the Province of France," in *Report of What Happened in New France in the Year 1647*.

A brief account of the double martyrdom.

1. "Mais à peine avoit-il [St. Isaac] mis pied à terre que … il fut traitté de captif par ces barbares: luy et son compagnon [St. Jean de Lalande], qui estoit un jeune François séculier, battus, despouillez et mis à nud et conduits en cet estat au prochain bourg, où le lendemain de leur arrivé, dix-huictiesme du mesme mois d'octobre, le Père Jogues fut massacré et son compagnon pareillement." [*MNF* 7.71]

Translation. "But hardly had he [St. Isaac] disembarked than … he was treated as a captive by these barbarians: him and his companion [St. Jean de Lalande], who was a young French secular, beaten, robbed, stripped naked and led in this condition to the next big village, where the day after their arrival, the 18th of the same month of October, Fr. Jogues was slaughtered and his companion as well."

Document 13. Fr. Jérôme Lalemant, *Relation de ce qui s'est passé en la Nouvelle-France en l'année 1647*, chapitre I, or *Report of What Happened in New France in the Year 1647*, chapter 1.

From a brief and incomplete account.

1. "Le 24 de septembre de l'an passé, le Père Isaac Jogues partit des Trois-Rivières pour aller au païs des Hiroquois Agnéronons, afin d'entretenir la paix qu'ils avoient solemnellement conclue et pour cultiver et augmenter la semence de l'evangile ... Le sujet de cette perfidie [of the Mohawks] provient à mon advis de leur humeur guerrière ... et de plus, de leur superstition et de la haine que les Hurons captifs leur ont donné de la doctrine de Jésus-Christ ... Si bien qu'ils accusèrent le Père Jogues, en son premier voyage depuis la paix faite, d'avoir caché des sorts dans un coffret ou dans une petite caisse qu'il laissoit à son hoste pour gage de son retour." [*MNF* 7.73]

Translation. "The 24th of September last year, Fr. Isaac Jogues departed from Trois-Rivières to go to the country of the Iroquois Mohawks, in order to maintain the peace that they had solemnly concluded, and to cultivate and augment the seed of the Gospel ... The cause of this perfidy [of the Mohawks] comes in my opinion from their warlike disposition ... and moreover from their superstition, and from the hatred that the Huron captives have conveyed to them of the doctrine of Jesus Christ ... So that they accused Fr. Jogues, on his first journey since the peace was made, of having hidden some spells in a coffer or in a little box that he left with his host as a pledge of his return."

Document 14. Fr. Jérôme Lalemant, *Relation de ce qui s'est passé en la Nouvelle-France ès années 1647 et 1648*, chapitre II, or *Report of What Happened in New France in the Years 1647 and 1648*, chapter 2.

Martyrdoms of St. Isaac Jogues and St. Jean de Lalande

1. "Il [a Mohawk captive[2]] a, dis-je, protesté que depuis ce temps-là il avoit eu de l'amour et du respect pour Onontio [Governor Montmagny] et pour tous les François et qu'il avoit receu un coup au bras, dont il monstroit les marques, pour s'estre opposé à celuy qui malheureusement a massacré le Père Isaac Jogues; et qu'après la mort du Père, il s'estoit rendu protecteur du François [St. Jean] qui l'accompagnoit, qu'il luy avoit défendu de s'eloigner de luy, voyant bien que sa vie n'estoit pas en asseurance. 'Mais ce jeune homme, disoit-il, s'estant écarté pour chercher je ne sçay quoi qu'il avoit apporté, fut assommé d'un coup de hache par ceux qui l'espioient.'" [*MNF* 7.302]

Translation. "He [a Mohawk captive] had, I say, protested that he had had for a long time love and respect for Onontio [Governor Montmagny] and for all the French, and that he had received a blow on the arm, of which he showed the marks, for opposing himself to that one who wickedly slaughtered Fr. Isaac Jogues; and that after the death of the Father, he made himself protector of the Frenchman [St. Jean] who was accompanying him, that he had prevented him from going away from him, seeing clearly that his life was not secure. 'But this young man,' he said, 'going astray to look for I don't know what that he had brought, was felled by a blow of a hatchet, by those who were spying on him.'"

2. Campeau, *MNF* 7.302n9, observes, "Par conséquent, c'est l'un des Agniers pris par Simon Piechkaretch en 1645, qui servirent à ménager la paix, cette même année." Talbot, *Saint among Savages*, 351, 356, 358, 415, 417, 431, and 432, identifies Honatteniate, the son of St. Isaac's adoptive aunt, a representative at the 1645 peace conference with Governor Montmagny (*MNF* 6.370), with this man who defended St. Isaac and tried to protect St. Jean. This carries the implication that Honatteniate was the Iroquois whom the French nicknamed Le Berger and who, in my opinion, can be considered a confessor of the Faith. Talbot's evidence, in addition to the Campeau passage cited above, can be found at *MNF* 6.360–62, 6.370, 7.769–76. Simon Piechkaretch, a Christian Algonquin and war chief who declined torturing his Iroquois prisoners, despite pressure from his comrades, might be considered a confessor, too.

Archeologists' Arguments against the Martyrdoms of St. Isaac and St. Jean at the Bauder Site, with Rebuttals

The Dutch Reformed minister at Rensselaerswyck, Johannes Megapolensis, reported the following in his correspondence about the clan structure of the neighboring Mohawk Indians:

> The Mohawk Indians are divided into three tribes, which are called *Ochkari*, *Anaware*, *Oknaho*, that is, the Bear, the Tortoise and the Wolf. Of these, the Tortoise is the greatest and the most prominent ... They have made a fort of palisades, and they call their castle Asserué. Those of the Bear are the next to these, and their castle is called by them Banagiro. The last are a progeny of these, and their castle is called Thenondiogo.[3]

Megapolensis was mistaken. Members of every clan dwelt in each village. This was known to the French. As Fr. Lalemant observed of the Mohawks (Document 9.2), members of the Turtle clan were "scattered in their three big villages." Moreover, this is a common notion among modern anthropologists.[4] By extension, of course, clan cantons did not exist.

Well into the twentieth century, however, Mohawk Valley archeologists believed in three Mohawk clan cantons, each with a

3. Megapolensis, *Short Account of the Mohawk Indians*, 46. The correlations of Asserué-Ossenrenon, Banagiro-Andagaron, and Thenondiogo-Theonontougen seem to be accepted.

4. Fenton, "Northern Iroquoian Culture Patterns," 309–12; Richter, *Ordeal of the Longhouse*, 20–21. In a later work, Fenton slightly qualified his view: "Each village band, or community, is composed of one or more clan segments, or lineages. The lineage is a core of mothers, sisters, and daughters who, in native theory, are a longhouse family, or residential group, together with a fringe of spouses of other lineages ... Its members identify with an eponymous animal ... which becomes their crest, which was anciently displayed on the gable ends of lodges and which might become the name of the community. It was in this sense that the three Mohawk clans were each identified with a particular town, or the town with a clan" (*Great Law and the Longhouse*, 24).

clan castle. For example, papers published in 1936 and 1937 by the Van Epps-Hartley Chapter of the New York State Archaeological Association, located in Fonda, perpetuated the fallacy.[5]

It is little wonder, therefore, that Donald A. Rumrill accepted this model of Mohawk social and political organization, nor that it led him astray. He noticed that St. Isaac was killed in the "lodge of the bear clan," which he took to be the Rumrill-Naylor Site.[6] His reasoning seems to be that since the Bear clan lived in the central canton of the three Mohawk clans, as he illustrates on his map of Mohawk country in his article,[7] and since the clan castle at that time was Andagaron at the Rumrill-Naylor Site, then St. Isaac and St. Jean could not have been martyred at Ossenrenon-Oneugiouré, which he placed at the Bauder Site, the location of the Turtle castle in the Turtle canton. Of course, one observes, too, that a "lodge" and a "village" are not the same thing.

Dean R. Snow agrees with Rumrill's conclusion, but for different reasons, since he accepts the consensus that clan castles and cantons did not exist.[8] First, Dr. Snow develops an argument from Fr. Lalemant's report that "ils arrivèrent en leur première bourgade appellée Oneugi8ré, jadis Osserrion" (Document 9.1). The translation is easily made: "they reached their first big village called Oneugiouré, formerly Osserrion." The adverb *jadis* is straightforward. It is used normally in the previous paragraph of this report by Fr. Lalemant: "Sa bonté fit faire ce destour pour donner quelque secours à la pauvre Thérèse, jadis séminariste des ursulines."[9] "His [God's] bounty caused this detour to be made

5. Hartley, "Position of the Mohawk Clans"; Lathers and Sheehan, "Iroquois Occupation."

6. Rumrill, "Mohawk Glass Trade Bead Chronology," 27. He cites a history and an anthology of sources, but not the original source. That source, however, must be the one cited in Document 7.3.

7. Rumrill, "Mohawk Glass Trade Bead Chronology," 6.

8. Snow, *Mohawk Valley Archaeology: Sites*, 300.

9. *MNF* 6.571.

to give some comfort to poor Thérèse, formerly a seminarian of the Ursulines." Thus the natural reading of Lalemant's statement is that the first big village of the Mohawks was now in 1646 called Oneugiouré, whereas it had been called Osserrion when St. Isaac was there in 1642, or in a slightly expanded translation, "their first big village called Oneugiouré, formerly called Osserrion."

For this reader the first question this statement raised was, Why did Lalemant write "Osserrion" when St. Isaac had written "Ossenrenon" in his letter to his provincial?[10] The problem is probably paleographical. Unfortunately, the original manuscripts and printers' copies of the *Jesuit Relations* (if they were different) seem to have been lost.[11] Therefore the following discussion must be speculative or conjectural in nature. In this discussion, we assume a legible hand in the *italienne bastarde* tradition,[12] as in the manuscript copy of St. Isaac's letter, Collection du P. Prat, S.J., PraA9, folio 373, and we seek assistance from Nicolas Buat and Evelyne Van den Neste's recent *Manuel de paléographie française*.

The two village names differ from each other only a little bit when written: *Ossenrenon* and *Osserrion*. Each word has four syllables, and they differ only by one in the number of letters each contains. In the seventeenth century, a tilde was often placed over a vowel to represent a following *n* or *m*.[13] In PraA9, for example, although the tilde was not much used, it did sometimes occur over a vowel at the end of a line, always representing *m*, however. Thus

10. See "A Preliminary Note on Ossenrenon" in the introduction to this volume and Document 1.9.

11. I have been able to find no mention of the original manuscripts or of the printers' copies of the *Relations* in Pouliot, *Étude sur les Relations*. Also, the "Bibliographical Data" provided in many volumes of Thwaites's *Jesuit Relations and Allied Documents* never mention a manuscript source or printer's copy for the various volumes of the *Relations* themselves, at least in the several volumes that I own.

12. See the plate of the alphabet near the beginning of Barbedor, *Éscritures financiere*. The volume is not paginated. I accessed the copy at the website of the Newberry Library at the University of Toronto, paleography.library.utoronto.ca, 4 March 2022.

13. Buat and Van den Neste, *Manuel de paléographie française*, 59, 196.

if the name Ossenrenon had been divided by the scribe at line-end after the third syllable (or if this scribe was not so sparing of tildes as the scribe of PraA9), and if a tilde had been drawn over the *e* to represent *n*, then the compositor's eye might have taken the name as having nine letters just as *Osserrion* does, that is, *Ossenrēon*. In this case, the only difference remaining between the words would be ***nrē*** and ***rri***. What could the eye have done to change the former into the latter?

At the time we are considering, two forms of *r* were used, the curled *r* and the angular *r*. A curled *r* was like a circle, but open on top. In fact, the curled *r* and the hastily made *o* sometimes looked identical.[14] An angular *r* was rather like our cursive *r*, but without the initial upstroke. In some cases, it resembled a modern minuscule italic *r*. As we have seen, an *n* with a short second leg (or minim), which makes the letter look like an *r*, can be seen in PraA9 on folio 372, on the second line in the word *remitterent*. The second minim was shortened a bit by the too early upward movement of the scribe's pen toward the next letter. The scribe who made the printer's copy for Fr. Lalemant's *Relation* could have done the same. One also finds in Buat and Van den Neste an example of an angular *r* that resembles an *n*. Thus, *mutatis mutandis*, one might also have found an *n* that resembles an angular *r*.[15] Thus it is quite conceivable that an *n* could have been misread as an *r*.

The misreading of *i* for *e* with a tilde is harder to explain because the latter had a more complex form. There were three types of *e* in use in St. Isaac's time. One form was made with a rightward semicircle on the bottom with, on top, a short downward curved stroke with a tick. The top stroke was often detached and modified to connect with the following letter or to function as a tilde. The second form of *e* was adapted from the first and made with a single stroke. It looked like a circle with an open top with

14. Buat and Van den Neste, *Manuel*, 204, nos. 7–9.

15. Buat and Van den Neste, *Manuel*, 197, no. 1.

the righthand side curling back on and crossing itself rather like a fat, cursive, classical Greek *theta*. The curling tail was often made quite lofty, and sometimes was turned into a tilde, too. The third form, used in PraA9, was the modern *e*.[16] And on the very folio on which the name of this village—Ossenrenon—is written twice, the reader also finds the word *monendo* written with the loop of the (modern) *e* almost closed and with a stray pen stroke over it, so that the word appears to be *monindo*. If the *ē* in the village name was written with a nearly closed loop and a carelessly drawn tilde, it could have looked like an *i*.

Moreover, Buat and Van den Neste do have one example of the first type of *e* that is reduced to its first stroke alone and could be misread as an *i*.[17] Thus even the complex letter *e* was subject to misreading as an *i*.

Therefore this conjectural argument leads one to conclude that Ossenrenon was the name written by St. Isaac and by Fr. Ragueneau, and that whoever made the printer's copy or composed the type for the original volume of the *Jesuit Relations* for this year misread the name and spelled it *Osserrion*.

The second question that occurred to this reader on pondering this passage further was whether the subsequent peace conference took place at Ossenrenon-Oneugiouré or at another village that was not named. The text continues: "they reached their first big village called Oneugiouré, formerly Osserrion. There it was necessary to stay two days to be gazed on and welcomed by these peoples who were coming from all parts to see them … The 10th of June, honored by the Feast of the Holy Trinity, he [St. Isaac] gave this sacrosanct name to this big village. At the same time, was

16. Buat and Van den Neste, *Manuel*, 42; 196, nos. 4–5; 197, no. 2; 217, nos. 3, 8, and 11. The second form of the *e* almost looks like a rightward facing seahorse with its tail curled up behind it.

17. Buat and Van den Neste, *Manuel*, 250, no. 5. Cf. 275, no. 1, where the top stroke of the *e* is so light that the bottom stroke could be read as an *i*.

held a general assembly of all the chief captains and of the elders of the country" (Document 9.1: "ils arrivèrent en leur première bourgade appellée Oneugi8ré, jadis Osserrion. Là il fallut demeurer deux jours pour estre considérez et bienveignez de ces peuples qui venoient de toutes parts pour les voir . . . Le 10 de juin, honoré par le feste de la saincte Trinité, il [St. Isaac] donna ce nom sacrosainct à cette bourgade. Il se fit en mesme temps une assemblée générale de tous les principaux capitaines et des anciens du pays"). Later, we read: "To conclude, the Father, our French, and their guides departed from the village of the Holy Trinity the 16th of June" (Document 9.5: "Pour conclusion, le Père, nos François et leurs guides partirent du bourg de la Sainte-Trinité le 16 de juin").

Did St. Isaac mean that the ambassadorial party had to stay at Ossenrenon-Oneugiouré for a couple of days to be welcomed, and then went elsewhere for the peace council? This was the opinion of Fr. Talbot, who supposed that the council took place at Theonontougen.[18] Or did St. Isaac mean that they stayed at Ossenrenon-Oneugiouré for the peace conference after the welcoming? The coincidence in the narrative between the naming of the village for the Holy Trinity and the holding of the general assembly seems to preclude a move to another village for the assembly. Moreover, people came "from all parts" to welcome the French at Ossenrenon-Oneugiouré, which presumably means from all major villages and the various hamlets. Thus the members of the assembly were probably already in the village. Finally, the departure of the French was made from Ossenrenon-Oneugiouré. Why from there, if the council had not been held there, too?

For Snow, however, the big problem with this passage is that he finds the meaning of *jadis* confusing. To understand what he is getting at, it is necessary to quote his entire argument, though long.

18. Talbot, *Saint among Savages*, 386.

On his return to Canada during the summer, he [St. Isaac] wrote an account that referred confusingly to "*Oneugi8ré, jadis Osserrïon*" (JR 29:51).[19] This seems to imply that the village he had called "Ossernenon" in 1642 he was now calling "Osserrïon." Further, he might have been implying that the community had moved and that the name of the new village was Oneugi8ré.[20] The key problems in any interpretation are that the same Mohawk village names were heard differently at different times, even by the same source, and that Mohawk village names sometimes moved with the relocating communities. I infer in this case that "Canagere,"[21] "Banagiro," "Andagaron," and "Oneugi8ré" are all versions of the same village name. The most important consequence of this interpretation of place-names is that Ossernenon (= Osserrïon) could not have in any sense become Andagaron (= Oneugi8ré) between Jogues's visits. To put it in his terms, "Oneugi8ré, jadis Osserrïon" cannot mean that Andagaron was a new village that had formerly been known as Ossernenon. Thus, Jogues probably meant that while he had been held previously in Ossernenon (or Osserrïon), his 1646 visit took him to Oneugi8ré, which he had previously called "Andagaron." This would have been identical with Megapolensis's "Banagiro" and van den Bogaert's "Canagere." Mohawk words never begin with a "B," and the phonemically equivalent "K" or "G" are often soft. Van den Bogaert heard it as a "K," Megapolensis heard it as a "B," and Jogues heard it not at all. Of course, this interpretation implies that Jogues heard the

19. The report does not exist, as far as I know. Lalemant refers, a few lines before the passage under consideration, *au rapport du Père*, indicating that his own narrative was based on a report of St. Isaac's, presumably written. See *MNF* 6.571.

20. This was Fr. Campeau's opinion. See *MNF* 6.571n15.

21. Harmen Meyndertsz van den Bogaert (1612–47), a barber-surgeon at Fort Orange, led a trading company expedition into Mohawk country in 1634. He kept a journal of the expedition, which was rediscovered in 1895. See Gehring and Starna, *Journey into Mohawk and Oneida Country*, xix–xl. Van den Bogaert gives the name "Canagere" to the second Mohawk castle. See Gehring and Starna, *Journey into Mohawk and Oneida Country*, 6 and 38n32.

> same place-name as "Andagaron" in 1642 and as "Oneugi8ré" in 1646, an implication that some scholars might not be willing to accept. The sound shift is, however, not much greater than that implied by his reference to the first village as Ossernenon in 1642 and to the same place as Osserrïon in 1646.[22]

One feels that this argument should fail on the principle of parsimony or Occam's razor. It is difficult to follow because of all its parts. But the main problem with the argument is that it is circular, which is a material, not a logical, fallacy. Snow's first two observations are correct. The problematic *jadis* statement "seems to imply" a name change, and possibly it implies a relocation of the community. Snow drops these implications, however, and makes an observation on the difficulty Europeans had with hearing Mohawk names correctly, and the added difficulty that names sometimes were relocated with their communities. While these observations are true, they are really beside the point, and they ensnare Snow in "the falsity, or, at least, undue assumption of a Premiss"[23] with his inference—really a guess—that certain rather differently sounding town names recorded by Megapolensis, van den Bogaert, and St. Isaac all denominated the same town, which was not Ossenrenon at the Bauder Site (or perhaps its successor site), but rather Andagaron at the Rumrill-Naylor Site.

To supply the middle premise between his unduly assumed major premise and his conclusion, Snow asserts that the phrase under consideration—*Oneugi8ré, jadis Osserrion*—was meant to show that Ossenrenon could not have begotten a successor village

22. Snow, *Mohawk Valley Archaeology: Sites*, 299–300. This argument, even if it had real weight, would fail because the spelling *Osserrion* was a result of paleographical confusion, as we have seen.

23. Whately, *Elements of Logic*, 228. See also: "It may be better, therefore, to drop the name [*non causa pro causa*] which perpetuates this confusion [the taking of cause for reason], and simply to state (when such is the case) that the premiss is unduly assumed, *i.e.*, without being either self-evident, or satisfactorily proved" (233–34).

named Andagaron. The phrase was meant to clarify the fact that St. Isaac had reached Andagaron, not Ossenrenon. The argument takes the form $A = B$ *but* $B \neq C \therefore A \neq C$. This is logically valid, but it contains the material fallacy of a false or an unduly assumed premise, namely, that Oneugiouré was Andagaron. Only from that major premise, which has not been proven, does it follow through the minor premise—Andagaron was not Ossenrenon (which is true)—that Oneugiouré was not Ossenrenon. Snow adds a brief discussion of the initial vowels of the town names at issue here, but the discussion does not validate the defective syllogism.

Moreover, Snow's interpretation of the phrase *Oneugi8ré, jadis Osserrion* adds another difficulty. The original sentence read more completely, "[T]hey reached their [the Mohawks'] first big village called Oneugiouré, formerly Osserrion." Thus we must understand that, according to Snow's argument, the first big village was now Andagaron. But Andagaron was the middle castle of the Mohawks. How could the first castle also be the castle in the middle? This is absurd.

Snow does adduce certain artifacts discovered at Rumrill-Naylor to support this conclusion. In his discussion of the site, he says, "Rumrill (1991: 27) guesses that this is the site of the village called "Oneugi8ré" by Jogues in 1646 ... This argument is convincing in light of the religious artifacts found."[24] In fact, this reader can find only one religious artifact listed in Snow's discussion of the artifacts dug up at Rumrill-Naylor: a "Catholic grotto medal."[25] He does mention "'Cassock' buttons," but he says elsewhere that these are not indicative of Jesuit presence.[26] Also, he mentions the discovery of a "hinged locking hasp ... which might have been part of a Jesuit coffer."[27] Rumrill himself uses these arti-

24.Snow, *Mohawk Valley Archaeology: Sites*, 309.

25. Snow, *Mohawk Valley Archaeology: Sites*, 318 (fig. 8.17), 319.

26. Snow, *Mohawk Valley Archaeology: Sites*, 315 and 300.

27. Snow, *Mohawk Valley Archaeology: Sites*, 320 (fig. 8.21) and 321. If Snow means

facts in a different way: to demonstrate that Bauder, Rumrill-Naylor, and Oak Hill #1 were of the right epoch to be the locations of the villages where the afflictions of the martyrs and confessors happened in the 1640s. He says, "The items include a small rosary medal, a silver chalice and a pewter bottle cap at Oak Hill #1; a late 16th or early 17th-century Catholic French Grotto souvenir pin ... and a hinged locking clasp at Rumrill-Naylor; and a pewter cup at Bauder."[28] If we count the evidence, Oak Hill #1 has a better claim to be Oneugiouré. If we weigh the evidence, we find that it does not tip the scale.

Therefore neither Rumrill's attempt to make Oneugiouré into Andagaron nor Snow's attempt is successful. And so the martyrdoms of St. Isaac and St. Jean did take place at the village that was formerly called Ossenrenon, but now was called Oneugiouré.

Moreover, evidence of another sort supports the conclusion that St. Isaac and St. Jean were martyred at Ossenrenon-Oneugiouré. We saw above that the peace conference of the spring of 1646 took place at this village. St. Isaac left a small chest behind as a pledge that he would return for mission work. This caused consternation among certain of the Mohawks at the conference who thought the box contained a devil (Document 8.1). After a summer of disease and crop failure, a conspiracy was formed of the mutinous Bear clan (see Document 7.2) and the most superstitious of the traditionalists against St. Isaac upon his return in the fall.

> Before the Father had arrived in the country, the most mutinous and the most superstitious had resolved to kill him. The former not wishing peace with the French nor the Hurons nor

to imply that this might have belonged to the chest St. Isaac left behind after the peace conference, he must have forgotten that the chest was reported to have been thrown away in the water (Document 11.1).

28. Rumrill, "Bead Chronology," 27. Lenig, "Bauder," 5, figure on 6, suggests that this cup or goblet might have been a chalice for the Mass. He also mentions a pewter finial from "a covered mug or chalice [that] could have similar Christian connections."

> the Algonquins, and the latter believing that the sickness which reigned in the country and the caterpillars that were eating their grain had been brought in the coffer of Fr. Jogues, who had left [it] nevertheless with the Iroquois as a pledge of his affection. This coffer was thrown into the water without being opened and more than one month before the Father arrived in the country (Document 11.1: "Avant que le Père fust arrivé dans le pays, les plus mutins et les plus superstitieux avoient résolu de le tuer. Ceux-là ne voulant pas de paix avec les François, ny Hurons, ny Algonquins, et ceux-cy croyant que la maladie qui régnoit dedans le pays et les chenilles qui mangeoient leurs bleds avoient esté aportées dans le coffre du Pére Jogues, qu'il avoit laissé néanmoints aux Iroquois comme gage de son affection. Ce coffre fut jetté à l'eau sans estre ouvert et plus d'un moys avant que le Père arrivast au païs.")

The principle of parsimony or Occam's razor leads to a conclusion. Since the conspiracy against St. Isaac was launched in the village where he left the chest which the Mohawks feared, it follows that he was also killed there, that is, in Ossenrenon-Oneugiouré.

Moreover, as Fr. Jacques Buteux reported, "The Iroquois of the first village who ought to have defended Fr. Jogues, and even the brother of his aunt or hostess, were complicit in his death" (Document 11.1: "Les Iroquois du premier village qui devoient deffendre le Père Jogues, et mesme le frère de sa tente ou hostesse a esté complice de sa mort").[29] This implies that his aunt's brother dwelt in

29. The man called St. Isaac's "host" (Document 5.10) and his "aunt's" brother were probably the same person. Iroquoian society was matriarchal in crucial aspects. Women of a kin group occupied their own longhouse with their children, brothers, and other maternal relatives. Their husbands did not always make a permanent home in their longhouse, while their brothers often spent more time with their female kin than with their wives' kin. The women were the leaders of the longhouse. However, their brothers might have appeared to Europeans as the leaders of the home, and they were indeed sometimes chiefs. Nevertheless, the longhouse was the space of the women, as were the cultivated fields. Except for the council fire, the forest was the men's domain See Fenton, "Northern Iroquoian Culture Patterns," 309–14; Richter, *Ordeal of the Longhouse*, 20–21.

the same village where the conspiracy and the murder took place, that is, in Ossenrenon-Oneugiouré.

Finally, a young Mohawk warrior tried to help St. Isaac when he was murdered, and to protect St. Jean from the same fate. It is quite plausible that this man was Honatteniate, the son of St. Isaac's adoptive aunt. If so, then this is more evidence for the murder of the two saints at Ossenrenon-Oneugiouré.

We are left with two questions. Why did the residents of Ossenrenon change the name of their village? Was it because they had built a new village to replace the old?

On the one hand, the first question is imponderable, for we have no way of gauging the villagers' thinking. On the other, the Mohawks did sometimes change the names of their villages when they relocated them. Iroquoian villages usually were inhabited for only about twelve years, according to William N. Fenton. For one thing, the ground supports of the village structures decayed over time, even though supporting timbers were often added at some point during their existence. For another, the fertility of the fields diminished seriously. Finally, the forests were cut back as much as a mile, making it difficult for the women to cut or gather firewood, and to carry it home. Therefore removal inevitably became necessary, and sometimes the village name was used over again. At other times a new name was adopted.[30]

St. Isaac recorded his aunt's concern for him in his account of St. René's death. "The next day, as they were seeking to kill me, my aunt sent me to her field to avoid [the danger], as I think" (Document 3.6: "Le lendemain, comme on me cherchoit pour me tuer, ma tante m'envoya à son champ pour esquiver [the danger], comme je pense.") She also saved him once from being beaten to death by a madman with a warclub (*MNF* 6.295, 7.119). Apparently, she admired his virtues (*MNF* 7.118).

30. Fenton, "Northern Iroquoian Culture Patterns," 302: "In general, when the soil was exhausted and firewood became scarce, about twice in a generation, the town was moved. Removal was a gradual process, one town going up while the other was decaying, as commemorated in the place-name theme: "New Town" and "Old Town." The final removal was marked by the Feast of the Dead." See also Richter, *Ordeal of the Longhouse*, 23–24; Grumet, *Historic Contact*, 329. It is possible that village names were changed for other

Therefore we must ask whether the Ossenrenon community removed from the Bauder Site to another site during 1646 and renamed its village Oneugiouré. It appears that Ossenrenon, Andagaron, and Theonontougen were all built after the 1634 smallpox epidemic to house diminished populations. The date for their establishment is therefore about 1635.[31] Each village would have been nearing its approximate twelve-year lifespan in 1646. In fact, 1646 is the date Snow proposes for the termination of occupation at Bauder and Rumrill-Naylor.[32] Apparently, the former community moved to the so-called Printup Site about 1646, while the latter moved to the Van Evera-McKinney Site.[33]

How did the removal of a Mohawk village from one location to another occur? A pattern can be derived from Daniel K. Richter's description of the use of its territory by a Mohawk community.

> Iroquois groups, therefore, required an extensive homeland that at any given time encompassed a current town and its associated hamlets, perhaps a new village being constructed and gradually occupied, several former sites in process of natural reclamation marked by decaying palisades and cemeteries containing the remains of past generations, a variety of fishing and fowling camps, and various hunting territories.[34]

Thus when it became clear that the village buildings and palisades were decaying beyond repair, that the fields were yielding a seriously diminishing return, and that the forest had been cut down to such a distance from the village that it was difficult to retrieve

---

reasons than removal to a new site. Sagard, *Grand voyage*, 141n2, gives three names for the same Huron village without a suggestion of a change of place. One must remember that the Huron were also an Iroquoian people with similar cultural patterns to the Iroquois.

31. Snow, *Mohawk Valley Archaeology: Sites*, 37, 301, 304.

32. Snow, *Mohawk Valley Archaeology: Sites*, 304, 307, 308, 309 (Bauder); 309, 310, 312, 320, 321 (Rumrill-Naylor).

33. Snow, *Mohawk Valley Archaeology: Sites*, 309, 322.

34. Richter, *Ordeal of the Longhouse*, 24.

firewood, then the villagers would choose a new site within their territory. Ground would be cleared by the men for planting and for the materials for building the new village.[35] Then the village would be built. Tools, utensils, stocks of food, and other goods would be carried to the new site, fields planted, and life would be begun anew over time. It would have been "a gradual process," as Fenton says, "one town going up while the other was decaying."[36]

It seems most logical to this reader to suppose that the controversial phrase *Oneugi8re, jadis Osserrion* encapsulates this process, and that two scenarios are possible. Perhaps St. Isaac and Jean Bourdon arrived at the Bauder Site in the spring of 1646 to find the village well decayed and a new village already under construction, and that the community had chosen a new name for it: Oneugiouré. Nevertheless, the community was still largely lodged at the Bauder Site, which remained the locus of the community. Alternatively, the two Frenchmen could have arrived to find that the community had already pretty well finished its move to the Printup Site, with the result that they conducted their negotiations there.

Logically speaking, the least that the controversial phrase implies is that the name of the community at the Bauder Site had been changed, perhaps in anticipation of a move. The most it implies is that a new village with a new name was now housing the community that had formerly dwelt at Ossenrenon or the Bauder Site. On the principle of parsimony or Occam's razor, one must choose the former alternative and think that St. Isaac and St. Jean were martyred not only by the same community as St. René but also at the same location, the Bauder Site.

Historically speaking, given that the village at the Bauder Site was built circa 1635 and that it was only just reaching its natural term of viability, it is safe to assume that the process of building a new village was in its early stages and that the community still

35. Richter, *Ordeal of the Longhouse*, 23.

36. See note 30 above.

resided chiefly at the Bauder Site, although the name of the new town was already being used. Thus it is probable that the historical reality that met the French ambassadors lay between the two logical poles established in the last paragraph.

Conclusion

Depending as it does on the explicit application of logic to arguments about fragmentary and perplexing evidence, the conclusion of this chapter may seem weak to the contemporary reader. Though we use logic all the time in our daily lives, rarely do we use it expressly, and we tend to be persuaded by the accumulation of "facts" or the violence of passion. To the contemporary mentality, therefore, chapter 3 may seem more persuasive than the present chapter.

Nevertheless, the arguments are as conclusive as historical and scientific arguments can be. First, the names *Ossenrenon* and *Osserrion* are variants based on paleographical confusion. Second, Oneugiouré can be associated with Andagaron only by a mistaken interpretation of Mohawk clan organization or by a logical argument in which the major premise is unduly assumed. Third, the identification of Oneugiouré with Andagaron also leads to a manifest absurdity. Fourth, it is simpler to assume that the peace conference in the spring of 1646 and the martyrdoms later that year took place at the Bauder Site, while the fields for the new village at the Printup Site was being cleared. Fifth, certain pieces of evidence must be overestimated—the number of Catholic artifacts—or ignored—the holding of the peace conference at Ossenrenon, St. Isaac's coffer, his aunt with her brother and son—to make the association of Oneugiouré with Andagaron work.

Therefore one can say with great confidence that St. Isaac and St. Jean were martyred not only by the same community that martyred St. René—the people of Ossenrenon-Oneugiouré—but also at the same location, the Bauder Site.

CHAPTER 5

The Locations Where St. Catherine Tekakwitha Lived in the Mohawk Valley

THE EVIDENCE we have for St. Catherine's life is abundant. It is contained in biographies written by her Jesuit pastors at the Mission de Saint-François-Xavier-du-Sault, on the opposite bank of the St. Lawrence from La Chine on Montreal Island. The first biography was written by Fr. Claude Chauchetière probably between 1685 and 1695.[1] The second biography was written by Fr. Pierre Cholenec around 1696.[2] Fr. Cholenec also wrote a let-

1. Greer, *Mohawk Saint*, 23. Martin, *Catherine Tegakouïtha*, 1 (French text), dates it definitively to 1695. The French text of Fr. Martin's work was apparently never published until this edition. Fr. van Rensselaer's translation was published in *Pilgrim of Our Lady of Martyrs*, 1898–99. See Martin, *Catherine Tegakouïtha*, ii, v.

2. Greer says that Cholenec's revised version of this manuscript "appeared in print" in 1717 (*Mohawk Saint*, viii and 24). I found no record of this book in a search of WorldCat on 10 February 2022. But Rigal-Cellard, "Kateri Tekakwitha and Saint Kateri's Shrine," lists in her references section "Cholenec, Pierre. 1717. *La vie de Catherine Tegakouita Première Vierge Iroquoise*. Manuscrit conservé par les Hospitalières de Saint Augustin à Québec. Lettre publiée dans *Lettres édifiantes et curieuses écrites des missions étrangères*. Paris." Does Rigal-Cellard mean that the Hospitalières' manuscript was published in 1717 in the *Lettres édifiantes*? Or that the date 1717 is written on the

ter in 1715 containing a shorter version of the saint's life.[3] These priests only knew St. Catherine at the Sault, however. They did collect evidence from Mohawk informants about her life in her homeland, but they were not interested in the kinds of historical facts that we need for our inquiry. The documentary evidence gathered below will show this. Bibliographical information, as the reader now knows, can be found in the introduction.

Documentary Evidence with Translations

Document 15. Claude Chauchetière, SJ, *La Vie de la B[ienheureuse]. Catherine Tegakoüita, Dite à Present La Saincte Sauuagesse*, or *The Life of the Blessed Catherine Tekakwitha, Called Currently the Holy Woman of the Wilds.*

Details regarding St. Catherine's childhood.

1. "[C]ette algonquine [St. Catherine's mother] dont le nom de baptesme m'est inconnu eut aussy un garçon [in addition to Catherine] et demeura auec son mari et ses enfants a gandaouagué petit uillage des Aniés." [Chauchetière, *Vie*, 19]

Translation. "[T]his Algonquin woman [St. Catherine's mother], whose baptismal name is unknown to me, also had a boy [in addition to Catherine], and lived with her husband and children at Gandaouagué, a little village of the Mohawks."

2. "La petite uerrole rauagea ce village et enleua petits et grandes ce qui obligea puet estre ces Sauuages a faire la paix auec les francois." [Chauchetière, *Vie*, 19–20]

Translation. "Smallpox ravaged this village and took off small

Hôtel-Dieu manuscript? In addition, Loyzance, "Kateri Tegewitha," 5, mentions a Latin life of St. Catherine by Father Cholenec. I have found no trace of such a book. At any rate, as we have seen, the version of Cholenec's *Vie de Catherine* used below is based on the autograph copy in the Archives de l'Hôtel-Dieu de Québec. See the introduction to Document 16, p. 13*ff.* above.

3. Document 17 below.

and great, which obliged perhaps these Savages to make peace with the French."

Details of St. Catherine's teenaged years, during which she was converted, catechized, and baptized.

3. "[L]a paix se fit entre les sauuages et les françois et plusieurs peres Jesuittes furent enuoyés chez les sauuages pour y prescher la foy les peres arriuerent aux uillages des iroquois dans un temps d'yurognerie ainsy comme on estoit pas en estat de les receuoir au grand uillage comme on deuoit on les arresta dans le uillage de gandaouagué ou Catherine demeuroit."[4] [Chauchetière, *Vie*, 25]

Translation. "[P]eace was made between the savages and the French, and many Jesuit Fathers were sent among the savages to preach the faith there. The Fathers reached the Iroquois villages in a time of drunkenness, such that they [the Mohawks] were not in a state to receive them [the Jesuits] at the big village as they ought. They stopped them at the village of Gandaouagué where Catherine was living."

4. "Le pere [Jacques de Lamberville] passant par le uillage et estant arriué ala cabane de Catherine fut poussé a y entrer, il y trouua Catherine; une rencontre ne fut iamais plus heureuse du costé de la fille qui uouloit parler au pere et qui n'osoit l'aller chercher, du costé du pere qui trouua un thresor ou il croyoit ne trouuer personne." [Chauchetière, *Vie*, 43–44]

Translation. "The Father [Jacques de Lamberville], passing through the village and having arrived at Catherine's longhouse,

4. See *JR* 57.88, in the 1672–73 *Relation* under the title "De la mission de Gandaouagué ou de Saint Pierre dans la Pais d'Agnié." Fr. Boniface reports there, "On a donné a cette mission Le nom de Saint Pierre, a cause que depuis qui les armes de sa maiesté ont assuietté Les Iroquois inferieurs, ce fut a Gandaoüagué, ou la foy fut plus constamment embrassee qu'en aucun autre pais d'agnié: ce fut la proprement qu'on vit d'abord vne Eglise naissante" ("One has given to this mission the name of St. Peter, because, since his Majesty's arms subjected the lower Iroquois, it was at Gandaouagué where the faith was more steadily embraced than in any other region of the Mohawks. It was there properly that one first saw a nascent Church").

was pressed to go in there. He found Catherine there, an encounter that was never happier on the girl's side, who wished to speak to the Father and who did not dare to go to look for him, than on the Father's side, who found a treasure where he did not think he would find anyone."

5. "Le pere choisit le iour de pasques [1675] pour faire un baptesme si solennel et le lieu ou elle fut baptisee fut la chapelle." [Chauchetière, *Vie*, 46]

Translation. "The Father chooses the day of Easter [1675] to do a baptism so solemn, and the place where she was baptized was the chapel."

Catherine's flight to the Sault.

6. "Catherine ne put se separer de ces nouueaux uenus[5] elle tesmoigna au pere quil falloit quelle s'en allast quand il deuroit luy en couter la uie le pere Lamberuille en parla a la poudre chaude et a ses compaignons la poudre chaude dit quil y auroit place pour elle dans le canot puisquil auoit dessein daller a onneiout et de passer par toutes les nations Iroquoises en preschant la foy; la resolution ne fut pas plustost prise quelle fut executee et les deux compaignons de la poudre chaude embarquerent Catherine en cachette et prirent le chemin qui conduit aux flammants." [Chauchetière, *Vie*, 76]

Translation. "Catherine was not able to separate herself from these newcomers. She gave witness to the Father that it was necessary that she go with them, though it should cost her her life. Fr. Lamberville spoke of it with Hot Powder and his companions. Hot Powder said that he had a place for her there in the canoe, since he had the design of going to Oneida territory, and of

5. The Oneida war chief Ogératarihen or Garonhiagué had been converted and baptized Louis. He dwelt now at the Sault and made evangelical missions to his homeland. He was known for his hot temper, and the French nicknamed him "Hot Powder." He had recently arrived with two companions at Gandaouagué. See Chauchetière, *Vie*, 58–76. Cf. note 7 below.

passing through all the Iroquois nations in preaching the Faith. The resolution was no sooner taken than it was executed, and the two companions of Hot Powder embarked Catherine secretly and took the way that leads to the Flemish."

Document 16. Pierre Cholenec, SJ, *La Vie De Catherine Tegakouita Première Vierge Irokoise*, or *The Life of Catherine Tekakwitha, First Iroquois Virgin*.

St. Catherine's childhood.

1. "Catherine Tegakoüita … naquit aux Irokois, l'an mil six cents cinquante six dans un village des Agniers nommé Gahnaouagé." [Cholenec, *Vie*, 1]

Translation. "Catherine Tegakoüita … was born among the Iroquois, the year sixteen hundred fifty-six in a village of the Mohawks named Gahnaouagé."

2. "La petite vérole s'étant glissée parmi les Irokois et y ayant fair des grands ravages, elle [Catherine's mother] fut enveloppée dans le malheur commun." [Cholenec, *Vie*, 1]

Translation. "Smallpox having crept among the Iroquois and made great ravages, she [Catherine's mother] was involved in the common evil."

St. Catherine's conversion, etc.

3. "Il y avait déjà quelque temps que le Père Jacques de Lamberville était venu demeurer dans le village de Ganaouagé … C'est donc en ce temps là [Autumn 1676] que le missionnaire faisant un jour la visite ordinaire par les cabanes et ayant passé déjà la sienne, parcequ'il croyait n'y trouver personne, se sentit inspiré de retourner sur ses pas et d'y entrer; il le fit et il y trouva la jeune fille qui témoigna une joie extraordinaire de cette visite qu'elle souhaitait si fort." [Cholenec, *Vie*, 3]

Translation. "It had already been some time that Fr. Jacques de Lamberville had come to dwell in the village of Ganaouagé … It was therefore at that time [Autumn 1676] that the missionary, one day making his ordinary visit through the longhouses and already having passed hers, because he believed he would not find anyone there, felt himself inspired to return on his steps and enter there. He did it and found there the young girl who witnessed an extraordinary joy at this visit that she wished so strongly."

4. "Le Père de Lamberville ... le [baptism] lui [Catherine] voulut conférer avec solennité et se servit pour cela de celle de la fête de Pâque ... il la baptisa et lui donna le nom de Catherine." [Cholenec, *Vie*, 4]

Translation. "Fr. de Lamberville ... wished to confer it [baptism] on her [Catherine] solemnly, and for this availed himself of that of the feast of Easter ... he baptized her and gave her the name of Catherine."

Her flight.

5. "C'est là [the Sault] où le Père Lamberville jugea que Dieu voulait notre Catherine, elle-même en avait un grand désir depuis quelque temps ... l'envie que celle-ci [Catherine's adoptive sister at the Sault] avait de faire part de leur bonheur à sa cadette, l'avait poussée á faire partir son mari avec plusieurs autres qui allaient chercher leurs parent, pour lui amener aussi Catherine ... le Ciel se mêlant de son affaire, cet oncle [her guardian at Gandaouagué] était alors en traite chez les Anglais à Orange, ce qui les obligea pour profiter d'une si favorable conjoncture à se mettre incessamment en chemin." [Cholenec, *Vie*, 5]

Translation. "It was there [the Sault] that Fr. Lamberville reckoned that God wished our Catherine, she herself had a great desire for it for some time ... the longing that this woman [Catherine's adoptive sister at the Sault] had to share her happiness with her younger sister, had pushed her to make her husband depart with many others who were going to look for their relatives, in order to conduct Catherine also to her ... Heaven taking a hand in her affair, this uncle [her guardian at Gandaouagué] was then trading among the English at [Fort] Orange, which obliged them to profit from a conjuncture so favorable to put themselves without interruption upon the road."

Document 17. "Lettre du Père Cholenec, missionnaire da la Compagnie de Jésus, au Père Augustin le Blanc, de la même Compagnie, Procureur des missions du Canada," or "Letter of Father Cholenec, Missionary of the Society of Jesus, to Father Augustin le Blanc, of the Same Society, Procurator of the Missions of Canada."

St. Catherine's childhood.

1. "Tegahkouita ... naquit l'an 1656 à Gandaouagué, l'une des bourgades des Iroquois inférieurs appelés Agniez." [Cholenec, "Lettre," 26]

Translation. "Tegahkouita ... was born the year 1656 at Gandaouagué, one of the big villages of the lower Iroquois named Mohawks."

2. "Une petite vérole qui ravageoit le pays des Iroquois, l'enleva, elle [Tegahkouita's mother] et son fils en peu de jours: Tegahkouita en fut attaquée comme les autres, mais elle ne succomba point à la violence du mal." [Cholenec, "Lettre," 26]

Translation. "A smallpox that was ravaging the country of the Iroquois carried her off, her [Tegahkouita's mother] and her son, in a few days; Tegahkouita was attacked by it like the others, but she did not succumb to the violence of the illness."

3. "M. de Tracy ayant été envoyé de la cour pour mettre á la raison les nations iroquoises qui désoloient nos colonies, porta la guerre dans leur pays, et y brula trois villages des Agniez ... On saisit cette occasion ... pour envoyer des missionnaires aux Iroquois. Ils avoient déjà quelque teinture de l'évangile qui leur avoit été prêché par le père Jogues, surtout ceux d'Onnontagué,[6] parmi lesquels ce père avoit fixé sa demeure." [Cholenec, "Lettre," 28]

6. Cholenec appears to have confused Gandaouagué with Onnontagué.

Translation. "Monsieur de Tracy, having been sent from the court to bring some sense to the Iroquois nations that were laying waste our colonies, carried the war into their country and there burned three villages of the Mohawks … We seized this opportunity … to send some missionaries to the Iroquois. They already had some tincture of the Gospel, which had been preached to them by Fr. Jogues, especially those of Onondaga, among whom this Father had fixed his abode."

St. Catherine's conversion, etc.

4. "Ils [the missionaries] y arrivèrent dans le temps que ces peuples ont accoutumé de se plonger dans toute sorte de débauches, et personne ne se trouva en état de les recevoir. Ce contre-temps procura à la jeune Tegahkouita l'avantage de connoître de bonne heure ceux dont Dieu vouloit se servir … elle fut chargée de loger les missionnaires." [Cholenec, "Lettre," 29]

Translation. "They [the missionaries] arrived there at the time that these peoples were accustomed to plunge themselves into every sort of debauchery, and no one found himself in a condition to receive them. This contretemps procured for the young Tegahkouita the advantage of knowing early those of whom God wished her to avail herself … she was charged with lodging the missionaries."

5. "En ce temps-là, le père Jacques de Lamberville fut conduit par la Providence au village de notre jeune iroquoise, et il reçut ordre de ses supérieurs de s'y arrêter." [Cholenec, "Lettre," 31]

Translation. "At that time, Fr. Jacques de Lamberville was led by Providence to the village of our young Iroquois woman, and he received an order from his superiors to stay there."

6. "Le missionnaire prit ce temps-là pour faire sa tournée, et pour instruire à loisir ceux qui étoient restés dans leurs cabanes. Il entra dans celle de Tegahkouita. Cette bonne fille ne put retenir sa joie à la vue du missionnaire." [Cholenec, "Lettre," 32]

Translation. "The missionary took that time to make his

rounds and to instruct at leisure those who were resting in their longhouses. He entered Tegahkouita's longhouse. This good girl could not retain her joy at the sight of the missionary."

7. "Elle le [Holy Baptism] reçut le jour de Pâques de l'année 1676." [Cholenec, "Lettre," 33]

Translation. "She received it [Holy Baptism] the day of Easter of the year 1676."

Catherine's flight to the Sault.

8. "Ce zèle [of the Christians at the Sault] ne se bornoit pas à ceux qui venoient les trouver, il les portoit encore à faire des excursions dans les différentes bourgades de leur nation, et ils renvoient toujours accompagnés d'un grand nombre de leurs compatriotes. Le jour que Catherine reçut le baptême, le plus considérable des Agniez, après une excursion semblable, retourna à la mission du Sault en compagnie de trente Iroquois de sa nation . . . La néophite [Catherine] eùt bien voulu le suivre . . . Ce ne fut que l'année suivante qu'elle trouva les facilités qu'elle souhaitoit pour l'exécution de son dessein."[7] [Cholenec, "Lettre," 37–38]

Translation. "This zeal [of the Christians at the Sault] did not restrict itself to those who came to find them, it carried them besides to make some excursions to the different villages of their nation, and they always returned accompanied by a large number of their compatriots. The day that Catherine received baptism, the most considerable of the Mohawks, after such an excursion, returned to the mission of the Sault in the company of 30 Iroquois of his nation . . . The neophyte [Catherine] had really wished to

7. Cholenec relates that Catherine's adoptive sister's husband made the trip from the Sault to Gandaouagué to rescue her (Cholenec, "Lettre," 38–39). This cannot be readily reconciled with Chauchetière's account, but Cholenec does embed the story of Catherine's rescue within the story of a famous Iroquois's preaching mission to Gandaouagué. Perhaps different Native informants got the details of the story mixed up in their memories. Greer, *Mohawk Saint*, 58, conflates the two stories, having Catherine's brother-in-law and another man accompany Hot Powder to Gandaouagué. Greer may well be right to do this.

follow him … It was only the following year that she found the opportunity that she wished for the execution of her design."

Archeological Evidence

Since the documentary evidence tells us so little about place, we must turn to the archeological evidence to locate the village sites where St. Catherine grew up. We have seen that Catholic tradition, following the research of John S. Clark, has held that Ossenrenon stood at Auriesville from 1642 to 1659. Those years included the three Jesuit martyrdoms and the birth of St. Catherine. Following Gen. Clark, the tradition also holds that the people of Ossenrenon reestablished themselves a mile or so west in a new village above Auries Creek about 1659, which they renamed Gandaouagué, and which the archeologists know as the Milton Smith Site.[8] After that village was burned by the Seigneur de Tracy in 1666, continues the tradition, the villagers rebuilt north of the river on a bluff above Cayadutta Creek in what is now western Fonda, at what the archeologists call the Veeder Site but is better known as the Saint Kateri National Shrine and Historic Site. The residents called the village Gandaouagué or Caughnawaga.

The traditional account does not fit the archeological evidence at all. As we saw in chapter 2, Auriesville #2 at most contains evidence of a mid-seventeenth-century Mohawk hamlet. By that very fact, it cannot have been the location of events that happened in Mohawk castles.

The arguments of chapters 3 and 4 have shown that the Bauder Site was the most likely location for the martyrdoms of St. René, St. Isaac, and St. Jean. In addition, in chapter 4 the so-called Printup Site was introduced as the new village location of the

8. See chap. 2, note 10, in this volume. At a distance of a mile and a third, the Milton Smith Site was too close to Auriesville #2 to be the successor site. The forest would already have been cut down that far for firewood.

community that had been dwelling at the Bauder Site. It is now time to examine the evidence for that claim.

The old Printup house, built in 1829 or 1830, stands on Dillenbeck Road in Stone Ridge, Township of Glen, Montgomery County, New York, at the intersection with Borden Road. (William Maring kindly pointed out the house to me in 2019.)[9] The Printup Site, as I discovered, lies roughly a mile east of this historic structure. Snow, writing in 1995, identified the site also as the Jim Francis Site, after its then owner. The only land in that area owned by Jim Francis at that time was at 3761 NY-5 South, a parcel of ninety-two acres. That land is now owned and farmed by Joseph and Ella Keim. James Francis and his wife Helena bought the land from A. Dewey and Inez Moore in 1967, while the Moores purchased the parcel from Joseph and Alice Komarzanski in 1960.[10] In these deeds one notices the reservation of access to a spring on lands formerly owned by Stephen Wormuth. This is interesting because Frey and Clark located Andagaron on land owned by a Mr. Wormuth. Looking further back in the deed books, we find that in 1865, William H. and Martha Printup sold nearly twenty-one acres of land at this locale to Stephen Wormuth, bordering on lands he already owned, with the reservation that the Printups might draw water from the spring mentioned above.[11] Thus we see that the Francis property was formerly Printup land, invested with rights to a spring of water on the twenty-acre parcel bought

9. Maring also drove me 0.3 miles west on Dillenbeck Road to the New York State Historical Marker for the Cromwell House. The marker stands at the corner of a gravel drive that goes up the hill to the old Cromwell House, now owned by an Amish farmer. Maring thought that the Printup Site might be on the hill near the farmhouse, but he was not sure. It seems more likely, however, that this is the location of the large village, possibly called Onekagonka, that Rumrill, "Interpretation and Analysis," 8–9, describes as belonging to the years 1624–36. Thus it would have been the predecessor site to the Bauder Site.

10. Montgomery County (NY) Deed Book 372, p. 409; 331, p. 270.

11. Montgomery County (NY) Deed Book 78, pp. 470–71.

by Wormuth in 1865. It may well be that Wormuth later bought the Francis parcel, too, but I did not have the time in Fonda to determine this.

On 21 June 2022, I drove to 3761 NY-5 South and motored up a twisting dirt road to the top of a steep ridge, where I found the Keim farmstead. Mr. Keim, an Amishman, was talking to a non-Amishman in the barnyard. I parked, joined the pair, and listened until there was a break in the conversation. Keim's visitor was leaving in his truck, so I was able to speak to Keim next. I explained my research to him, and he volunteered that the hill that rose behind us, enclosed as a pasture, might have been an Indian village. A man had, not too many years ago, asked his permission to use his metal detector on the hill, as he was convinced that an Indian village had stood up there long ago. Keim said that all the man ever found, after several attempts, was "a French penny." Of course, this interested me, since a French coin in what was a very remote area in the seventeenth century could only mean an Indian village with contact with the French.

Keim kindly directed me to the gate into the pasture, assuring me that the horses would be inquisitive at most but not aggressive. I entered the pasture while he went off on his chores, and I found that the two buggy horses and four draught horses were a little afraid of me, curious but not willing to approach too closely. The single cow in the pasture was indifferent to my presence, affording me one brief glance. As I walked up to the top, I felt strongly that this was the right place. The hilltop was certainly perfect for a Mohawk village of the time: a ravine on the west, steep downhill slopes to the north and east, plenty of land for tilling and gathering wood, large enough for a village at the top, well back and high up from the Mohawk River. I felt strongly that this was St. Catherine's birthplace, and could imagine her playing in the field, now pasture, as a little child.

Rumrill reckons that the site lies roughly 450 meters (0.28

miles) from the Mohawk River. Measured against the US Geological Survey map of the area, this fits with the Keim farm's location. Snow's estimate for the elevation of the site is 152 meters (500 feet) above sea level.[12] An examination of the US Geological Survey map of the area[13] shows the terrain rising above 500 feet of elevation behind the Keims' pasture where I walked. The elevation given on the map for the middle of the hilltop in the pasture above the barnyard is between 460 and 480 feet.

Artifacts gathered at the site establish that the village was occupied in the period 1646/47 to 1659/60. The dates are a conflation of the dates given by Rumrill and Snow.[14] These dates are consistent with the presence of "R mouth harps ... Jesuit rings ... [and] EB pipes ... [and with] the absence of funnel bowl pipes ... [and of r]ound red beads" at the site.[15]

Therefore one concludes, with Rumrill and Snow, that the Printup Site was the location where the Bauder Site community resettled in 1646–47, and that it was later abandoned at the end of the usual roughly twelve-year period in 1659–60.[16] Snow speculates that the name of the village was Ossenrenon-Osserrion. We have argued, however, that the name of the village was probably

12. Rumrill, "Interpretation and Analysis," 18; Snow, *Mohawk Valley Archaeology: Sites*, 365.

13. See chap. 3, note 53 in this volume.

14. Rumrill, "Interpretation and Analysis," 21; Snow, *Sites*, 369.

15. Snow, *Mohawk Valley Archaeology: Sites*, 367 and 369. It should be noted here, too, that evidence exists of a Mohawk hamlet in the Yatesville watershed that was contemporary with the Bauder Site village. It is "unregistered," called the Harris Site, and lies "a mile to the southwest" of the Bauder Site. See Lenig, "Bauder," 7.

16. See chap. 4, note 30 in this volume, and text at that point, as well as Rumrill, "Interpretation and Analysis," 21; Snow, *Mohawk Valley Archaeology: Sites*, 366. Snow, *Mohawk Valley Archaeology: Sites*, 415, says that the Printup Site was St. Catherine's birthplace, but on p. 431 he says she was born at the Freeman Site. This contradiction must have been an oversight. This may be the place to notice, too, that Snow remarks, Catherine "would not have spent much time at the Veeder site (now usually called Caughnawaga) before leaving for Canada" (415). In fact, she left for Canada before Caughnawaga was built.

Oneugiouré.[17] This is by far the most likely locus of the eastern Mohawk castle in this period.

Was this, then, the birthplace of St. Catherine Tekakwitha? One cannot say for sure. The archeological evidence is not yet, and may never be, complete. But the documents assert that she was a daughter of the castle of Gandaouagué, that she suffered the smallpox at Gandaouagué, and that she was received into the Church at Gandaouagué (above Documents 15.1, 16.1, 16.3, and 17.1–3). These assertions associate her with the eastern castle of the Mohawk at three different periods. Her birth in 1656 associates her with the eastern castle at the time the Printup Site was flourishing. Her affliction with the smallpox associates her with the Freeman Site during its ill-fated existence, as we shall see. Finally, her conversion associates her with the Fox Farm Site, as we shall also see. Therefore one can say with considerable assurance that the Printup Site was the birthplace of St. Catherine.

At any rate, in 1659–60, the community at the Printup Site moved west along what is now NY-5 South (more or less), and west-southwest up the present Dillenbeck Road (more or less) to what the archeologists call the Freeman Site. This site is easily located, as it lies under the modern house at 162 Dillenbeck Road in the Town of Root, near the intersection with Argersinger Road. The house was still owned by the Freeman family when I visited the location in 2019. I spoke to a nice lady in the front yard of the house, who confirmed that archeological digging had taken place before the house was built, and that her son had later found arrowheads on the property. Snow calls the digging "salvage excavations" and notes that evidence of the burning of the palisade was discovered. Additionally, the bead types indicate occupation during the 1660s, as do other artifacts discovered on the site.[18] This village was the first to bear the name Gandaouagué.

17. See chap. 4, "Archeologists' Arguments."

18. Snow, Mohawk Valley Archaeology: *Sites*, 371–75. Rumrill, "Interpretation and

Gandaouagué was an ill-starred location, as this village was where St. Catherine's community suffered the smallpox epidemic of 1661–63, and which was burned down by the Seigneur de Tracy in 1666. St. Catherine's community rebuilt north of the Mohawk River in 1666–67. They took the name Gandaouagué with them. However, they did not build their new village above Cayadutta Creek, as Catholic tradition supposes, but at the location where tradition says that the people of Andagaron resettled, which archeologists call the Fox Farm Site.[19]

At first, I was deceived as to Fox Farm's location by a New York State Historical Marker on NY-5 about fifteen feet west of the intersection with Reservoir Road west of Fonda. The marker reads, "Can-a-gor-ha, 1666–1693, Mohawk Indian Castle burned by French and Indians 1693." I took this to signal the location of the Fox Farm Site, explored the area, and spoke to the present owner of the property, Frank Jennings. I also checked the transfers of the property in the twentieth century and found that the parcel had long been known as the Levi J. Dillenbeck farm.[20] I could find no record of Fox ownership, however. This should have alerted me that something was wrong, but I convinced myself that this had to be the Fox Farm Site. (This mistake of mine should be a cautionary tale for all researchers.) There is a large pond on the site, which I took to be an old gravel or sand pit since filled up with water, and the location of the village.[21] At the pond, the altitude was 413.39

Analysis," 25, observes, "Where once proud Mohawks lived and traded, and yes, probably witnessed the vengeance of the French from Canada under the Marquis De Tracy in October 1666, there is now a modern ranch style house surrounded by a well groomed [*sic*] lawn and a farm pond."

19. See chap. 2, note 12 in this volume.

20. See Montgomery County (NY) Deed Books 410, pp. 271–72; 279, p. 482; and 166, pp. 353–54.

21. The County Real Property Tax Office printed for me the aerial tax survey of the Jennings property (49.-2–8.2), which includes the pond. The identity of the pond—viewed from the air—with the sand pit was startlingly clear when compared to the 1980 USGS map. On returning home to Ohio, I checked the 1944 USGS map for Randall

feet. The pond is almost at the center of a basin formed by higher ground encircling it.

At any rate, what I had stumbled upon was the Levi Dillenbeck Site, of the existence of which I was unaware. The Mohawk locus stood on the southern rim of the basin overlooking the Mohawk River on about 1.5 acres of land. Wayne Lenig estimates that four to six longhouses could have stood on the site.[22] Artifacts gathered there suggest "a small Early Woodland component" (200 to ca. 1000) and demonstrate a "mid to late 17th century Mohawk hamlet."[23] Lenig speculates that the site

> most likely represents a splinter population that separated from the main eastern village at the Fox Farm site (Fda 20-1), perhaps due to friction caused by the presence of the Jesuits. While the *Jesuit Relations* do not specifically mention this settlement, the presence of *six or seven* Mohawk villages is noted in several places. Clearly, there was more to Mohawk demography than the three or four main towns or "castles" named in the historical record during the 1660s and 1670s.[24]

The site has not been excavated.

As to the Fox Farm Site, Gen. John S. Clark discovered it in 1877. The site was destroyed by gravel mining, Snow says,[25] but this is a mistake. Wayne Lenig reproduces an aerial photograph of the site with the locations of the old gravel pit and the Mohawk

---

and found no trace of a sand pit or gravel pit at the location of the present pond. Therefore the hole that now contains the pond was dug at some point between 1944 and 1980, and the pit was abandoned and filled up with water after 1980. People today call it Turtle Pond.

22. Lenig, "Dillenbeck," 4 and 5.

23. Lenig, "Dillenbeck," 1.

24. Lenig, "Dillenbeck," 5. Richter, *Ordeal of the Longhouse*, 46, notices that in the case of extreme disagreement on issues within a village, the dissenters might leave and establish themselves elsewhere.

25. Snow, *Mohawk Valley Archaeology: Sites*, 415.

site outlined. The overlap is not great.[26] The outline of the village was roughly square and occupied about two acres on a terrace 140 feet above the level of the Mohawk River and set back 925 feet from its bank.[27] It has not been excavated.

Rumrill and Snow date the site to 1666–79 ± 1683.[28] Their dating is based on the artifacts discovered at the site. As Snow summarizes, "[T]he redwood beads, cross and orb kaolin pipes, and stamped Jesuit rings would seem to put this site clearly in the series established after 1666 on the north bank of the Mohawk River. The lack of HG kaolin pipes, large numbers of black beads, or wire-wound beads leads to the conclusion that the site was abandoned by 1679."[29] These dates correspond nicely with the usual roughly twelve-year occupation of an Iroquoian village. Lenig says that the site has three components: circa 1700 BC; circa 1400 BC, and 1666–86 AD. The basis for his judgment on the last year of occupation is the possible *terminus post quem* of 1686 provided by a "Cross and Orb clay pipe."[30]

This site corresponds well with the description of Gandaouagué left by the Englishman Wentworth Greenhalgh in 1677.[31] He called the village Cahaniaga and wrote, "[I]t is situate upon the Edge of an Hill, about a bow shott from the river side."[32] Thus the

26. Lenig, "Fox Farm," 3.

27. Lenig, "Fox Farm," 1 and 4.

28. Rumrill, "Interpretation and Analysis," 31; Snow, *Mohawk Valley Archaeology: Sites*, 415.

29. Snow, *Mohawk Valley Archaeology: Sites*, 418. On "HG pipes," see Snow, *Mohawk Valley Archaeology: Sites*, 43: "Hendrick Gerdes married Edward Bird's widow in 1668 and took over her late husband's pipe business. Pipes bearing his initials (HG) appear only on sites occupied after this date. Indeed, there appears to be a ten-year lag in either the production or distribution of pipes with the HG hallmark, for it seems not to arrive in the Mohawk Valley until after the Jesuits and the last of the Catholic Mohawks left in 1679." Lenig, "Fox Farm," 3, prefers the dates 1666–86.

30. Lenig, "Fox Farm," 1 and 3.

31. Snow, *Mohawk Valley Archaeology: Sites*, 442–43, 418.

32. "Observations of Wentworth Greenhalgh in a Journey from Albany to the Indyans Westward" (Snow et al., *Mohawk Country*, 189).

preponderance of evidence favors the Fox Farm Site for the second castle named Gandaouagué and the site of St. Peter's Mission.

Therefore the Fox Farm Site was the location of the village which the documentary evidence cited above calls Gandaouagué, where the most successful Jesuit mission developed in the 1670s under the title of St. Peter, where St. Catherine was catechized and baptized by Fr. Jacques de Lamberville, and from which a steady emigration flowed to the Mission de Saint-François-Xavier-du-Sault.

In fact, when the villagers rebuilt their village a couple of miles east on the bluff above Cayadutta Creek, most of the Christians had probably already left the Mohawk Valley, with the result that the village was predominantly traditionalist in religion.[33] This village, also called Gandaouagué or Caughnawaga, existed from 1679 or ±1683 to February 1693, when it was burned down in a French raid from Canada during King William's War (1688–97).[34] Snow summarizes the indicative artifacts. "HG kaolin pipes have been found at Caughnawaga. These were not available in the Mohawk Valley until around 1682. Redwood beads are relatively few. In their place we see a sharp increase in small round black beads. Although variants of the type were around for over a century, they predominate only after 1679." Radiocarbon dating of corn kernels does yield a mean date of 1662, but Snow notes that "the radiocarbon technique is not reliable for samples postdating 1650."

Caughnawaga is unique among Iroquois sites in having been entirely excavated. One can walk the site today and see the outlines of the palisade and the longhouses marked by stakes planted by the excavators. One only needs a little bit of historical imagination to reconstruct the village and to imagine the people. For this

33. Snow, *Mohawk Valley Archaeology: Sites*, 40.

34. Richter, *Ordeal of the Longhouse*, 173–74, says the burning of the villages occurred in January. From Schuyler, "Report of the French Attack," 226, it appears that the destruction happened in early February.

excavation we have Thomas Grassmann, OFM, Conv., to thank, for his order owned the site, and he himself inspired and led the excavation of the site by members of the Van Epps-Hartley Chapter of the New York State Archaeological Association from 1950 to 1956.[35]

After the destruction of Caughnawaga in 1693, the villagers relocated back to the south side of the Mohawk River. The Milton Smith Site in the Town of Glen is the likely location of their resettlement. As we have seen, this was the site identified by Clark as the location of Gandaouagué from 1659 to 1666.[36] The village stood at 128 meters (420 feet) of elevation, a mile or so west of the Auriesville Shrine.[37] Milton Smith owned land at the northern end of Ingersoll Road west of the Village of Auriesville and Auries Creek. His old house stands just south of NY-5 South at 739 Ingersoll Road, Glen Township. The house at 763 Ingersoll is also built on property that used to belong to him. Rising to the west-southwest of these houses is a hill of 420 feet of elevation and standing roughly one and a third miles from the Auriesville Shrine, according to the USGS map of the area.[38] There can be little doubt that this is the location of the Milton Smith Site. In fact, Clark's 1881 map of the Auriesville vicinity shows a hill with an "Indian Castle" on top in the very location I have described.[39]

Snow's remarks on the dating of the site must be quoted at length.

35. Snow, *Mohawk Valley Archeology: Sites*, 432. Note also, "The Caughnawaga site was crucial in establishing the ratio of 1 person per 20 m² of Mohawk village space for most periods" (433). Thus one sees that the excavations at Caughnawaga have been important for archeology and history.

36. See chap. 2, note 10 in this volume.

37. Snow, *Mohawk Valley Archaeology: Sites*, 454. In Egan, "The General and the Professor," 2, there is a photograph taken in 1898 from the Auriesville Site looking up the Mohawk River. An arrow indicates the hill on which the Milton Smith Site stands. The hill lies the other side of Auriesville in the location described above in the text.

38. USGS Historical Map, Tribes Hill, chap. 3, note 50 in this volume.

39. Lenig, "Auriesville I," fig. 1.

> Rumrill ... says that this is a two-component site dating to A.D. 1643–1657 and A.D. 1694–1712 respectively. However, all of his evidence for the earlier component could be fallout from periods previous to the main occupation. He is struck by the absence of Jesuit rings, and he uses this to set the end of the first occupation to no later than 1657. However, the occupants of this site were probably the non-Catholic half of the Caughnawaga population that relocated in 1693. The abundance of seed beads puts this site into the A.D. 1710–1755 period. Although there are clearly scattered bits of evidence relating to the A.D. 1635–1655 period, there is not enough here to justify claims for a component dating to that time. The site was probably abandoned in 1712 as Rumrill suggests, due to the construction of Fort Hunter nearby. Its single component should be dated A.D. 1693–1712.[40]

Snow notices, too, "The site has a single residential locus. In addition, the Auriesville #3 cemetery site might be associated with either this site, the Auriesville #1 site, or both."[41] Auriesville #1, #2, and #3 were discussed in chapter 3, "Archeological Evidence." We saw there how full of mistakes Snow's account of the various sites at Auriesville was. Yet his analysis of Milton Smith itself seems to be sound, although he may be too dismissive of an earlier component.

Conclusion

A clear sequence of villages associated with St. Catherine's life in Iroquoia has emerged in this section. She was born and lived her toddler years at the Printup Site (Oneugiouré) on the south side of the Mohawk River. She spent her childhood at the Freeman Site

40. Snow, *Sites, Mohawk Valley Archaeology:* 459. Snow is citing Rumrill, "Interpretation and Analysis," 21.

41. Snow, *Mohawk Valley Archaeology: Sites,* 458. The village was probably called Ogsadaga, according to Snow (456).

(Gandaouagué), also on the south side of the river, where she lost her family and her own good health to smallpox. She spent her teenaged years, converted to Catholicism, was catechized, and was baptized at the Fox Farm Site (also Gandaouagué) on the north side of the river. At last, she fled from this same village to the Sault. A few years after her departure, the remaining villagers, many of them her relations, moved to the Veeder Site (Caughnawaga), also on the north side of the Mohawk. They had to abandon this village after its destruction in 1693, when they moved back across the river to the Milton Smith Site (Ogsadaga).

CHAPTER 6

A Narrative Presentation of the Research Results

A CRITICALLY INFORMED and up-to-date narrative of the events we have been examining was promised in the introduction to this book. Many of the details given in the noncommittal narrative in chapter 1 need not be repeated. Here we need simply follow the martyrs through their ordeals, and St. Catherine through her young life, in the places where we have argued they actually happened. Such a narrative will provide a good summary of what has been argued above.

On 14 August 1642, after a three- or four-day march overland from the head of Lake Champlain, the Mohawk war party that had captured St. Isaac, St. René, and their companions on the St. Lawrence reached the north bank of the Mohawk River a little west of the modern Yosts, Montgomery County, New York. This location is just east of the famous Mohawk Valley landmark of the Noses, mountainous bluffs north and south of the river that resemble the jutting feature of the human face. The party stood opposite the mouth of what we call the Yatesville Creek, the gateway to their cantonal village or castle, Ossenrenon. The large party was ferried across the river in canoes. When these elm-bark craft entered the mouth of the Yatesville, the prisoners were roughly disembarked into the shallow waters of the creek, where they were insulted and beaten by Mohawks leaping into the water from both sides of the creek, while Huron slaves shouted warnings and threats to the captives.

Ossenrenon stood about a mile away from the mouth of the Yatesville on the other side of a steep ridge that ran parallel to the river. The ridge was the northeastern end of the mountain that rose to eight hundred feet of elevation just east of Little Nose and was divided from it by Lashers Creek. The Yatesville flowed from the south, cutting a very deep ravine or gorge along the eastern flank of the ridge, and then turned northwest and cut its way around the low northern end of the ridge to the river. To reach the village, one could either climb a path along a ledge from the creek up the steep western side of the ridge and cross over the top to the village, or one could walk upstream a few hundred yards to the point where a shallow ravine ran downhill from the south from the gently sloping terrain on the eastern flank of the ridge where the village stood. Today's Currytown Road follows this ravine. The Indian path probably diverged from the bed of the modern road at the top of the ravine and cut southeast through the woods and across the cleared fields to the village. Since St. Isaac and his companions were already in such poor physical condition from their ordeals, they were led to the village by the easier route and then "welcomed" with the gauntlet.

After a day of torture,[1] the captives were led to the second Mohawk castle, Andagaron, which stood on the western flank of Little Nose above the modern village of Sprakers, a little northeast of the intersection of the present CR-108 and NY-162. The party's route would have followed the southern flank of the mountain

1. *MNF* 6.283 and 7.106 say they were kept at Ossenrenon for three days.

next to Little Nose, much as Moyer Road does today, until it reached a point where the Lashers Creek ravine could be easily crossed and a beeline made for Andagaron. After two more days of torture, the prisoners were led to the third Mohawk castle, Theonontougen. Their route would have lain to the west somewhere below the gorge cut by Flat Creek to the location of the modern Canajoharie. There the route would have followed the river flats to a point northwest of Fort Plain where the intervale narrows almost to nothing. There they would have climbed the ridge to Theonontougen, which stood probably at 680 feet of elevation, on a large shelf where the Fort Plain Airport now lies. After two more days of torture, the captives were led back to Andagaron (21 August), where deliberations took place regarding their fate. St. Isaac and St. René were sent back to Ossenrenon at the conclusion of the debate.

On 29 September, St. Isaac and S. René walked west from the village through the modestly rising fields to what woods remained on the steep slopes of the ridge above Ossenrenon. As they returned to the village from their prayerful seclusion in the woods, they were accosted by two young warriors at or near the village gates, one of whom chopped St. René down with a hatchet. The warriors stripped St. René's body and, accompanied by the village children and dogs, dragged it through the village and down the precipitous bed of the brook that started just north of the palisade to the Yatesville. They abandoned the body on an islet of scree clear of the tree canopy, where it could be seen by vultures and crows, which would finish what the dogs were already starting. There St. Isaac found the body, dragged it into the main channel of the Yatesville, and covered it with stones, intending to return the next day to bury it.

St. Isaac escaped to the Dutch in 1643 and was back in New France in 1644. In the late spring of 1646, he accompanied Jean Bourdon on a peace mission to the Mohawk authorized by the governor of New France. They reached Ossenrenon 8 June 1646. People flocked from the three cantonal villages and from the hamlets to see them, and the negotiations for peace were conducted at Ossenrenon by a council of elders from the chief villages and hamlets. St. Isaac ministered to the pastoral needs of the Mohawks and Huron captives gathered at Ossenrenon and learned that the name of the village had been changed to Oneugiouré in anticipation of a necessary move to a new village site. The French diplomats departed 16 June.

St. Isaac and St. Jean de Lalande set out for Mohawk territory again on 24 September on a supplemental peace embassy and religious mission. On 14 October, near the head waters of the Hudson River, the small group—two Frenchmen and one Huron—was attacked and taken captive by a party of Mohawk warriors of the Bear Clan. The Bears had rejected the peace treaty with the French. The warriors haled the three captives to Ossenrenon-Oneugiouré, which they reached 17 October. A council was called for the next day at Theonontougen, in which it was decided to spare the French prisoners. On the evening of 18 October, however, a Bear warrior invited St. Isaac to a feast held in a Bear longhouse in Ossenrenon. St. Isaac was murdered in the cabin's lean-to porch. St Jean was murdered later that night, when he left the longhouse where he was staying, probably to find St. Isaac.

In the next year or so, at the end of the roughly twelve-year life expectancy of an Iroquoian village, the people of Ossenrenon-Oneugiouré moved completely to the new village site, which they had been preparing for a couple of years. It stood on a high ridge well above the Mohawk River intervale and was surrounded by plenty of arable land, once the woods were chopped down. This new village, Oneugiouré, thus became the easternmost castle of the Mohawk, as Ossenrenon had been before it. Here St. Catherine was born in 1656. In time, a new village was built for the community and renamed Gandaouagué. This was done toward the end of the usual twelve-year period in 1659–60. The new castle was in a glorious spot well back from the Mohawk and high above it, with easily accessible arable land on all sides, but this castle was unlucky. The population was decimated by smallpox in 1661–63, and the village was burned down by the French in 1666.

Along with the communities of the other cantonal villages, the community of Gandaouagué relocated to the north bank of the Mohawk River. The people of Gandaouagué chose to rebuild on a shelving ridge overlooking a wide intervale and the Mohawk River about three miles west of present-day Fonda, Montgomery County. This became in its turn the easternmost Mohawk castle. A couple of years after St. Catherine fled to Canada in 1677, the community, following the roughly twelve-year pattern of removal to a new village, moved east and settled on a ridge that abutted the deep ravine of Cayadutta Creek and overlooked the Mohawk River some distance away. This village was named Caughnawaga. After the French burned this village down in 1693, the community moved back across the river to what is known as the Milton Smith Site, in the modern hamlet of Auriesville, and renamed the village Ogsadaga.

Conclusion

The Continuing Significance of the Shrine of Our Lady of Martyrs and the St. Kateri National Shrine

IN HIS 1934 article on St. Catherine, Fr. Joseph Loyzance posed the question, "Why Do We Insist so Much on Locating the Three Mohawk Castles up to 1666 on the South of the River?" He answered in three parts.

> 1. Because it is a fact of history, now proved beyond any doubt, Rev. Father Walwaorth [*sic*], Dr. J. G. Shea, General Clark, Father Felix Martin, S.J. vouch for it. 2. Because these three villages are holy places, sanctified by the blood of many martyrs, among who [*sic*] were Rene Goupil, S.J., Father Bressani, S.J., [*sic*] and Father Isaac Jogues, S.J. 3. Because it is very important to know the very spot of these villages, that we may venerate them and invoke the protection of those martyrs in our temporal and spiritual wants.[1]

While it is universally admitted today that the Mohawk villages of that period were located south of the Mohawk River, nevertheless it is clear that the evidence and arguments in this book have been at variance with Fr. Loyzance's conviction that

1. Loyzance, "Kateri Tegewitha," 6.

Gen. John S. Clark's village identifications were correct. However, the investigations undertaken in this book have been entirely in the spirit of Fr. Loyzance's second and third points. It is vital for Catholics to know the true locations of the heavenly birthdays of the martyrs, places sanctified by affliction and by death. Christianity is historical. Just as the knowledge of the actual location of Golgotha is critical for Christian faith, so is the knowledge of the actual locations of the torments of the martyrs critical for life in the Communion of Saints and for popular piety. If it is meaningful and uplifting for Americans to walk the fields at Gettysburg, how much more moving and purifying must it be for Catholics to tread the sites the saints and martyrs trod? Moreover, Catholic devotion is led to the spiritual through the physical. It needs the inspiration of things and places sanctified by grace to approach God. It is strengthened by martyrs' shrines and the relics of the saints in its prayer. Critical it is therefore to know where St. René, St. Isaac, and St. Jean made their witness to the Faith, and where St. Catherine grew up, converted, and was baptized.

Nonetheless, the arguments in this book could be perceived as a threat by those who maintain the Martyrs Shrine at Auriesville and the St. Kateri Shrine in Fonda. They could also be seen as threatening by Catholics who have sanctified these shrines with their faith and devotions. But let us review the arguments of this book before we address these concerns.

Archeological discoveries in the Mohawk Valley and the scientific study of artifacts, especially in the second half of the twentieth century, have driven the argument of this book. The accurate dating of beads, clay pipes, and other European trade goods has shown that the easternmost Mohawk castle was not at the Auriesville Site in the second, third, and fourth quarters of the seventeenth century. Instead, it was at the Bauder Site (Ossenrenon) from circa 1635 to circa 1646, then at the Printup Site (Oneugiouré) from circa 1647 to circa 1659, next at the

Freeman Site (Gandaouagué) from circa 1660 to 1666, at the Fox Farm Site (also Gandaouagué) from 1666 to circa 1679, at the Veeder Site (Caughnawaga) from circa 1679 to 1693, and finally at the Milton Smith Site (Ogsadaga), the last palisaded castle,[2] from 1693 to circa 1712. These dated periods also reflect the known necessity of the Iroquoian peoples to build a new village every twelve years or so, except in the two cases where the French burned the villages in 1666 and 1693.[3]

Moreover, the archeological evidence is supported by the documentary evidence in the accounts of the martyrdoms of St. René, St. Isaac, and St. Jean. (The written records concerning St. Catherine, however, add only one crucial point to the archeological record.)

First, all the written accounts make more sense if the party that captured St. Isaac and St. René reached the northern bank of the Mohawk River on foot in the vicinity of the modern village of Yosts and crossed to the mouth of Yatesville Creek by canoe. The configuration of the mouth of the creek suits the "greeting" of the captives better than the easy riverbank at Auriesville, as do the alternative routes to the Bauder Site, one extremely steep, the other more negotiable for captives disabled by torture. Second, the distance to the Rumrill-Naylor Site from the Bauder Site fits the narratives better than that from Auriesville to Printup. Third, the dramatic hill, ravine, and creek at the Bauder Site reflect the documents better than the same features at the Auriesville Site.

Turning our eyes from St. Rene's martyrdom to the martyrdoms of St. Isaac and St. Jean, we see in the documents strong

2. Snow, *Mohawk Valley Archaeology: Sites*, 456.

3. Milton Smith is another exception, but as it was the last palisaded castle and represented the end of an epoch, perhaps the inhabitants let it decay around them while they moved ahead piecemeal into the new era of separate family cabins. Cf. Snow, *Mohawk Valley Archaeology: Sites*, 454.

evidence that the deaths of these two martyrs occurred at the Bauder Site, and not at Rumrill-Naylor, as certain archeologists believe. For one thing, the archeologists' arguments are easily rebutted. Rumrill's argument rested on a false idea of clan cantons and castles. Snow's argument failed because its premise was not adequately proved. In addition, both arguments rested on a fatal absurdity. Moreover, the details in the documents about St. Isaac's coffer, and about his adoptive aunt and her family, confirm that the deaths of St. Isaac and St. Jean occurred at the Bauder Site. Finally, it is highly unlikely that the Bauder Site community had yet moved to Oneugiouré at the Printup Site.

As far as the documents associated with St. Catherine go, we find that they confirm the name of her village as Gandaouagué, the location of the Jesuits' Mission of St. Peter. They do not confirm the name of her birthplace as Oneugiouré, nor are they consistent in mentioning the Seigneur de Tracy's raid in 1666. In fact, one gets little sense from the documents of the geographical peripeties of Catherine's life in Mohawk country. The documents do show, however, that Catherine spent her life in the Mohawk Valley in a castle and not in an outlying hamlet.

So, to return to our question, do those committed to the Auriesville and Veeder Sites as shrines to the Jesuit Martyrs and to St. Catherine Tekakwitha need fear the diminution of the significance of the shrines they tend and love? No, I do not think so.

First, the shrines have already been sanctified by more than a dozen decades of pilgrimage and devotion and Masses. Second, they have the infrastructure in place to continue to serve as foci for pilgrimage, devotion, and Mass. Third, as the Jesuits said about the Auriesville ravine, that it is itself a reliquary, so one could say about this whole stretch of the Mohawk Valley: it is one giant reliquary. We have none of the bones of the martyrs. They are scattered in the woods and creeks of the area, and St. Catherine is buried in Kahnawake, Quebec. Therefore the two Mohawk Valley shrines can quite legitimately serve as focal points for the veneration of these saints.

Beyond this, the shrines could be proactive and purchase some or all of the sites associated with the martyrs. They could also build outdoor chapels, such as the one that stands on the site of the martyrdoms of St. Jean de Brébeuf and St. Gabriel Lalemant near Midland, Ontario. It is just a simple structure with no walls and a stone altar at the edge of a mown field where the village stood in which Brébeuf and Lalemant suffered and died, Taenhatenteron/Saint-Ignace II. Furthermore, the shrines could provide transportation for pilgrims to the sites, perhaps even volunteer guides. And Masses could be said at special times in the chapels at the sites.

The faithful would surely donate generously, while Catholic lawyers could make contracts and liability arrangements, and negotiate whatever claims the Mohawk Nation might have on burial sites and artifacts. Short of purchasing the sites, perhaps agreements could be reached with the owners of the properties for visits to be made to the sites by pilgrims.

At any rate, I would encourage those most closely associated with the shrines, as well as all the faithful, to pray fervently for guidance about the way forward to the enhancement—not the diminution—of the significance of the shrines at Auriesville and Fonda, and to the deepened experience of these saints by Christ's faithful people.

APPENDIX

What Did St. Isaac Do with St. René's Bones?

This question does not pertain to our inquiry, though it does arise from it. It is important for the martyrs' stories, however, and will answer to the method we have been employing.

Documentary Evidence

A. St. Isaac's Letter to His Provincial, Document 1.17

1. "Verum ubi liquefactae sunt nives, audivi ab adolescentibus videri sparsa defuncti Galli ossa. Itaque eo me conferens semirosa ossa, reliquias canum, vulpium et corvorum, et praecipua ea terrae mandavi."

Translation. "But when the snows had melted, I heard from the young men that the scattered bones of the dead Frenchman were being seen. And so, going there, I committed to the earth these eminent things, the half-gnawed bones, the leavings of the dogs, foxes, and crows."

B. Father Bressani's Translation of the Preceding, Document 2.14

1. "[E] non ne posso haver nuova prima della primavera seguente, quando liquefatte le nevi, i giovani del paese m' avvertirono haver visto le sue ossa nell' istessa riva del fiume, le quali insieme con il capo riverentemente baciate, all' hora finalmente sepellii al meglio che potei."

Translation. "[A]nd I was not able to have news of him before next spring, when, the snows having melted, the young men of the canton told me they had seen his bones on the same bank of the river, the which together with the head, reverently kissed, I buried then finally the best I could."

C. St. Isaac's Brief Account of St. Rene's Martyrdom, Document 3.8

1. "Le printemps, comme on me dist que c'estoit là qu'on l'avoit traisné, j'y allé plusieurs foys sans rien trouver. Enfin, la quatriesme fois, je trouve la teste, quelques os demy rongés, que j'enterray … Je les baisé bien dévotement par plusieurs foys, comme les os d'un martyr de Jésus-Christ."

Translation. "In the spring, as they told me that it was there that they had dragged it, I went there many times without finding anything. At last, the fourth time, I find the head, some half-gnawed bones, which I buried … I kissed them very devoutly many times, as the bones of a martyr of Jesus Christ."

D. Fr. Lalemant's Account Taken from St. Isaac, Document 4.12

1. "Le printemps suivant, quelques enfans rapportans qu'ils avoient veu le François dans un ruisseau, le Père s'y transporte sans dire mot, retire ces sacrez despouilles, les baise avec respect, les cache dans le creux d'un arbre."

Translation. "The following spring some lads reporting that they had seen the Frenchman in a stream, the Father betakes himself there without saying a word, he withdraws these sacred remains, he kisses them with respect, he hides them in the hollow of a tree."

E. Fr. Buteux's Account Taken from St. Isaac, Document 5.11

1. "Il fault attendre jusques au printemps. Ce fut pour lors qu'il aprit de quelques jeunes enfants que le corps du François estoit

proche d'un petit boccage dans un ruisseau. Il se transporte sur le lieu, cherche longtemps et enfin le trouve, c'est-à-dire les os, qu'il ramasse décemment, les baise et les cache dans trois ou quatre creux d'arbres."

Translation. "It is necessary to wait until springtime. It was then that he learned from certain young lads that the corpse of the Frenchman was near a little wood in the stream. He betakes himself to the place, he searches a long time and at last finds it, that is to say, the bones, which he gathers decently, he kisses them and he hides them in three or four hollows of trees."

Commentary

A contradiction certainly does seem to exist. In his semiofficial accounts of his treatment of the holy bones, St. Isaac himself says, *ea terrae mandavi*, "I committed them to the earth," and that he found the bones *que j'enterray*, "which I buried." In the first case, however, St. Isaac may have been emphasizing that he performed the Absolution of the Dead.

Thinking as a priest, and writing to his superior—a priest, too—he may have been trying to intimate that he did what he could to perform the burial rites for his friend. In the second case, although *enterrer* certainly means "to bury," again St. Isaac's emphasis may have been on the performance of the appropriate ritual and ceremony.[1]

Fr. Bressani's alteration of St. Isaac's text to *sepellii al meglio che potei*, "I buried [them] finally the best I could," may support the interpretation given above. He may mean that St. Isaac performed the burial rites of the Church as well as he was able. In addition,

1. St. Isaac did intend to inter the body. That is why he took a hoe (not a shovel; see chap. 3, note 22) with him when he first went in search of the body. This does not mean that the following spring he would have been committed to burying the bones in the earth.

sepellire, at least in the eighteenth century, could mean "to hide, to conceal, to keep quiet,"[2] which is not unlike English idiom, of course. It may be that Bressani had heard that the bones were hidden, not buried in a grave, and that he was trying to suggest this here.

Fr. Lalemant and Fr. Buteux, each of whom had heard the story of the martyrdom in private conversations with St. Isaac over a long Montreal winter, say that the bones were hidden in the hollows of trees. This makes good sense, as St. Isaac hoped to be repatriated to New France from Iroquoia, and to bring the bones back with him.[3] It would have been easier to retrieve the bones quickly from tree hollows than from a grave, especially during the winter. Moreover, in a tree the bones would have been safer from scavenging animals than in a shallow hole in the earth. Perhaps, too, he thought he could conceal the relics in trees with less risk of observation by his captors than if he went through the longer process of burying them in the ground.

In conclusion, having weighed the witnesses, not counted them, we can say it is possible to hold these several accounts together as complementary, and that St. Isaac, after performing the burial rites as well as he could, concealed the relics in the hollow of a tree or in the hollows of a couple of trees. Is it possible that these trees have survived to this day?

2. Baretti, *Dictionary of the Italian and English*, s.v. "spellire."

3. E.g., *MNF* 5.612: "ut ea si vellet aliquando Deus in terram sanctam et christianorum tanquam ingentes divitias exportarem" ("in order that, if God ever wished it, I might carry them [the bones] out as great riches to holy ground and ground belonging to Christians").

BIBLIOGRAPHY

Primary Sources

Archival Sources

County Clerk's Office. Montgomery County, Fonda, NY. Various deeds.

County Surrogate's Court. Montgomery County, Fonda, NY. Various wills.

County Tax Maps and Real Property Office. Montgomery County, Fonda, NY. Various property tax records.

[Frey, Samuel L.] "Work with Gen. Clark re: 3 Towns." HF 14-A-5. Photocopy of a handwritten document. Montgomery County Department of History and Archives, Fonda, NY.

Jogues, St. Isaac, SJ. "Epistola Patris Isaaci Jogues in noua Francia inter Iroheos captiui ad Prouincialem Francię." In Collection du Père Prat, SJ, PraA9, folios 361–92. Archives françaises de la Compagnie de Jésus, Vanves, France.

Printed Sources

Alegambe, Philippe, SJ. *Mortes Illustres et Gesta Eorum de Societate Iesu.* 3 vols. Rome: Typographia Varesii, 1657, 1659, 1660.

Boniface, François, SJ. "De la mission de Gandaouagué ou de Saint Pierre dans la Pais d'Agnié." In *Relation de ce qui s'est passé en la Nouvelle France, les années 1672 et 1673*. Chapter 2 in Reuben Gold Thwaites, *Jesuit Relations and Allied Documents*. Vol. 57. Cleveland: Burrows Brothers, 1899, 88–111.

Bressani, Francesco Gioseppe, SJ, trans. *Breve Relatione d'alcvne missioni de' PP. della Compagnia di Giesù nella Nuoua Francia*. In Lucien Campeau, *Monumenta Novae Franciae* VIII. *Au bord de la ruine*

(*1651–1656*). Rome: Institutum Historicum Societatis Iesu, 1996, Document 103 III, 483–502.

Buteux, Jacques, SJ. "Narré de la prise du Père Isaac Jogues, par le P. Jacques Buteux." In Lucien Campeau, *Monumenta Novae Franciae* VI. *Recherche de la paix* (*1644–1646*). Rome: Institutum Historicum Societatis Iesu, 1992, Document 67, 273–306.

———. "Le Père Jacques Buteux au P. Jérôme Lalemant, Sup." In Lucien Campeau, *Monumenta Novae Franciae* VII. *Le Témoignage du sang* (*1647–1650*). Rome: Institutum Historicum Societatis Iesu, 1994, Document 20, 43–44.

———. "Le P. Jacques Buteux au P. Jérôme Lalemant, Sup." In Lucien Campeau, *Monumenta Novae Franciae* VII. *Le Témoignage du sang* (*1647–1650*). Rome: Institutum Historicum Societatis Iesu, 1994, Document 24, 48–51.

Campeau, Lucien, SJ, ed. *Monumenta Novae Franciae* V. *La bonne nouvelle reçue* (*1641–1643*). Rome: Institutum Historicum Societatis Iesu, 1990.

———. *Monumenta Novae Franciae* VI. *Recherche de la paix* (*1644–1646*). Rome: Institutum Historicum Societatis Iesu, 1992.

———. *Monumenta Novae Franciae* VII. *Le Témoignage du sang* (*1647–1650*). Rome: Institutum Historicum Societatis Iesu, 1994.

———. *Monumenta Novae Franciae* VIII. *Au bord de la ruine* (*1651–1656*). Rome: Institutum Historicum Societatis Iesu, 1996.

Chauchetière, Claude, SJ. *La Vie de la B*[*ienheureuse*]. *Catherine Tegakoüita, Dite à Present La Saincte Sauuagesse*. Manhattan: Presse Cramoisy de Jean-Marie Shea, 1887.

———. "Narration annuelle de La Mission du Sault depuis la Fondation iusques a l'an 1686." In *Jesuit Relations and Allied Documents*, vol. 63, edited by Reuben Gold Thwaites. Cleveland: Burrows Brothers, 1900, 139–245.

Cholenec, Pierre, SJ. "Lettre du Père Cholenec, missionnaire da la Compagnie de Jésus, au Père Augustin le Blanc, de la même Compagnie, Procureur des missions du Canada." In *Lettres édifiantes et curieuses écrites des missions étrangères*. Vol. 4. *Mémoires d'Amérique*, new ed., edited by Charles Le Gobien, SJ, et al., 1703–76. Lyon: J. Verneral & Étienne Cabin, 1819, 25–61.

———. *La Vie de Catherine Tegakouita Première Vierge Irokoise*. In Pierre Cholenec, *Catherine Tekakwitha: Her Life*. Translated by William Lonc, SJ. Hamilton, ON: William Lonc, 2002. Appendix with French text, separately paginated, 1–67.

Gehring, Charles T., and William A. Starna (trans. and ed.). *A Journey into Mohawk and Oneida Country, 1634–1635: The Journal of Harmen Meyndertsz van den Bogaert*, rev. ed. The Iroquois and Their Neighbors. Syracuse, NY: Syracuse University Press, 2013.

Greenhalgh, Wentworth. "Observations of Wentworth Greenhalgh in a Journey from Albany to the Indyans Westward." In *In Mohawk Country: Early Narratives about a Native People*, edited by Dean R. Snow, Charles T. Gehring, and William Starna. Syracuse, NY: Syracuse University Press, 1996, 188–92.

Jogues, St. Isaac, SJ. "Epistola Patris Isaaci Jogues in Nova Francia inter Irohaeos captivi ad Provincialem Franciae." In Lucien Campeau, *Monumenta Novae Franciae* V. *La bonne nouvelle reçue (1641–1643)*. Rome: Institutum Historicum Societatis Iesu, 1990, Document 115, 592–625.

———. "Le martyre de René Goupil par les Iroquois." In Lucien Campeau, *Monumenta Novae Franciae* V. *La bonne nouvelle reçue (1641–1643)*. Rome: Institutum Historicum Societatis Iesu, 1990, Document 80, 284–91.

———. "Le P. Isaac Jogues au P. André Castillon." In Lucien Campeau, *Monumenta Novae Franciae* VI. *Recherche de la paix (1644–1646)*. Rome: Institutum Historicum Societatis Iesu, 1992, Document 121, 512–14.

———. "Lettera del Padre Isaac Iogues al Padre Provinciale della provincia di Francia." In Francesco Gioseppe Bressani, *Breve Relatione d'alcvne missioni de' PP. della Compagnia di Giesù nella Nuoua Francia*. In Lucien Campeau, *Monumenta Novae Franciae* VIII. *Au bord de la ruine (1651–1656)*. Rome: Institutum Historicum Societatis Iesu, 1996, Document 103 III, 483–502.

Jogues, Isaac, SJ, and Jérôme Lalemant, SJ. *Relation de ce qui s'est passé en la Nouvelle-France en l'année 1647*. Chapters 4–5 in Lucien Campeau, *Monumenta Novae Franciae* VII. *Le Témoignage du sang (1647–1650)*. Rome: Institutum Historicum Societatis Iesu, 1994, Document 35, 96–114.

Kieft, Willem. "Willem Kieft, Dir., à Charles Huault de Montmagny, Gouv." In Lucien Campeau, *Monumenta Novae Franciae* VI. *Recherche de la paix (1644–1646)*. Rome: Institutum Historicum Societatis Iesu, 1992, Document 137, 539–40. Also in VII, Document 35, 129.

Labatie, Jan. "L'Interprète Labatie à Jean de la Montagne." In Lucien Campeau, *Monumenta Novae Franciae* VI. *Recherche de la paix (1644–1646)*. Rome: Institutum Historicum Societatis Iesu, 1992, Document 132, 527–28. Also in VII, Document 35, 130.

Lalemant, Jérôme, SJ. "De la Mission des Martyrs commencée au pays des Iroquois." Chapter 4 in *Relation de ce qui s'est passé en la Nouvelle-France ès années 1645 et 1646*. In Lucien Campeau, *Monumenta Novae Franciae* VI. *Recherche de la paix (1644–1646)*. Rome: Institutum Historicum Societatis Iesu, 1992, Document 140 I, 568–76.

———. ["Lettre au R. P. Estienne Charlet, provincial de la Compagnie de Jésus en la province de France."] In *Relation de ce qui s'est passé en la Nouvelle-France en l'année 1647*. In Lucien Campeau, *Monumenta Novae Franciae* VII. *Le Témoignage du sang (1647–1650)*. Rome: Institutum Historicum Societatis Iesu, 1994, Document 35, 70–72.

———. *Relation de ce qui s'est passé en la Nouvelle-France en l'année 1647*. Chapter 1 in Lucien Campeau, *Monumenta Novae Franciae* VII. *Le Témoignage du sang (1647–1650)*. Rome: Institutum Historicum Societatis Iesu, 1994, Document 35, 72–82.

———. *Relation de ce qui s'est passé en la Nouvelle-France ès années 1647 et 1648*. Chapter 2 in Lucien Campeau, *Monumenta Novae Franciae* VII. *Le Témoignage du sang (1647–1650)*. Rome: Institutum Historicum Societatis Iesu, 1994, Document 77, 299–308.

Le Gobien, Charles, SJ, et al., eds. *Lettres édifiantes et curieuses écrites des missions étrangères*. Vol. 4, *Mémoires d'Amérique*, 1703–76. Lyon: J. Verneral & Étienne Cabin, 1819.

Megapolensis, Johannes. *A Short Account of the Mohawk Indians*. In *In Mohawk Country: Early Narratives about a Native People*, edited by Dean R. Snow, Charles T. Gehring, and William Starna. Syracuse, NY: Syracuse University Press, 1996, 38–46.

Padberg, John W., SJ, ed. *The Constitutions of the Society of Jesus and Their*

Complementary Norms: A Complete English Translation of the Official Latin Texts. Jesuit Primary Sources in English Translation I.15. St. Louis, MO: Institute of Jesuit Sources, 1996.

Ragueneau, Paul, SJ. *Mémoires: 1652, Touchant la Mort et les Vertus des Pères Isaac Jogues, Anne de Noüe, Anthoine Daniel, Jean de Brébeuf, Gabriel Lallement, Charles Garnier, Noël Chabanel et un Séculier René Goupil.* Transcribed by William Lonc, SJ, and edited by Steve Catlin. Ottawa: Early Jesuit Missions in Canada, 2013.

———. *Memoirs: 1652. Memoirs of the Death and Virtues of Fathers …* Edited by William Lonc, SJ, and Steve Catlin. Ottawa: Early Jesuit Missions in Canada, 2013.

Relations des Jésuites contenant ce qui s'est passé de plus remarquable dans les missions des Pères de la Compagnie de Jésus dans le Nouvelle-France. Québec: Augustin Coté, 1858.

Roustang, François, SJ, ed. *Jesuit Missionaries to North America: Spiritual Writings and Biographical Sketches.* San Francisco: Ignatius Press, 2006.

Sagard, Gabriel. *Le grand voyage du pays des Hurons*, new ed. Edited by Réal Ouellet and Jack Warwick. Quebec: Bibliothèque Québécoise, 2007.

Schuyler, Peter. "Report of the French Attack on the Mohawks, 1693." In *In Mohawk Country: Early Narratives about a Native People*, edited by Dean R. Snow, Charles T. Gehring, and William Starna. Syracuse, NY: Syracuse University Press, 1996, 225–30.

Snow, Dean R., Charles T. Gehring, and William Starna, eds. *In Mohawk Country: Early Narratives about a Native People.* The Iroquois and Their Neighbors. Syracuse, NY: Syracuse University Press, 1996.

Thwaites, Reuben Gold, ed. *The Jesuit Relations and Allied Documents, Travels and Explorations of the Jesuit Missionaries in New France, 1610–1791.* 73 vols. Cleveland: Burrows Brothers, 1896–1901.

Archeological Sources (Books)

Bradley, James W. *Onondaga and Empire: An Iroquoian People in an Imperial Era.* New York State Museum Bulletin 514. Albany: State University of New York, 2020.

Grumet, Robert S. *Historic Contact: Indian People and Colonists in Today's Northeastern United States in the Sixteenth through Eighteenth Centuries.* Contributions to Public Archeology 1. Norman: University of Oklahoma Press, 1995.

Lenig, Wayne. *Prehistoric Mohawk Studies: The Mohawk Valley Project and Beyond.* Unpublished monograph. 1998. Revised 2013. Available at the Montgomery County Department of History and Archives.

Lepper, Bradley T. *Ohio Archaeology: An Illustrated Chronicle of Ohio's Ancient American Indian Cultures.* Wilmington, OH: Orange Frazer Press, 2005.

Ritchie, William A. *The Archaeology of New York State.* Rev. ed. Harrison, NY: Harbor Hill Books, 1980.

Snow, Dean R. *Mohawk Valley Archaeology: The Collections.* Occasional Papers in Anthropology 22. University Park: Matson Museum of Anthropology, Pennsylvania State University, 1995.

———. *Mohawk Valley Archaeology: The Sites.* Occasional Papers in Anthropology 23. University Park: Matson Museum of Anthropology, Pennsylvania State University, 1995.

Trigger, Bruce G., ed. *Handbook of North American Indians.* Vol. 15. *Northeast.* Washington, DC: Smithsonian Institution, 1978.

Archeological Sources (Articles)

Ewing, J. Franklin, SJ. "First Note on the Archaeology of the Mohawk Town of Ossernenon." *American Antiquity* 18 (1953): 389–91.

Fenton, William N. "Northern Iroquoian Culture Patterns." In *Handbook of North American Indians.* Vol. 15, *Northeast,* edited by Bruce G. Trigger. Washington, DC: Smithsonian Institution, 1978, 296–321.

Hancock, John E. "Earthworks." In *Ohio Archaeology: An Illustrated Chronicle of Ohio's Ancient American Indian Cultures,* edited by Bradley T. Lepper. Wilmington, OH: Orange Frazer Press, 2005, 162–69.

Fitting, James E. "Regional Cultural Development, 300 B.C. to A.D. 1000." In *Handbook of North American Indians.* Vol. 15, *Northeast,* edited by Bruce G. Trigger. Washington, DC: Smithsonian Institution, 1978, 44–57.

Lenig, Wayne. "Patterns of Material Culture during the Early Years of New Netherland Trade." *Northeast Anthropology* 58 (1999): 47–74.

———. "Site Name: Auriesville Shrine I." Seven unnumbered pages. Private communication by email, 17 July 2022.

———. "Site Name: Auriesville Shrine II." Eight unnumbered pages. Private communication by email, 17 July 2022.

———. "Site Name: Auriesville Shrine III." Six unnumbered pages. Private communication by email, 17 July 2022.

———. "Site Name: Bauder." Eight pages. Private communication by email, 8 September 2022.

———. "Site Name: Fox Farm." Seven unnumbered pages. Private communication by email, 8 September 2022.

———. "Site Name: Levi Dillenbeck." Six pages. Private communication by email, 12 September 2022.

Rumrill, Donald A. "An Interpretation and Analysis of the Seventeenth Century Mohawk Nation: Its Chronology and Movements." *Bulletin and Journal of Archaeology for New York State* 90 (1985): 1–39.

———. "The Mohawk Glass Trade Bead Chronology: ca. 1560–1785." *Beads: Journal of the Society of Bead Researchers* 3 (1991): 5–45.

Tuck, James A. "Northern Iroquoian Prehistory." In *Handbook of North American Indians*. Vol. 15, *Northeast*, edited by Bruce G. Trigger. Washington, DC: Smithsonian Institution, 1978, 322–33.

———. "Regional Cultural Development, 3000 to 300 B.C." In *Handbook of North American Indians*. Vol. 15, *Northeast*, edited by Bruce G. Trigger. Washington, DC: Smithsonian Institution, 1978, 28–43.

Secondary Sources

Archival Sources

Hartley, [Robert M.] "The Position of the Mohawk Clans." *Van-Epps-Hartley Bulletin* 1 (1936): 3–4. HF 102-A-17. Copy. Montgomery County Department of History and Archives, Fonda, NY.

Lathers, William, Jr., and Edward J. Sheehan. "The Iroquois Occupation of the Mohawk Valley." *Van-Epps-Hartley Bulletin 2* (1937): 5–9.

HF 102-A-15. Copy. Montgomery County Department of History and Archives, Fonda, NY.

Melançon, Artur, SJ. Undated letter to an unnamed fellow priest re Ossenrenon. BO-80-K. Jesuit Archives of Canada, Montreal.

Reference Works

Barbedor, Louis. *Les escritures financiere et italienne bastarde dans leur naivete* ... Paris: Nicholas Langlois, ca. 1660.

Baretti, Giuseppe, comp. *A Dictionary of the Italian and English Languages*. London: C. Hitch and L. Hawes, 1760.

Bieler, Ludwig. *The Grammarian's Craft: An Introduction to Textual Criticism*, 3rd ed. Classical Folia. Edited by Martin R. P. McGuire. New York: Catholic Classical Association of Greater New York, 1965.

Buat, Nicolas, and Evelyne Van den Neste. *Manuel de paléographie française*. Paris: Les Belles Lettres, Collection Sources, 2016.

Garraghan, Gilbert J., SJ. *A Guide to Historical Method*. Edited by Jean Delanglez, SJ. New York: Fordham University Press, 1951.

Lewis, Charlton T., and Charles Short. *A Latin Dictionary*. Oxford: Clarendon Press, 1975.

Maas, Paul. *Textual Criticism*. Translated by Barbara Flower. Oxford: Clarendon Press, 1958.

Meyer-Lübke, W. *Romanisches Etymologisches Wörterbuch*. 5th ed. Heidelberg: Carl Winter Universitätsverlag, 1972.

Provencher, Jean, *Chronologie du Québec depuis 1534*. 4th ed. Montreal: Éditions du Boréal, 2017.

Reynolds, L. D., and N. G. Wilson. *Scribes and Scholars: A Guide to the Transmission of Greek and Latin Literature*. 3rd ed. Oxford: Clarendon Press, 1991.

Rowlett, Russ. *How Many? A Dictionary of Units of Measurement*. Chapel Hill: University of North Carolina Press, 2012.

Whately, Richard. *Elements of Logic*. 7th ed. London: B. Fellowes, 1840.

Other Books

Fenton, William N. *The Great Law and the Longhouse: A Political History of the Iroquois Confederacy*. Civilization of the American Indian Series 223. Norman: University of Oklahoma Press, 1998.

Greer, Allan. *Mohawk Saint: Catherine Tekakwitha and the Jesuits.* Oxford: Oxford University Press, 2005.

Hooker, Richard. *Of the Laws of Ecclesiastical Polity*. Book V, *The Folger Library Edition of The Works of Richard Hooker*, vol. 2, edited by W. Speed Hill. Cambridge, MA: Belknap Press of Harvard University Press, 1977.

Innes, Harold A. *The Cod Fisheries: The History of an International Economy*. Rev. ed. 1940. Toronto: University of Toronto Press, 1954.

Lynch, Beth. *Our Lady of Martyrs Shrine: A Brief History of Auriesville, the Holy Ground of the Sacrifice of the North American Martyrs and the Birthplace of St. Kateri Tekakwitha*. Amsterdam, NY: Friends of Our Lady of Martyrs Shrine, 2020.

Martin, Felix, SJ. *Catherine Tegakouïtha: Iroquois Maiden/Une Vierge Iroquoise.* Translated by Henry van Rensselaer, SJ. Revised by William Lonc, SJ. Montreal: Les Archives Jésuites, 2006.

Martin, Joel W. *The Land Looks after Us: A History of Native American Religion*. New York: Oxford University Press, 2001.

Pauketat, Timothy R. *Cahokia: Ancient America's Great City on the Mississippi*. Penguin Library of American Indian History. New York: Penguin, 2010.

Pouliot, Léon, SJ. *Étude sur les Relations des Jésuites de la Nouvelle France (1632–1672)*. Paris: Desclée de Brouwer, 1940.

Richter, Daniel K. *The Ordeal of the Longhouse: The People of the Iroquois League in the Era of European Colonization*. Chapel Hill: University of North Carolina Press; Williamsburg, VA: Institute of Early American History and Culture, 1992.

Sioui, Georges E. *Pour une autohistoire amérindienne*. Quebec: Les Presses de l'Université Laval, 2018.

Snow, Dean R. *The Iroquois*. Peoples of America. Oxford: Blackwell, 1994.

Talbot, Francis, SJ. *Saint among Savages: The Life of Isaac Jogues.* New York: Harper & Brothers, 1935.

Articles

Codignola, Luca. "CAMPEAU, Lucien, s.j., éd., *Monumenta Novae Franciae*. Tome IV: *Les grandes épreuves (1638–1640)*. Rome/

Montréal, Institutum Historicum Societatis Iesu/Les Éditions Bellarmin, 1989, 48–808 p." *Revue d'histoire de l'Amérique française* 44 (1990): 97–103.

Egan, Thomas F., SJ. "The General and the Professor—Identification of Ossernenon." *Pilgrim from the Martyrs Shrine* 84, no. 2 (1973): 6 unnumbered pages.

"How We Know: Auriesville Is Ossernenon." *Auriesville Pilgrim* (1945): 10–11.

Loyzance, Joseph, SJ. "Kateri Tegewitha, Lily of the Mohawks, Born on Site Where Goupil and Fr. Jogues Shed Their Blood, Methods Employed to Determine Exact Location." *Auriesville Pilgrim* (July 1934). Reprinted in *St. Johnsville Enterprise and News*, 28 November 1934.

Smith, Richard Upsher, Jr. "Preludes and Points—Part I. On the Trail of the Jesuit Martyrs of North America and St. Catherine Tekakwitha." *New Oxford Review* (June 2019): 18–26.

———. "Preludes and Points—Part II. The Final Journey of the Jesuit Martyrs of North America and the Birthplace of St. Catherine Tekakwitha." *New Oxford Review* (July–August 2019): 20–26.

True, Micah. "Is It Time for a New Edition of the Jesuit Relations from New France? Campeau vs. Thwaites." *Papers of the Bibliographical Society of Canada* 51, no. 2 (2013): 261–79.

Maps

Clayburn, Paul H., Commissioner of Public Works. *Montgomery County Highway Map* (Erlanger, KY: Universal Map Enterprises, 2007).

US Geological Survey Historical Map. Canajoharie, NY, N4252.5—W7430/7.5. 1944.

———. Carlisle, NY, N4245—W7422.5/7.5. 1945.

———. Randall, NY, N4252.5—W7422.5/7.5. 1944. Photo revised 1980.

———. Tribes Hill, NY, N4252.5—W7415/7.5. 1944. Photo revised 1980.

Bibliography

Online Sources

Elswick, Albert. "Bauder Burial Lot, Town of Root, off Currytown Road on the Land of Winford Peck, Randall, Root Twp." Written in 1967 for the Caughnawaga Chapter of the Daughters of the American Revolution. Accessed 27 August 2019, montgomery.nygenweb.net/cemeteries/rootcems.html.

Rigal-Cellard, Bernadette. "Kateri Tekakwitha and Saint Kateri's Shrine." Accessed 10 February 2022, https://wrldrels.org/2016/10/08/kateris-shrine/.

INDEX

abscendo, neologism, 59n43
Adena, 47. *See also* mound building, Native American
Adirondacks, 25
Agniers. *See* Mohawk
agriculture, Mohawk, 87, 121, 123
Airport Road. *See* CR-67
Albany, NY, 22, 57n42
Algonquin, 21, 22, 26–27, 106; helper of St. Isaac Jogues, 66–67. *See also* Catherine Tekakwitha, St.; Simon Piechkaretch
Alston Creek, 98
amnis, 54n38
Andagaron, 24, 35, 37, 38, 40, 49, 51, 55, 56, 62, 70, 75–76, 122, 135, 139, 147–48; distances from other castles, 84–86; not Ossenrenon-Oneigiouré, 115–19. *See also* Banagiro; Canagere; Rumrill-Naylor Site
Annapolis Royal, NS. *See* Port-Royal, Acadia
archeology, 1–2, 4, 20; repositories for artifacts, 43, 52; summary of impact on this inquiry, 152–53, 154. *See also* houses, archeological traces, Mohawk; palisades, Mohawk; post molds
Argersinger Road, 138
artifacts: Auriesville Site, 43, 45; Bauder Site, 52, 119; beads, 38, 51, 137, 141, 142, 144, 152; cassock buttons, 118; Catholic, 118–19; Caughnawaga, 142; Fox Farm Site, 141; Freeman Site, 138; Jesuit rings, 137, 144; Levi Dillenbeck Site, 140; and location of Ossenrenon-Oneugiouré, 118–19; Milton Smith Site, 144; Oak Hill #1, 52, 119; pipes, 52, 137, 141, 142, 152; Printup Site, 136, 137; Rumrill-Naylor, 52, 118–19; summary of impact on this inquiry, 152. *See also* archeology, repositories for artifacts; Bird, Edward; Gerdes, Hendrick; Iroquois Mission (Jesuit), artifacts; relics, Native American
Asserue, 110. See also Ossenrenon; Ossenrenon-Oneugiouré
aunt/hostess, St. Isaac's Mohawk, 25, 26, 29, 67, 106, 109n2, 120, 121, 124, 154. *See also* brother of St. Isaac's Mohawk aunt/St. Isaac's host; Honatteniate; mercy shown by Mohawk
Auries Creek, 38, 134, 143
Auriesville, NY, 19, 36, 82, 143, 150
Auriesville Site, 36, 40, 53, 57n42, 97–98, 134, 152, Fig. 1; Auriesville Hill, 37, 86–89, Fig. 4; Auriesville #1, 36–37, 42–43, 96, 144, Fig. 2; Auriesville #2, 36–37, 42, 44–49, 87, 89, 98, 100, 134, 144, Fig. 3;

Index

Auriesville Site (*cont.*)
Auriesville #3, 42–43, 144; ditches and earthworks, 44–45, 46–49; elevation, 84; evidence it was the martyrdom site, 33–41; ravine, 37, 89–90, 94, 99–100, 154, Fig. 5; ravine brook, 37, 89, Figs. 5–6; Ravine Creek, 37, 83, 89–90, 94, 95, 96, 100, Figs. 7–8; ravine meadow, 83, 89–90; riverbank, steep, 40, 80–81, Fig. 1; summaries of argument against St. Rene's place of death, 98–100, 153. *See also* Mohawk River; mound building, Native American; Victor Putnam Site; villages, Mohawk

Auriesvile Shrine. *See* National Shrine of the North American Martyrs and Birthplace of St. Kateri Tekakwitha

Banagiro, 110, 116. See also Andagaron; Canagere

Baptism, Holy, 101–2, 105, 128, 130, 133

Bauder family, 50; cemetery and well, 49–50, 90n63, Fig. 9

Bauder Site, 3, 48, 49–53, 85, 86, 96, 98, 111, 117, 122–24, 134, 135n9, 137, 152; artifacts, 119; elevation, 84; middens, 52; ravine, north, 51, 90–93, 94, 148, Fig. 11; ravine, south, 50, 90; ridge near Yatesville mouth, 81, 147, Fig. 13; ridge west of site, 51, 86–89, 147, 148, Fig. 12; summaries of argument for St. René's place of death, 98–100, 153; summary of argument for place of St. Isaac's and St. Jean's deaths, 153–54. *See also* Currytown Road; Ossenrenon; villages, Mohawk; Yatesville Creek

beads. *See* artifacts

Bear clan (Mohawk), 25, 29, 110–11, 149; and the deaths of St. Isaac and St. Jean, 102, 106, 119, 149. *See also* Francophobes (Mohawk)

Beaver Wars, 22

Bentley, Richard, 98

Berger, Le. *See* Honatteniate

Bird, Edward, 52n34, 141n29

booty, 15, 23, 80

Borden Road, 135

Bourdon, Jean, 27–28, 80, 101, 103–5, 123, 148

Brébeuf, Jean de, SJ, St., 21, 30, 155

Bressani, Francesco Gioseppe, SJ, 8, 15, 26, 30, 85–86, 151

brother of St. Isaac's Mohawk aunt/St. Isaac's host, 78–79, 106, 120n9, 120–21, 124, 154. *See also* aunt/hostess, St. Isaac's Mohawk; Honatteniate

Buteux, Jacques, SJ, 9, 10, 26, 105, 106; interpretation of arrival narrative, 80–82

Cahaniaga. *See* Fox Farm Site

Camp Dudley, NY, 53n37

Campeau, Lucien, SJ, 6n9, 18, 80n49, 116n20

Canagere, 116

Can-a-gor-ha, 139

Canajoharie, NY, 34n5, 37n10, 148

cannibalism: and religious belief, 14–16; instance of, 25. *See also* mourning war

captives: of Mohawk, 15, 23–24, 54, 57, 63, 149; unassigned, status of, 70–71. *See also* slaves of Mohawk

Index

Cartier, Jacques, 20
Castillon, André, SJ, 11, 28
castles, Mohawk, 16n49, 19, 48, 49, 52, 62, 80, 98, 140, 146, 147, 148, 149, 150, 154
Catherine Tekakwitha, St., 3, 19–20, 30, 31–32, 49, 97, 125, 136, 152, 154; adoptive sister, 130–31, 133n7; Algonquin mother, 126; and Gandaouagué, 126, 127, 129 130, 131, 138; and smallpox 126–27, 129, 131, 138, 139; baptism, 128, 130, 133, 142, 145; birth at Printup Site, 138; family, 126, 129, 131; flight to the Sault, 128–29, 130–31, 133–34; lodges missionaries, 132; residences, summary of sequence of, 144–45; summary of this research, 149–50; uncle of, 130–31. *See also* Freeman Site; Fox Farm Site; Kateri Tekakwitha, St.; Lamberville, Jacques de, SJ; Printup Site
Catholicism, 25, 145; devotional practices of, 151–52, 155. *See also* artifacts, Catholic
Caughnawaga, 20, 48n23, 97, 134, 137n16, 145, 150, 153; burned by French (1693), 142, 150; excavations, 142–43. *See also* artifacts; Gandaouagué; Veeder Site
Cayadutta Creek, 33–34, 38, 39n13, 134, 139, 142, 150
Cayuga, 22, 30
Chabanel, Noël, SJ, St., 30
Champlain, Lake, 21, 24, 29, 53, 57, 61, 65, 68, 80, 146
Champlain, Samuel de, 21
Chauchetière, Claude, SJ, 32, 125–26
Cholenec, Pierre, SJ, 32, 125–26
Clark, John S., Gen., 33–38, 42, 85, 97, 99, 134, 135, 140, 143, 151, 152. *See also* "Work with Gen. Clark re, 3 Towns"
coffer, St. Isaac's, 27, 103, 104, 106, 108, 118–19, 124, 154. *See also* magic; traditionalists, Mohawk religious
condolence ceremonies, 15
Coûture, Guillaume (Guillelmus), 23–24, 56, 58, 63, 70–71, 76
Cromwell Site/House, 50n27, 135n9. *See also* Onekagoncka
CR-67, 85
CR-108, 85, 86, 147
CR-164, 36, 43, 44, 49, 89. *See also* Noeltner Road
Currytown, NY, 49
Currytown Road, 49, 50, 81–82, 85–86, 88, 90, 147

Daniel, Antoine, SJ, St., 30
demographic decline, 15, 16, 122. *See also* diseases
devil. *See* magic
Dieppe, France, 28
Dillenbeck, Levi J., 139
Dillenbeck Road, 135, 138
diseases, 20; smallpox, 30, 32, 122, 126–27, 131, 138, 139, 145, 150. *See also* demographic decline
documents: review of, 7–14; summary of impact on this inquiry, 153–54; use of, 3–4, 98–99
donné, 23, 28, 56n41
Dutch, 8, 11, 22, 25–26, 30, 57, 63, 148. *See also* Dutch Reformed; Dutch West India Company; New Netherland; *Novum Belgium*
Dutch Reformed, 26, 103n1
Dutch West India Company, 52n34

Index

Egan, Thomas, SJ, 33
Elswick, Albert, 49
English, 21, 22, 30, 130. *See also* Second Anglo-Dutch War
"Epistola Patris Isaaci Jogues in Nova Francia inter Irohaeos captivi ad Provincialem Franciae," Document 1, 7–8, 26, 36, 40, 53–60, 80, 82, 84, 87, 88, 93, 96, 97, 157
Erie Canal: bike path, 80; towpath, 36, 37
Eustace Ahatsistari, 24, 56, 63
evidence: types of, 3–5; assessment of, 98–99, 160
Ewing, J. Franklin, SJ, 36, 37, 43, 44, 46, 47, 49

Fenton, William N., 121. *See also* villages, Mohawk
Filleau, Jean, SJ, 26
fishing: cod, 20; Mohawk, 25, 27, 122
fiume, 82
Five Nations. *See* Iroquois
Flat Creek, 37n10, 148
Flat Creek Ravine. *See* Flat Creek
flats, Mohawk. *See* intervale/flats, Mohawk River
Flemish. *See* Dutch
fluvius, 54n39
Fonda, NY, 20, 39n13, 97, 134, 139, 150
Fort Hunter, 144
Fort Orange, 11, 22, 25–26, 130
Fort Plain Airport, 148. *See also* CR-67; Fort Plain, NY
Fort Plain, NY, 34, 49, 85, 148. *See also* Fort Plain Airport
Fort Richelieu, 27, 28
Fox Farm Site, 3, 38n12, 48n23, 138, 139–42, 145, 153. *See also* Gandaouagué; villages, Mohawk
France, 8, 26. *See also* French; New France
Francis, Jim and Helena, 135. *See also* Printup Site
Francophobes (Mohawk), 25, 31. *See also* Bear Clan (Mohawk)
Freeman family, 138
Freeman Site, 137n16, 138–39, 144, 153. *See also* Gandaouagué; Tracy, Seigneur (Marquis) de; villages, Mohawk
French, 22, 30, 31, 63–64, 106, 109n2, 127, 136, 150. *See also* France; New France
French River, 21
Frey, Samuel Ludlow, 34–37, 99, 135. *See also* "Work with Gen. Clark re; 3 Towns"
frize, 77n48
Fultonville, NY, 37, 85

Gandaouagué, 30–33 passim, 37n10, 38, 97, 126, 129–31 passim, 134, 138, 139, 141–43 passim, 145, 149–50, 153, 154. See also Caughnawaga; Fox Farm Site; Freeman Site; Veeder Site
Garnier, Charles, SJ, St., 30
Garonhiagué. *See* Louis Ogératarihen
gauntlet, 24, 55, 62, 69–70, 74–75, 147. *See also* torture
genre of this book, 5
George, Lake, 27, 29, 80
Georgian Bay, 21
Gerdes, Hendrick, 141n29
Glen (township), 3, 135, 143
glory, warrior's, 15
Goupil, René (Renatus), SJ, St., 2, 23–25, 35, 39–40, 53, 56–57, 63, 70, 76, 84, 86–89 passim, 91, 92–93,

Index

98, 151, 153–54; Bauder Site, and, 42–100, 134; burial, 25, 60, 65, 68, 72–73, 79, 157–60; hidden bones argument, 159–60; lie about the location of St. Rene's body, 60, 68, 97–98; martyrdom, 25, 57–60, 63–65, 66–68, 71–72, 76–79, 123, 124; summary of this research, 146–48. *See also* Jogues, Isaac (Isaacus), SJ, St.
Grassman, Thomas, OFM, Conv., 143
gravel pits, 139–41
Greenhalgh, Wentworth, 141–42
Greer, Allan, 1n1, 133n7
Grider, Rufus A., 43n8, 44

habit, religious, 28, 77n48
harquebuses, trade in, 22
Harris Site, 137n15
historical markers, 85, 86, 97n70, 135n9, 139
Holy Circle of life, 15, 16
Honatteniate, 26, 29, 109n2, 121, 124, 154. *See also* aunt/hostess, St. Isaac's Mohawk
Hopewell (culture), 47. *See also* mound building, Native American
Hot Powder. *See* Louis Ogératarihen
houses, archeological traces, Mohawk, 43–45 passim, 52, 142. *See also* archeology; post molds
"How We Know, Auriesville Is Ossernenon," 39–40
Hudson River, 22, 25–27 passim, 29, 80, 149; Jogues and party cross at rapids (1642), 74
hunting camps, Mohawk, 25
Huron, 14, 21, 22, 26–27, 30, 106; ambassadors to Mohawk, 28; Huron Confederacy, 30; Huronia, 21, 23; Huron Mission, 23, 30; Jacques Buteux's informant, 106; captives/slaves, 54, 61–62, 69, 74–75, 108; Catholics, 23, 24, 31; traders, 21, 23.

imminet, 87
Ingersoll Road, 143
"Interprète Labatie à Jean de la Monagne, L'," Document 7, 11, 102, 119
intervale/flats, Mohawk River, 80–81, 85, 148–50 passim
Iroquoian. *See* Huron; Iroquois; mourning war
Iroquois, 14, 19, 22, 23, 30; Catholics, 31, 128–29, 133. *See also* Iroquoia; Iroquois League of Peace; Mohawk; mourning war; Oneida; Onondaga; Cayuga; Seneca
Iroquoia, 27, 30, 31
Iroquois League of Peace, 30
Iroquois Mission (Jesuit), 19, 31, 127, 131–32, 142; artifacts of, 118–19, 137, 141, 142, 144; friction caused by, 140. *See also* Mohawk dissenters; villages, Mohawk
Iroquois, River of the, 23. *See also* Richelieu River

jadis, 111–12, 115–18. *See also* "Mission des Martyrs commencé au pays des Iroquois, De la," Document 9
Jennings, Frank, 139
Jesuit Relations, 5–7, 112n11. *See also* Society of Jesus
Jesuits. *See* Society of Jesus
Jim Francis Site, 135. *See also* Printup Site
Jogues Island, NY, 24, 27, 53n37, 73

Index

Jogues, Isaac (Isaacus), SJ, St., 2, 9–10, 19, 21, 35, 38, 51, 53, 56–57, 63, 70, 76, 85–89 passim, 91–93 passim, 98, 101, 116, 132, 134, 151–54 passim; arrival in Ossenrenon (October 1646), 102; martyrdom of, 102, 105–9, 121, 123; ministry to Native Americans, 73, 101, 104–5, 149; overview of his part in story, 23–29; peace mission with Jean Bourdon, 103–5, 114–15, 123; St. Rene's burial, and, 60, 65, 68, 72–73, 79, 157–60; St. Rene's martyrdom, and, 57–60, 63–65, 66–68, 71–72, 76–79; summary of this research, 146–49. *See also* aunt/hostess, St. Isaac's Mohawk; Goupil, René (Renatus), SJ, St.
Jolliet, Louis, 34, 39, 40

Kahnawake, QC. *See* Mission de Saint-François-Xavier-du-Sault
Kateri Tekakwitha, St., 1n1. *See also* Catherine Tekakwitha, St.; St. Kateri National Shrine and Historic Center
Keim, Joseph and Ella, 135, 136, 137. *See also* Printup Site
Kentake. *See* La Prairie-de-la-Magdeleine
Kieft, Willem, 11, 102–3
King William's War, 142
Komarzanski, Joseph and Alice, 135. *See also* Printup Site

Labatie, Jan, 11, 102, 103
La Chine, Montreal Island, QC, 125
Lachine Rapids, 31
Lalande, Jean de, St., 2, 28–29, 101, 134, 152; arrival in Ossenrenon (October 1646), 102; martyrdom of, 102, 105, 107–9, 123; summary of this research, 149. *See also* Jogues, Isaac (Isaacus), SJ, St.
Lalemant, Gabriel, SJ, St., 30, 155
Lalemant, Jérôme, SJ, 8, 9, 26
Lamberville, Jacques de, SJ, 32, 142; and St. Catherine's flight, 128–29, 130–31; baptizes St. Catherine, 128, 130, 133; meets St. Catherine, 127–28, 129–30, 132; posted to Gandaouagué, 132
languages, classical and modern, knowledge of, 4, 6n9
La Prairie-de-la-Magdeleine, 31
La Rochelle, France, 26
Lashers Creek, 147, 148
league. *See leuca, leuga*
Le Gobien, Charles, SJ, 14n44
Le Jeune, Paul, SJ, 10
Lenig, Donald, 43
Lenig, Wayne, 36–37, 42n1, 43–46 passim, 140–41
"Lettera del Padre Isaac Jogues al Padre Provinciale della provinia di Francia," Document 2, 8, 30, 35–36, 39, 61–65, 80, 82, 84, 85, 87, 94–95, 96, 157–58
"Lettre au R.P. Estienne Charlet, provincial de la Compagnie de Jésus en la province de France," Document 12, 12, 107–8
"Lettre du Père Cholenec, missionnaire de la Compagnie de Jésus, au Père Augustin le Blanc, de la même Compagnie, Procureur des missions du Canada," Document 17, 14, 131–34, 138
leuca, leuga, 57n42
Levi Dillenbeck Site, 139–40

Index

lieue. *See leuca, leuga*
Little Nose, 147, 148. *See also* Noses
logic in arguments: absurdity, 118, 124, 154; circular, 40, 117; Occam's Razor, 117, 120, 123; persuasiveness of, 124; undue assumption of premise, 117, 124, 154
Lonc, William, SJ, 13
Louisiana mound builders, 46. *See also* mound building, Native American
Louis Ogératarihen, 128n5, 128–29, 133n7
Loyzance, Joseph, SJ, 38–39, 99, 151–52
Lynch, Beth, 43n8

magic, 27–28, 103, 104, 106, 108, 119. *See also* coffer, St. Isaac's; traditionalists, Mohawk religious
Mahicans, 22
Maring, William, 49, 86, 135
Mary the Virgin, St., 24, 54–55, 61–62, 69
Martin, Felix, SJ, 13, 151
martyrdom, 22, 49; Huron Catholics', 24–25, 76. *See also* Eustace Ahatsistari; Goupil, René (Renatus), SJ, St.; Jogues, Isaac (Isaacus), SJ, St.; Lalande, Jean, St.; Paul Ononchouraton; Stephen (Huron martyr)
"Martyre de René Goupil par les Iroquois, Le," Document 3, 8, 26, 36, 39, 65–68, 84, 87, 89, 91, 93, 94, 96, 97, 120n29, 158
Mass, Holy, 23, 26, 27, 38
Mattawa River, 21
McCashion, John, 52
Megapolensis, Johannes, Dominie, 26, 103, 110, 116–17
Melançon, Artur, SJ, 39n13, 97
Melious, Earlene, F., 81n50
mercy, of Mohawk, 74–75, 77, 120n29. *See also* aunt/hostess, St. Isaac's Mohawk; brother of St. Isaac's Mohawk aunt/St. Isaac's host; Honatteniate
metal artifacts/detectors, 52, 136
middens. *See* Bauder Site
Midland, ON, 155
Milton Smith Site, 37n10, 97, 134, 143–44, 145, 150, 153. *See also* Ogsadaga; villages, Mohawk
Minch, Robert, 50
miracle, 32
Mission de Saint-François-Xavier-du-Sault, 14, 31–32, 125, 142, 145, 154
Mission de Saint-Pierre. *See* St. Peter's Mission
"Mission des Martyrs commencé au pays des Iroquois, De la," Document 9, 11, 103–5, 110, 111–15. *See also jadis*
Mississippian culture, 47. *See also* mound building, Native American
Mitchell Site, 37n10
Mohawk Nation, 155
Mohawk: burning of castles, 131–32, 142, 150; capture of Jogues and party (1642), 53; Catholics, 31, 130–31, 133–34, 141n29, 142; clan structure, 110–11, 124; dissenters, 140n24; drunkenness/debauchery, time of, 127, 132; lived south of Mohawk River, 34–35, 39, 40; men's roles, 120n29, 123; people, 22–28 passim, 49, 99, 101, 102; rebuilt north of Mohawk River, 30–31, 134, 139, 150; removed back south of the river, 143, 145;

Mohawk (*cont.*)
warlike disposition, 108; women's roles, 91, 120n29, 121. *See also* Bear clan (Mohawk); castles, Mohawk; Iroquois; Turtle Clan (Mohawk); villages, Mohawk; Wolf Clan (Mohawk)
Mohawk River, 19, 33, 34, 37, 39, 40, 48, 49, 89, 97, 136, 137, 140–41, 144–45, 150, 151, 153; and the arrival of Jogues and his party at Ossenrenon (1642), 80–82, 146–47. *See also* intervale/flats, Mohawk River
Mohawk Valley, 34, 38, 44, 47, 49, 142, 154. *See also* reliquary, this section of Mohawk Valley
Mohawk Valley Project, 42
Montagnais, 21, 22, 27
Montagne, Jean de la, 11
Montgomery County Department of History and Archives, 34–35
Montgomery County, NY, 3, 33, 135, 146, 150. *See also* Montgomery County Department of History and Archives
Montmagny, Charles Huault de, 11, 26, 28, 102, 109, 148–49
Montreal, QC, 9, 21–22, 26, 28, 31, 80
Moore, A. Dewey and Inez, 135. *See also* Printup Site
mortuary practices, Native American, 47. *See also* mound building, Native American
mound building, Native American, 46–47, 48. See also Auriesville Site, ditches and earthworks; mortuary practices, Native American
mourning war, 14–16. *See also* cannibalism; Holy Circle of life; torture
Moyer Road, 85–86, 148

"Narré de la prise du Père Isaac Jogues, Par le P. Jacques Buteux," Document 5, 10, 26, 39–40, 73–79, 80, 83, 87, 94, 96, 120n29, 158–59
National Shrine of the North American Martyrs and Birthplace of St. Kateri Tekakwitha, 1–3, 19, 33, 38–39, 80, 83, 98, 99, 143; colosseum, 87; continuing significance of, 2, 152, 154–55; 1885 chapel, 43, 43n8, 81; Martyrs/Kateri Chapel, 43, 43n8; shrines, 89; Stations of the Cross pathway, 45. *See also* Auriesville Site; Society of Jesus
New Amsterdam, 11
New France, 8, 23, 26, 29, 31, 148. *See also* France; French
New Netherland, 22, 28, 30. *See also* Dutch; *Novum Belgium*
New York Thruway, 81, 99
Nipissing, Lake, 21
Noeltner Road, 36. *See also* CR-164
Noses, 146. *See also* Little Nose
Novum Belgium, 22; St. Isaac's book of this title, 28. *See also* Dutch; New Netherland
NY-5, 139
NY-5 South, 80, 85, 86, 99, 135, 136, 138, 143
NY-162, 37n10, 85, 86, 147

Oak Hill #1, 48, 49, 52, 85; artifacts, 119. *See also* Theonontougen
Ogsadaga, *See* Milton Smith Site

Index

old clothes, Jogues's. *See* coffer, St. Isaac's

Oneida, 22, 30, 31, 52, 128. *See also* Louis Ogératarihen

Onekagoncka, 50, 135n9. *See also* Cromwell Site/House

Oneugiouré, 27, 29, 122–23, 137–38, 144, 149, 152, 154. *See also* Printup Site; Ossenrenon-Oneugiouré

Onondaga, 22, 30, 31, 52, 132

Onontio, 109. *See also* Montmagny, Charles Huault de

Ossenrenon, 19, 24, 25, 27, 42, 44–45, 49, 51, 52, 56, 65, 81, 90, 95, 97, 103, 122, 134, 147n1, 148, 149, 152; argument for this spelling, 16–18; arrival of Jogues and party (1642), 54–55, 61–62, 69–70, 74–75, 80–83, 146–47; distance from Mohawk River, 83–84, 147; distances from other castles, 84–86; Osserrion, a misspelling of, 112–14, 124. *See also* Asserue; Auriesville Site; Bauder Site; Mohawk River; Ossenrenon-Oneugiouré; Oneugiouré; peace conferences, French and Aboriginal; Victor Putnam Site

Ossenrenon-Oneugiouré, 29, 30, 103–4, 106, 107, 111, 137, 149; named after Holy Trinity, 104, 105, 114–15; not Andagaron, 114–19, 124. *See also* Asserue; Ossenrenon

Osserrion. *See* Ossenrenon

Ossernenon. *See* Ossenrenon

Otrihouré, 29, 105

Ottawa River, 21

Our Lady of Martyrs, Shrine of. *See* National Shrine of the North American Martyrs and Birthplace of St. Kateri Tekakwitha

Palatine Bridge, NY, 34–36 passim

paleography, 16–18, 112–14, 124

palisades, Auriesville #1, 43; Auriesville #2, 44–49 passim, 84; Auriesville #3, 43; Bauder Site, 84, 148; Caughnawaga, 142; Freeman Site, 138; Iroquois, 48; Milton Smith Site, 153

passus, 55n40

Paul Ononchouraton, 24, 56, 63

peace conferences, French and Aboriginal, 26–28 passim, 103–5, 109n2; held at Ossenrenon-Oneugiouré (1646), 114–15, 124, 148–49

Peck, Winford, 50

"Père Isaac Jogues au P. André Castillon, Le," Document 6, 11, 28, 101–2

"Père Jacques Buteux au P. Jérôme Lalemant, Sup., Le," Document 10, 12, 105

"P[ère]. Jacques Buteux au P. Jérôme Lalemant, Sup., Le," Document 11, 12, 106–7, 118n27, 119–20

petite rivière, 82

Polheimus, Mr., 36n6

Port-Royal, Acadia, 21

post molds, 44–45

PraA9, manuscript, 17–18, 59n43, 112–14, frontispiece

printing practices, English Renaissance, 16–17; possible French parallels, 17, 112

Printup Site, 3, 37n9, 122–24 passim, 134–38, 144, 152–54 passim. *See also* Andagaron; Francis, Jim and Helena; Jim Francis Site; Keim, Joseph and Ella; Komarzanski, Joseph and Alice; Oneugiouré;

Printup Site (*cont.*)
Ossenrenon-Oneugiouré; Printup, William H. and Martha; Moore, A. Dewey and Inez; villages, Mohawk; Wormuth, Mr.; Wormuth, Stephen
Printup, William H. and Martha, 135. *See also* Printup Site
Putnam, Victor, 44. *See also* Victor Putnam Site

Quackenbush, David A., 36
Quebec, 12, 21, 23, 26, 28

radiocarbon dating, 142
Ragueneau, Paul, SJ, 8
Randall, NY, 37, 49, 50, 57n42
Ravine Creek. *See* Auriesville Site
Récollets, 21
Relation de ce qui s'est passé en la Nouvelle-France ès années 1645 et 1646, chapitre 4. *See* "Mission des Martyrs commencé au pays des Iroquois, De la," Document 9
Relation de ce qui s'est passé en la Nouvelle-France en l'année 1647, chapitre I, Document 13, 12, 108
Relation de ce qui s'est passé en la Nouvelle-France en l'année 1647, chapters 4–5, Document 4, 9, 26, 39, 68–73, 80, 82, 83, 84, 85, 87, 94, 96, 158
Relation de ce qui s'est passé en la Nouvelle-France en l'année 1647 et 1648, chapitre II, Document 14, 12, 108–9
relics, Native American, 36, 40–41
reliquary, this section of Mohawk Valley, 1, 154–55. *See also* Mohawk Valley
Rensselaerswyck, 8, 22, 25, 27
"requickening," 15–16, 22; Guillaume Coûture and, 71
Reservoir Road, 139
Richelieu River, 23–24, 27–29 passim, 53. *See also* Iroquois, River of the
Richmond, Adelbert G., 34n5, 37
Richter, Daniel K., 122
riverbank, steep. *See* Auriesville Site
Root, Township of, 3, 49, 138
Rosary of the Holy Virgin, 27, 58, 64, 66, 71, 77, 88
Rumrill, Donald A., 49, 51, 81, 95, 96, 111, 136–37, 141, 144, 154
Rumrill-Naylor Site, 37n10, 48, 49, 52, 55n40, 85–86, 111, 117, 122, 153; artifacts, 118–19; summary of arguments for and against place of St. Isaac's and St. Jean's deaths, 153–54. *See also* Andagaron; Banagiro; Canagere

Sacandaga River, 29
Saguenay River, 21
Saint-Pierre, Lac, 23, 26
Saint-Sacrement, Lac de. *See* George, Lake
saltus, 60n44
sand pits. *See* gravel pits
Saratoga Lake, 27
Sault Saint-Louis, 31
Sault. *See* Mission de Saint-François-Xavier-du-Sault
Schoharie Creek, 34, 39, 40, 98
Schoharie River. *See* Schoharie Creek
Second Anglo-Dutch War, 30
secco, 95
Seneca, 22, 30
sepellire, 160

Index

Shea, John Gilmary, Prof., 33–34, 38, 151
Shurtleff (site), 52. *See also* Onondaga
Simcoe, Lake, 21
Simon Piechkaretch, 109n2
Sioui, Georges E., Dr., 16, 22
slaves of Mohawk, 8, 22, 24, 26, 28, 56–57, 63, 147. *See also* captives of Mohawk
smallpox. *See* diseases
Smith, Milton, 143. *See also* Milton Smith Site
Snow, Dean R., Dr., 42–43, 111–12, 115–19, 122, 137, 140–41, 142, 143–44, 154
Society of Jesus, 21, 22; annual reports, 5–6, 23; National Shrine of the North American Martyrs and Birthplace of St. Kateri Tekakwitha, 38–39, 44 *See also* Iroquois Mission (Jesuit); *Jesuit Relations*. *See too* names of individual Jesuits
soutane, 77n48
Sprakers, NY, 37, 49, 85, 147
Sprakers Basin, NY. *See* Sprakers, NY
Sprakers Hill Road. See CR-108
Stephen (Huron martyr), 24, 56
St. Kateri National Shrine and Historic Center, 1–3, 19–20, 33, 97, 134; continuing significance of, 2, 152, 154–55
St. Lawrence River, 20, 21, 23, 31, 53, 68–69, 125, 146
Stone Ridge, NY, 37n10, 135
St. Peter's Mission, 127n4, 142, 154. *See also* Fox Farm Site
superstitious persons. *See* traditionalists, Mohawk religious
Susquehannocks, 30

Tadoussac, QC, 20, 26
Talbot, Francis, SJ, 29, 80n49, 109n2, 115
Teonontogen. *See* Theonontougen
textual criticism, 59n43
Thenondiogo. *See* Theonontougen
Theonontougen, 24, 29, 33, 37, 38, 40, 49, 51, 55–56, 62, 70, 75, 107, 110, 115, 122, 148, 149; distances from other castles, 84–86. *See also* Oak Hill #1
Thérèse, 23, 27, 111–12
Three Sisters. *See* agriculture, Huron and Mohawk
Thurston, 52. *See also* Oneida
Thwaites, Reuben Gold, 6n9
Ticonderoga portage, 27, 29, 80
Tionnontogen. *See* Theonontougen
tools: Hopewellian, 47; Louisiana, 46; Iroquois, 47, 159n1
torrens, 54n38
torture: and religious belief, 14–16; instances of, 8, 23–24, 54–55, 61–62, 65–66, 69, 74–75, 107, 147, 148. *See also* gauntlet; mourning war
Tracy, Seigneur (Marquis) de, 30, 38, 127n4, 131–32, 134, 139, 154
trade, 20–23 passim, 30
traditionalists, Mohawk religious, 31, 104, 106, 119–20, 142, 144. *See also* coffer, St. Isaac's; magic
Tribes Hill, NY, 36, 38
Trois-Rivières, QC, 12, 21, 23, 26–28 passim, 70–71, 76, 108
Turtle Clan (Mohawk), 38, 110–11
Turtle Pond, 139n21

Ursuline Order, 21, 23, 111–12

Van den Bogaert, Harman Meyndertsz, 26, 116–17

Index

Van der Donck, Adriaen, 40n15
Van Epps-Hartley Chapter, New York State Archaeological Association, 111, 143
Van Evera-McKinney Site, 37n10, 122
Veeder Site, 48n23, 134, 137n16, 145, 153. *See also* Caughnawaga; Gandaouagué; villages, Mohawk
Victor Putnam Site, 44, 45. *See also* Auriesville Site, Auriesville #2; villages, Mohawk
Vie de Catherine Tegakouita Première Vierge Irokoise, La, Document 16, 13–14, 129–31, 138
Vie de la B[ienheureuse]. Catherine Tegakoüita, Dite à Present La Saincte Sauuagesse, La, Document 15, 12–13, 126–29, 138
villages, Mohawk: establishment of new, 121–23; longevity, 121, 137, 141, 149, 150, 153; name changes, 121n30; names as heard by Europeans, 116–17; ratio of persons to square meters of space, 143n35; siting, 136, 149, 150. See also Auriesville Site; Bauder Site; Printup Site; Freeman Site; Fox Farm Site; Veeder Site; Milton Smith Site
Walworth, Ellen H., 1n1, 39n13
Walworth, Fr. Clarence A., 151
wampum, 104
warriors, party of 200, 24, 53–54, 57, 61, 63–64, 65, 68–69, 73
Wendat. *See* Huron
Westport, NY, 24, 53n37
"Willem Kieft, Dir., à Charles Huault de Montmagny, Gouv.," Document 8, 11, 102–3, 119
Wolf Clan (Mohawk), 102, 104, 110–11
"Work with Gen. Clark re, 3 Towns," 34–35
Wormuth, Mr., 37, 135. *See also* Printup Site
Wormuth, Stephen, 135–36. *See also* Printup Site

Yatesville Creek, 49–51 passim, 81, 83, 90n62, 98, 137n15, 147; below Bauder Site, 91–96, 148, Figs. 15–18; mouth, 83, 99, 146–47, 153, Fig. 14. *See also* Yatesville ravine
Yatesville, NY. *See* Randall, NY
Yatesville ravine, 90, 99–100, 147. *See also* Yatesville Creek
Yosts, NY, 37, 146, 153

Figure 1. Plateau of the Shrine of Our Lady of Martyrs, Auriesville, New York, taken from the Mohawk River and showing the easy access from the riverbank to the Shrine plateau. *Photo by Andrew Balet, 28 July 1986. Wikimedia Commons.*

Figure 2. Auriesville #1: Clark and Frey identified the field around the present shrine Visitor Center, the building in the middle distance, as the site of Ossenrenon. Father Ewing's 1950 excavations took place at several places in the field before the erection of the Visitor Center. In 1952 there was a cafeteria at the location from which this photo, looking north, was taken. *Photo by the author, 4 October 2024.*

Figure 3. Auriesville #2: the torture platform crucifix, pictured here, stands roughly in the center of the area, about two-thirds of an acre, that was once surrounded by square earthworks and ditches. Short earthworks also projected to the east. The photo looks north. Feather Ewing's 1952 excavations discovered houses only outside the earthworks, and did not discover evidence of a palisade associated with the earthworks. *Photo by the author, 4 October 2024.*

Figure 4. Auriesville Hill from the shrine plateau. Tradition says that St. René Goupil was martyred at the top of this hill. *Photo by the author, 22 June 2022.*

Figure 5. Ravine Road and brook at Auriesville. *Photo by the author, 22 June 2022.*

Figure 6. Brook as it flows through the meadow at Auriesville. *Photo by the author, 22 June 2022.*

Figure 7. Junction of the brook and Ravine Creek at the edge of the Auriesville meadow. *Photo by the author, 22 June 2022.*

Figure 8. Looking down Ravine Creek from the Auriesville meadow. *Photo by the author, 22 June 2022.*

Figure 9. Bauder Site and Bauder Graveyard fields. Field to the right of the middle tree contains the Bauder Site; field to the left, the Bauder graveyard. Taken near Currytown Road. *Photo by the author, 10 August 2021.*

Figure 10. Bauder Site field. *Photo by the author, 22 June 2022.*

Figure 11. View of the northern ravine down to Yatesville Creek from the Bauder Site. This is a view of the upper part of the ravine. The ravine drops off dramatically at the point where the channel cut by the stream disappears in the middle distance. This book argues that his murderers dragged St. René's corpse down this ravine. *Photo by the author, 24 October 2019.*

Figure 12. View from the Bauder Site up the field to the ridge. I believe that St. Isaac Jogues and St. René Goupil went to this ridge to pray the day René was martyred, and that he was killed when returning to the village through this field. *Photo by the author, 24 October 2019.*

Figure 13. Ridge between the mouth of the Yatesville and the Bauder Site. Taken a hundred yards west of the point the creek enters the intervale of the Mohawk River, this photo looks south. In this book I argue that the path over this ridge was the more difficult route to Ossenrenon, the climbing of which the prisoners were spared on their arrival in this Mohawk canton. *Photo by the author, 4 October 2024.*

Figure 14. Mouth of Yatesville Creek at the Mohawk River. This book argues that St. Isaac Jogues and his companions were first "welcomed" to Ossenrenon by the Mohawk in 1642 as they debarked from canoes in this stream. *Photo by the author, 22 June 2022.*

Figure 15. Side channel of the Yatesville below the Bauder Site looking downstream, with the islet of scree on the right. I argue that St. René's body was dumped on this islet. *Photo by the author, 20 June 2022.*

Figure 16. Main channel of the Yatesville below the Bauder Site looking upstream, with the island of scree on the right. Notice the pools. *Photo by the author, 20 June 2022.*

Figure 17. View downstream from the union of the two Yatesville channels below the Bauder Site. Notice the pools. Notice, too, the sheer wall of Utica shale carved out by the stream's violence when in spate. *Photo by the author, 20 June 2022.*

Figure 18. Union of the two Yatesville channels below the Bauder Site at the end of the island of scree. Notice the bed of the stream has been stripped down to the Utica shale. *Photo by the author, 20 June 2022.*

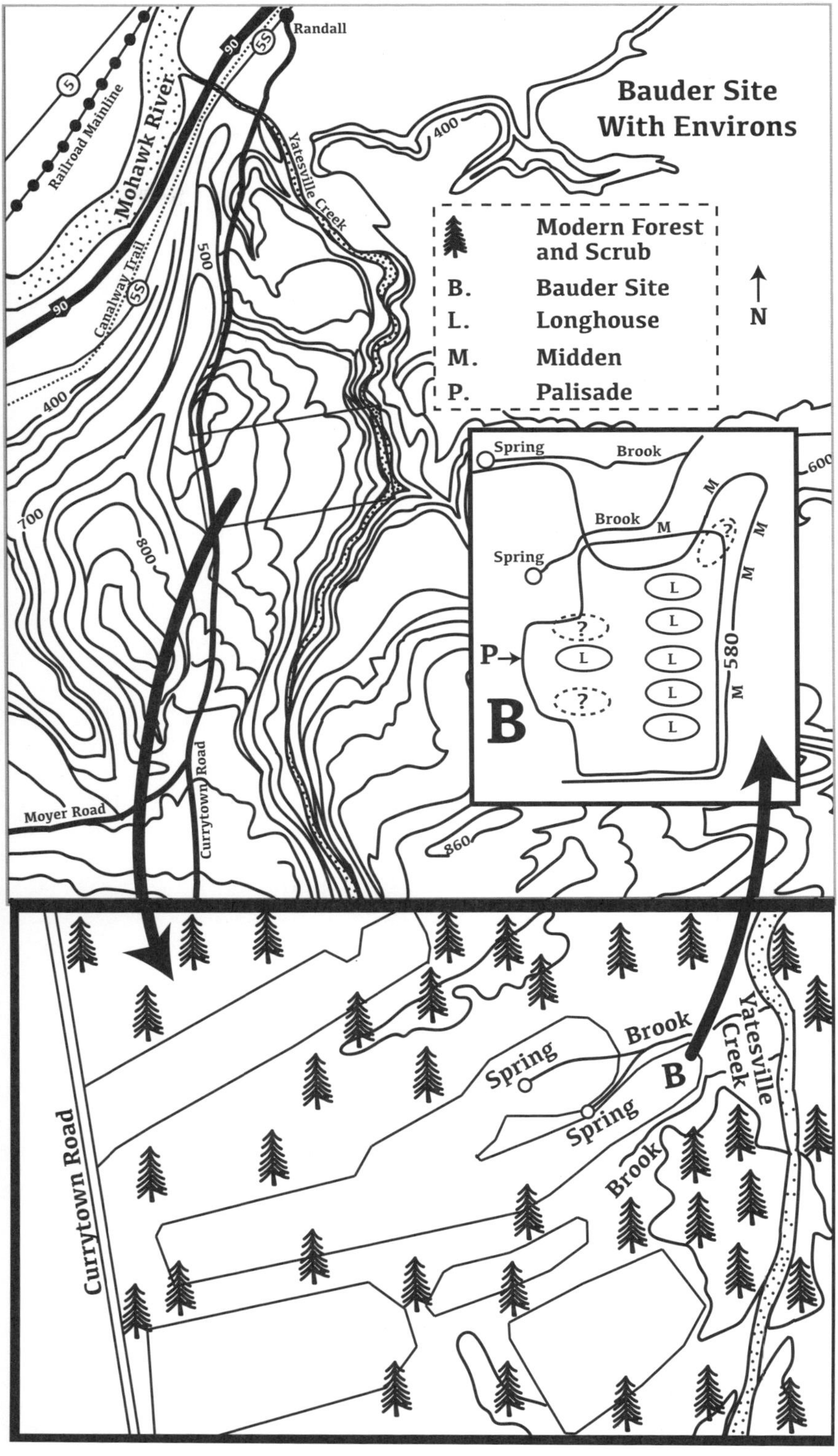

Bauder Site
With Environs
Modern Forest and Scrub
B. Bauder Site
L. Longhouse
M. Midden
P. Palisade
N
Randall
Railroad Mainline
Mohawk River
Yatesville Creek
Canalway Trail
Currytown Road
Moyer Road
400
500
600
700
800
860
580
Spring
Brook
P
B

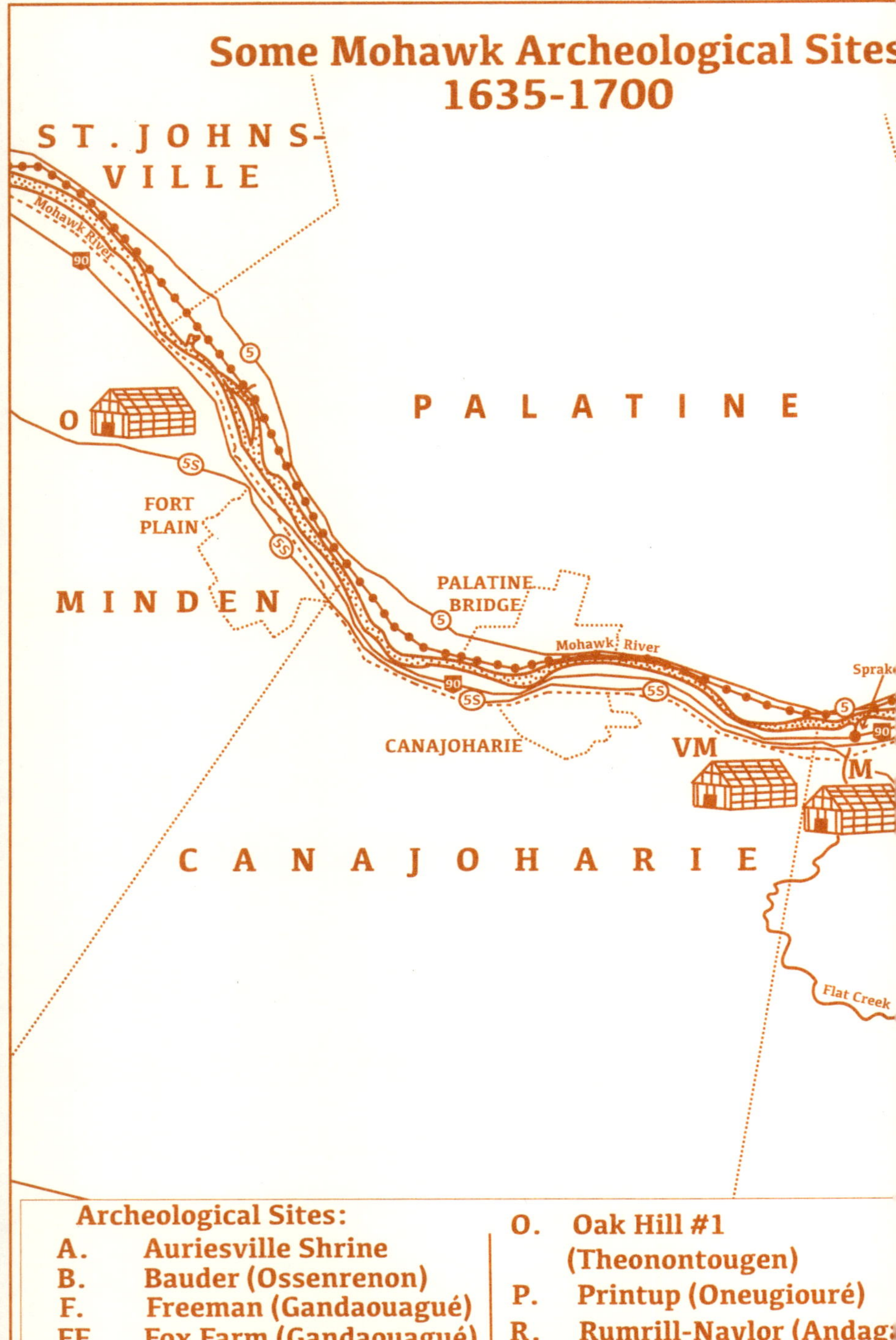

Archeological Sites:

A. Auriesville Shrine
B. Bauder (Ossenrenon)
F. Freeman (Gandaouagué)
FF. Fox Farm (Gandaouagué)
M. Mitchell (Andagaron)
MS. Milton Smith (Ogsadaga)
O. Oak Hill #1 (Theonontougen)
P. Printup (Oneugiouré)
R. Rumrill-Naylor (Andag
V. Veeder (Caughnawaga)
VM. Van Evera-McKinney (Andagaron)